BLAINEY

EYE ON AUSTRALIA

Dear Ray,

Merry Christmas
& Best Wishes always

Love Cameron
1991.

BLAINEY
EYE ON AUSTRALIA

SPEECHES AND ESSAYS OF
GEOFFREY BLAINEY

SCHWARTZ BOOKS

Published by
Schwartz Books
45 Flinders Lane
Melbourne VIC 3000
Telephone: (03) 654 6433
Fax: (03) 650 5418
Schwartz Books is an imprint of
Southern Media Corporation Pty Ltd

ISBN 1 86381 026 9

The National Library of Australia
Cataloguing-in-Publication entry

Blainey, Geoffrey, 1930–
    Blainey, eye on Australia.

    ISBN 1 86381 026 9

    1. Australia – social conditions – 1976–1990
    I. Title.

994.063

Cover design by Graphic Connection
Printed by Australia by Australian Print Group.

About the Author

Geoffrey Blainey is one of Australia's most distinguished authors and historians.

Professor Blainey was Dean of the Faculty of Arts, University of Melbourne 1982-87; Ernest Scott Professor of History 1977-88; Professor Harvard University 1982-83; Professor of Economic History 1968-77.

Geoffrey Blainey's twenty-two books include The Peaks of Lyell (1954), The Rush That Never Ended; A History of Australian Mining (1963), The Tyranny of Distance (1966), The Causes of War (1973), A Land Half Won (1980), The Great Seesaw: A New View of the Western World (1988), A Game of Our Own (1990).

Preface

This book is a selection of the commentaries I have made on the state of health of the nation during the last ten years. While it represents only a fraction of the speeches made at dinners and conferences, and maybe only one in five of the articles written for newspapers, it covers most of the main themes that concerned me or the audiences I spoke to. The commentaries included in these pages are those which seem to say something still worth saying about Australia's past and future. Occasionally an article or speech is included because it covered a symbolic event or an everyday happening.

The items are set out according to year. An endnote adds the place where each commentary first appeared. Changes have been made in the course of reviving the articles. The title or headline under which the articles originally appeared had been chosen, as is the custom, by newspaper sub-editors, but in re-publishing them I have often devised new titles. In re-reading them I occasionally edited a sentence that was repetitive or clumsily written. In a few articles I deleted passing references to events or people that were in the public eye on the day I wrote the article - references that now are irrelevant or confusing. In one or two long speeches, sections that were primarily of interest to the original audience have been deleted. Of course the spirit, the key paragraphs, the line of argument and the conclusions of all the commentaries gathered in this book are the same as those appearing in the original article or speech.

I thank *The Australian,* the *Herald & Weekly Times*, *The Age* and other newspapers for permission to re-publish articles first appearing in their pages. Indeed I owe a debt to the newspapermen who invited me to write regularly, not least to Pat Hinton, Les Carlyon and Neil Mitchell of the Melbourne *Herald* and to John Wheeldon and Frank

Devine of *The Australian*. I thank Michael Wilkinson, the publisher, who suggested that I put this book together.

Geoffrey Blainey

Contents

Part II — 1987 - 1988

Part III — 1989

Part IV — 1990

Part I

1981 - 1986

Ancient Rivals: Sydney v Melbourne

I know of only one book which concentrates on this central theme of Australian history: Melbourne v Sydney. It's only a booklet, and it's called the Constitution of the Commonwealth of Australia.

A century ago Australians perhaps exaggerated the rivalry between Sydney and Melbourne. But now there is a widespread view that either the rivalry doesn't exist or that the real differences between the cities are too mild to justify the rivalry.

It would be surprising if there was no rivalry, no competition and no outbursts of parochialism between the two cities. We don't quite realise that in world history it is unusual for two cities to run neck and neck for a long time.

In most nations the largest city is far larger than the second-largest city. In contrast, Melbourne and Sydney have been close rivals since 1851, and in that century-and-a-quarter the lead has changed twice. I don't know of any present pair of leading cities which have been locked together for so long.

During the last century the economic differences between Sydney and Melbourne have been numerous. Likewise, the social, cultural and political differences have been wide.

For decades there were strong religious contrasts between the two cities. For instance, the Anglicans were far stronger in Sydney than in Melbourne. The Methodists, Presbyterians and other Protestant denominations flourished in Melbourne, and that largely explains why that city even today is less tolerant towards certain kinds of gambling.

Whereas NSW opened a State lottery in 1931, Victoria waited another quarter-century before enticing Tatt's from

Tasmania. Even today Victorians who wish to play poker machines have to go north across the border.

Nonconformists have declined strongly in Melbourne in the past twenty years, and attitudes to gambling will probably be closer in the two cities by the year 2000. But when Melbourne reaches A.D. 2000, Sydney will be well into the twenty-first century.

The nonconformist religions also won that peculiar Melbourne strip of territory - the teetotal belt which embraces perhaps a quarter of a million people in the eastern suburbs.

There, since 1920, no hotels have existed. Even a recent attempt to provide a liquor licence for a pizza parlor was defeated by popular referendum. The garbage collectors say that people, nevertheless, drink in those suburbs running east of Camberwell.

The contrast between the two cities is now stronger in politics than in religion, though even in politics the contrast has no continuity.

Sydney was the less radical city in the period 1860 to 1890, and that may partly explain why the Labor Party gained an early stronghold in Sydney: it filled a political gap. Even in the period 1910 to 1929 Labor gained, in Federal elections, rather less support in Sydney than in Melbourne.

Thereafter, Melbourne and Victoria tended to be wary of Labor. This is especially visible in the leadership of parties, and since the Labor split in 1917, Victorians - mostly Melbourne politicians - have been Prime Minister in two of every three years.

In State politics in NSW a Labor Government in the past sixty years has been normal, but it is a quarter of a century since Labor held office in Victoria.

Why Sydney and NSW should be more sympathetic to Labor is not easily explained. Dramatic explanations are probably erroneous. We need different attitudes in only two or three per cent of the population to produce strong electoral differences.

One difference is that Melbourne people rely a little more on self-help. Traditionally they are keener on home ownership, life insurance, and private secondary schools, and this in turn may reflect attitudes partly derived from nonconformist religions. If so, these attitudes may well wane, bringing visible political effects.

Curiously, Sydney is widely said to be the cosmopolitan city of Australia, but of course it is not. Italians and Greeks form a much higher proportion of Melbourne's population than of Sydney's. So too do Yugoslavs, Germans, Poles, Dutch and Maltese.

Of the migrant groups which speak a foreign language, six of the seven largest are more prominent in Melbourne than in Sydney. In contrast, Sydney has been favored by many of the smaller migrant groups, especially those from the Middle East, the Pacific Islands and North America.

Now the economic omens for Sydney are probably the more favorable. It seems to be breaking loose again from Melbourne's challenge.

But the omen or indicator which is widely quoted in Sydney's favor seems to be a brittle one. In the past few years the value of real estate has been soaring in Sydney. This is confidently interpreted as the sign that Sydney has the real future.

Sometimes in Australian history soaring property values have been an assurance not of a glorious future but of a reckless present. Melbourne's hectic real-estate boom, in the late 1880s, marked the start of that city's eclipse, and for the following half-century Melbourne was outpaced by Sydney.

The relative rates of growth of large cities are not easily predicted. Did anyone in 1870 correctly predict, with reasoned arguments, that Sydney would pass Melbourne? And did anybody in 1940 correctly predict, with reasoned arguments, that in the next third of a century Melbourne would be growing much faster than Sydney? I doubt it.

The two cities have a different attitude to sport. That's an old difference and has persisted.

Melbourne by the 1880s could be counted as perhaps one of the three great sporting cities of the world. It was then only half a century old, but its major sports drew huge crowds.

The Melbourne Cup in 1888 was seen by 100,000 people, and they travelled to Flemington in 84 special trains. Big cricket in Melbourne had attendances such as London and Manchester could not match. Already footfall was a mania, and it seems likely that the football crowds were larger in Melbourne than in England and Europe in the early 1890s.

It is easy to think of reasons why so many spectators should be found in big Australian cities in comparison with, say, Paris or Vienna.

While the Australian cities of a century ago were smaller, many people had plentiful leisure, and ample ground near the centres of the cities was available for games and grandstands. Likewise, the proportion of single men in the population was high, and they had leisure and money.

All these factors favored the assembling of crowds of watchers. And our climate, by the standards of Copenhagen, was superb.

These reasons help to explain why sports meetings in Melbourne and Sydney should be swarming with people a century ago. But they don't explain why spectator sport was, generally, much more popular in Melbourne than in Sydney.

I'm not sure of the full reasons, but Sydney certainly in those days suffered from its warmer climate. Melbourne was believed to have the energetic climate.

In the era when everyone out of doors wore a hat - a wide-brimmed hat - many migrants in Sydney thought twice about standing in the sun and watching a game on very hot days.

Sydney did not have so much accessible parkland where games could be played. It was hillier and rockier than Melbourne, and so its sports grounds - especially those able to hold a large crowd - were not so plentiful within eight kilometres of the heart of the city.

Sydney's great parkland was the harbor itself. The harbor was spacious and cheap, requiring no rent, no rates, no ground curators, and not even a grandstand because the shores and headlands rose high. Sydney's warmer climate also fostered harbor sports. Thus Sydney was the Australian home of yachting and boating and that vanished sport, professional sculling.

Melbourne is more a city of the land and Sydney more a city of the sea. This is true emotionally as well as physically. You see the evidence in Sydney poems and paintings as well as in the press and on television.

Sydney's Opera House reflects this rich maritime tradition. I suspect that it caught the public's enthusiasm because it was envisaged as an aquatic temple as much as a house of culture. That is why, for all its magic, it has not been fully successful as a house of culture.

Melbourne built its equivalent of Sydney's Opera House in the 1920s. Called the Shrine of Remembrance, it stands on a rise in St Kilda Road, which is about as much as Melbourne can offer as a natural setting for grand architecture. It's a poor substitute for Bennelong Point.

In one sense the Shrine was Melbourne's answer to Sydney. It was designed when most Victorians were ashamed of Australia's convict background and were proud that Victoria had not been a convict colony, conveniently forgetting that thousands of convicts had come to Victoria from NSW in the pastoral era and from Tasmania in the gold era.

One powerful reason why Gallipoli became an instant legend was that it seemed to wipe out the memory of Botany Bay. At Gallipoli a nation had erased its prior convictions, and Melbourne's Shrine proclaimed that fact.

I imagine that in 1930 most Melbourne-born people of the age of 50 had not been to Sydney, not even once. Had most Sydney-born people of 50 visited Melbourne?

Interstate travel was to become more common after World War II, with higher living standards and cheap cars and petrol, Melbourne people at last had a chance to share in the beauty of the harbor, to see that Sydney was a special place. And television came - that too is a form of travel.

Contact does not necessarily make for concord, but sometimes it can eradicate the more absurd prejudices or weaken parochialism. One layer of the Melbourne-Sydney rivalry was simply ignorance. Another layer was the realisation that for a long time they had real differences.

I hope most of the differences persist. There is no magic in uniformity.

Sydney Morning Herald, 14 April 1981

2

A Great Tidal Wave

It is not easy to know whether to blame or praise technology. It is so pervasive; it covers so much. Technology is not only the latest compact computer and the latest insight into how this slip of land can be made fertile. It is also the creator of the wet-weather football and the fat phone book.

Every generation of Australians has probably been nervous of new technology, and in recent years we have been amongst the most nervous. New technology is widely seen as the destroyer of jobs, as the architect of permanent, massive unemployment. I hear some students say that by the late 1980s we will have 30 per cent unemployment. And when I ask why, they say that the new computers will abolish jobs with a ruthlessness not seen before in the world's history.

One can, one should, sympathise with their fears. And yet in all the debate about the role of technology in making or eroding jobs in Australia, one crucial point has not, to my knowledge, been stated. The growth of Australia is, in large part, the history of new technology. Nearly every job in Australia today was made possible by post-1850 technology. Sydney and Melbourne are largely the result of modern technology.

Fifteen million people live in this land, and their material standard of living is high - far higher than that of nearly all tribes and nations in the history of mankind. And yet, only two hundred years ago, perhaps only one fiftieth of our present population lived in this land. In the last two hundred years it is fair to say that the number of jobs in Australia has been multiplied by about fifty, and the great multiplier has been new technology.

The Aboriginal tribes which occupied the land had primitive weapons and implements and a patchy knowledge of the natural resources; and by our standards their technology was simple. But they had much to be proud of. They had, in the course of thousands of years, made discoveries of foodstuffs and raw materials which represented a great leap forward. They had found new techniques of hunting and fishing, building, gathering vegetables, of finding water, of curing illness. There were certainly Aboriginal Paddy Hannans, H.V. McKays, Floreys and Farrers and other discoverers and inventors. That we do not know their names is irrelevant. After all, most white Australians do not know the names of those innovators who in the last hundred years have helped to change our cities and countryside and way of life - through new technology.

Fifty thousand years ago, perhaps even longer ago, dark people crossed the seas and somewhere in the north west discovered this continent. No doubt they brought with them their own technology. They must have had some knowledge of the sea, of ocean fishes; they must have known how to find and how to cook those tropical plants which were common both to their ancestral islands and tropical Australia; and they must have had a small armoury of skills for manufacturing and using simple equipment of wood, fibre, stone and bone.

They moved across this continent and settled all habitable regions. They developed a diversity of economic skills and practices, each of which was adapted to the raw materials and seasons and resources in a particular Australian region. Their remarkable knowledge of the medicinal properties of plants was one of their contributions to technology. When the great armada of 1944 crossed the English Channel to the coast of Hitler's Europe, many of its soldiers and sailors were dosed against seasickness by an ancient Aboriginal drug, by hyoscine extracted from the leaves of an Australian *dubioisia* long used by Aboriginals.

Fire was the essence of Aboriginal technology: the widespread use of fire. They used fire to cook food, to manufacture implements and weapons, to provide warmth at night. They used fire and smoke to send messages: it was their two-way radio. They used fire to hunt animals and to control old vegetation and to stimulate new growth. They used fire-smoke as an insect repellent, and in many regions their fires cremated the dead.

In different regions Aboriginals must have used or tamed local conditions to improve their standard of living. Dr Peter Coutts and his teams from the Victorian Archaeological Survey have recently investigated the hundreds of earthen mounds in the mid-Murray Valley. They rarely use the word 'technology' in their reports but they describe how Aboriginals, long before the white people arrived, had developed their own technology to cope with the floods in the Murray Valley, downstream from Swan

Hill. Somehow, Aboriginals constructed hundreds of mounds, and many of them were more than a metre high and more than a thousand square meters in area. They probably used those mounds in flood-time as camping sites and as bases for collecting the abundant wildlife in the area.

Aboriginals, here, cooked their food in a steaming bed of pellets of burned clay, and many of the mounds hold scores of tonnes of these clay pellets, some of which formed the 'oven' for Aboriginal meals before William the Conqueror was alive. All this sounds like a numbingly simple way of life. But perhaps it represented another bold innovation - the decision to make clay pellets on alluvial plains which lacked the stone normally used 'as heat retainers for cooking'. Across Australia the widespread variations in the ways of hunting, fishing, the gathering and preparing of plant foods, the making of weapons, and the exploiting of local rocks and fibres, suggest that technological innovations were vital in Aboriginal societies.

We know more about the British than the Aboriginal history of this land. After 1788 the impact of new technology was quick and decisive. Australia was conquered, materially, with astonishing speed. There is no parallel in the history of the Americas, Asia, Europe and Africa for the speed with which immigrants placed their imprint on the land, transformed it and made it astonishingly productive.

Much of Australia's triumph was simply the bringing across the world of new livestock - sheep, cattle, horses, hens, dogs - and sufficiently altering the environment to enable that livestock to flourish. Another triumph was the bringing of seeds, seedlings, bulbs and tubers unknown to this land and cultivating them here on the large scale. Whereas the Aboriginals had their own remarkable variety of native rootplants, seeds, greens, nuts and fruits, they did not cultivate the soil and they did not strenuously encourage certain plant species rather than others. That Australia now grows enough food and fibre to feed and clothe 15 million people here and tens of millions more in other nations is very much an effect of specialisation, and the technological steps that required.

The transplanting of seeds and livestock was accompanied by the invention of new hardware. In 1900 the inland wheatfields of Australia would have been valueless without the steam railways which carried grain to the distant coast. They would have remained barren but for the devising of new strippers, harvesters, ploughs, and scrub-clearers and the emergence, by 1900, of a method of farming very dry lands with great efficiency. The rise of a strong dairying industry - at one time we were a heavy importer of barrels of Irish butter - depended on the increasing use of the Scandinavian cream separator on countless dairy farms from the 1890s.

The export of refrigerated meat and chilled butter and fruit depended on long experiments. Before 1880, when the steamship *Strathleven* successfully carried a small refrigerated cargo from Melbourne to London, much of Australia's rural potential was dead. Here was a land capable of producing an enormous output of perishable foods but - until new techniques were perfected - there was no way of shipping those foods to European markets which wanted them.

Our grasslands are suitable for countless flocks of sheep but the sheep would never have multiplied here but for a long line of new methods of caring for sheep: the lonely shepherd caring for a flock of a size unrecorded in any other land, and the development of wire fencing. The flocks would not have multiplied but for advances in breeding sheep and improving pastures and water-supply and washing and pressing wool, advances in carrying wool across the plains and seas, and, above all, the textile machines which began the industrial revolution. To an Australian, wool seems a simple Old Testament industry but if the pastoral and textile techniques of Abraham and Job still prevailed, Australia would not be producing wool.

Australia's cities would be small, but for the impact of technology. Urbanisation was made possible only by the efficient production of food, fibres, minerals, fuel. If the typical farmer could produce barely enough food to feed a few families, and if a wood-cutter or a miner could produce only enough wood or coal each year to support his own and a few other families, nearly everybody in the economy would be absorbed in the primary industries: in the simple tasks of producing food, warmth and primitive shelter. Urbanisation - the gathering of most of the nation's people in large cities - can usually happen only if the primary sector is very efficient, thus releasing most people for work in the secondary and tertiary sectors - in short, the jobs of the cities.

To exalt technology is to risk dethroning those natural resources which have been so important for our prosperity. Grasslands and arable lands, forest, mineral deposits and rivers have all been vital. In discussing national development, however, we tend to give too much weight to the resources and too little to the technology. Most of the resources we now use were present during the long Aboriginal history but were not used. They were potential resources, but became real resources only because advanced technology discovered them and was capable of extracting and using them. The oil beneath Bass Strait was unknown to the Aboriginals, and unknown to us until a technique of drilling in deep seas was developed after the 1939-45 war. Iron ore in the Pilbara was gouged by Aboriginals as a source of red ochre for their body cosmetics, but it was incapable of profitably feeding the blast furnaces of huge steelworks until the late 1950s or 1960s when large-scale methods of mining, mile-long railway trains, automatic loaders at ports and huge ocean carriers became available.

New technology can create: it can also dislocate. In the 19th century it shattered communities, it often dislocated a stable or staid way of life, and it brought pollution.

At times a new technology inflicted tragedy. The early rock drills or jackhammers in the Victorian gold mines in the

1890s filled the air with fine, sharp fragments of dust which damaged the lungs of miners. Appropriately the rock drills were called 'widow makers'. At Bendigo and other deep fields, hundreds of families lost their breadwinner before the cause of miner's disease was identified and a dangerous technology was tamed. And changes in technology revolutionised warfare. The new high-explosives which enabled Australians to blast roads and mine quarries and make new harbors with relative ease, performed the task of killing with the same ease at Gallipoli and in Flanders in the 1914-18 war. Likewise the iaircraft, which had eased loneliness, now created loneliness with bombs in the 1939-45 war.

In some districts the new technology came with a rush and created unemployment. The bullock-driver and his dray suffered from the new up-country railways. The small country brewery was edged out of business by the big city brewery and its modern plant. Many farm labourers lost their jobs when the new agricultural machines and heavy horses arrived. But these dislocating changes ultimately produced cheaper transport, cheaper beer, cheaper bread and a new set of jobs which paid higher wages than the old jobs.

It is usually easier to see specific jobs which have been eliminated by the new technology than it is to see the larger number of jobs which are created by new technology. I am not sure why this should be so, but part of the reason is that the loss of jobs is more visible, more newsworthy. When a factory or a mine closes, and families are driven out and townships die, the facts are reported on the news pages and made vivid on television. The loss of jobs often makes a headline: the creation of new jobs rarely occupies more than the classified ads.

In the last twelve months 150,000 more jobs were created in Australia than were eliminated. This must be one of the least-known facts in circulation. I do not mean that it is a cause for undue rejoicing: we need far more jobs. But it is a reflection of how we fail to notice the way in which new technology can give as well as take away.

The daily work of nearly every Australian has also been eased and lightened by new techniques. Back in 1881, hard manual work was the lot of the great majority of adult Australians. The pick and shovel, crowbar and axe were the common working tools of perhaps half of the working men. Railways were laid, farms were cleared, shafts were sunk, and machinery was made by sheer hard labour, day after day. Men were two-legged packhorses who performed Herculean feats in loading ships with coal and wheat, and in carrying supplies on their back into the mountains. Many children worked long hours, and in 1893 the NSW Government published a book called *Practical Dairying for Australia* which proudly explained how the South Coast dairy farms had been developed:

> *Each child took a share in the work, and learned how to milk just as ordinary children learn the ABC. The daily routine on the dairy farms was 5am to 8am, milking; 9am to 4pm, school; 5pm to 7pm, milking.*

Most housewives worked long hours, and the hours of domestic servants were usually longer. Households were little factories which made their own bread, jam, pickles, biscuits, preserved fruit, candles, soap, clothes, and herbal syrups and potions.

We have seen a revolution in daily work and vast increase in leisure. But not all has been gain, and we are not as fit, and we can't all cope with the glut of leisure.

One of the older axioms in economics is the law of diminishing returns. In the days of Ricardo and other pioneering economists it was often applied to labour. Economists argued that, after a certain stage, the more hours of labour which were applied, the lower was the output from each additional hour of labour. In short, weariness or exhaustion set in; and this was one of the arguments used to justify the reduction of daily hours of labour from twelve to eleven and from eleven to ten in the early factory era. I suspect that the law of diminishing returns also applies to leisure, and that after a certain stage the satisfaction which arises from each additional hour of leisure can be meagre and even negative.

I am not arguing that we should receive less leisure. I am suggesting rather that the impact of labour-saving technology has taken us by surprise, and that we do not yet realise that a steady increase in leisure is not necessarily a gain in human contentment. We will, eventually, have to think of education as equally a preparation for the sensible use of leisure time as for the sensible carrying out of work. We have barely begun to see what that will mean for teachers and schools.

So technology is like a great tidal wave which has crossed this land again and again. It has brought enormous gains, and losses too. I think the gains outweight the losses, but the margin of its victory would be even larger if we realised what had happened, what was unavoidable and what was preventible, and what can be done to make technology more our servant and less our imperious master.

It may well be that the greatest drawback of technology, ever-changing technology, is that it has made the world quick to change and difficult to understand. In a democracy the surrounding world must remain passably understandable or democracy will wilt. This is our dilemma.

B.H.P. Journal, 1981, No. 2

3

How Americans See Australia - and Thus Themselves

In the minds of many young Americans, Australia at present has an unusual glamour.

They see Australia as a last frontier in a shrinking world. They also see it as a land of opportunity at a time when opportunity, especially in business, seems to be wilting.

Australian movies in the last five years have become a minor cult in some American cities; and part of their fascination is that they often depict an outdoors way of life and a landscape which seems deserted.

In those wild ranges and those vast plains the camera has the appearance of being the first intruder. There, almost, is South Dakota, before the first sharp axe was heard.

"If President McKinley or Theodore Roosevelt were alive today, I sometimes think that they would be living in Melbourne, Australia." That comment came from a thoughtful American in his 70s, and he summed up one prominent attitude to Australia. "I sometimes imagine that Australia is like the United States was in sunnier days."

This quickening interest in Australia indirectly says much about what Americans think of their own nation, their own history. They have risen to success with an amplified sense of the importance of wide, open spaces.

Space meant plentiful resources: space meant breathing room and scope for individualism. Great space - when set out on a map of the world - helped to give an early sense of national security and importance. And great space fired the imagination of artists as well as immigrants.

Many young Americans, today, no longer believe they live in a spacious land. They feel hemmed in.

The heightened interest in Australia is possibly also a guide to the isolationist mood which continues to flourish in many American regions. There is still a hankering for that era - it surely ended at Pearl Harbor - when America could largely cut herself off from the outside world.

If Chicago and Des Moines can no longer hope to be Shangri-La, perhaps security can be sought in the isolation of Australia. That Australia is said to lie "down under" increases the impression that it is a safer retreat.

Australia is not only a mirror of moods and myths within America. Since 1945 its own economic development has been fast and its population has doubled, increasing at a faster rate than that of America.

During the quarter century 1945-70, Australians had little risk of being unemployed. A federal government almost lost an election when unemployment jumped over two per cent. In the last decade, however, unemployment steadily increased without reaching, in any one year, America's percentage.

Australia also generated wide optimism because of the run of mineral discoveries in the 1960s and 1970s. The opening of massive deposits of iron ore, black coal, bauxite, nickel, uranium and other minerals - mainly for the Japanese market - has produced huge revenues.

The palmy era of Californian gold, even when indexed for inflation, is proverty-stricken compared to Australian mining of the last few years.

These mineral finds often give the impression that Australia is still primarily in the pioneering era - a land of "forty-niners". But most of the new mining towns have a small population.

Despite the rise of new mining regions, most Australians continue to concentrate themselves in one part of the continent. Eight of every ten live in the southeast corner. Most Australians don't know the outback; they imagine it. Even they forget that most of it is dry, hot, lonely, infertile, and empty.

I think it is this great emptiness - this compound of space and mystery - which is primarily capturing the imagination of many young Americans. They are looking for the old America.

Christian Science Monitor, Boston, 4 February 1983

4

Australia and China: A Backward and Forward Glance

Back in the 1960s the typical Australian feared China much more than the Soviet Union. The Gallup polls made that clear. Similarly, the most popular justification for sending Australian troops to Vietnam was that they would halt the southwards march of the Chinese.

In the 1960s few Australians went to China as tourists. I went there on my own - not in a group - in 1966 and at times the atmosphere was not very welcoming. Of course Australia did not then recognise China, and as a tourist you had to collect your visa in Hong Kong and sign an affirmation that you had never been to Taiwan.

All this has changed. One of the first acts of Mr Whitlam's new government in 1972 was to grant diplomatic recognition to the People's Republic of China. We appointed an outstanding ambassador; and Stephen Fitzgerald, with his excellent knowledge of the Chinese language and his gift of theatre in speaking it, and his courtesy and sense of fun, did wonders for our name and our relations.

Many critics said - and some still repeat it - that Mr Fraser as Prime Minister would weaken our relationship with China but he greatly strengthened it. In his last years his stern anti-Soviet views delighted Chinese ears. Sometimes one reads in the press that the Chinese Government is naturally more sympathetic towards Labor than towards the Liberals and the National Party. Maybe, maybe not. Without doubt the Chinese are instinctively responsive to any Australian government which is burningly anti-Russian. I don't mean that the knowledge of such a fact should necessarily shape our foreign policy. Certainly it should affect our understanding of China, of how China sees us.

Our relations with China have blossomed and tourism is one of the fruits. Australia ranks third as the source of tourists in China. Moreover our tourism has risen by a third in the space of one year, a year of recession. We are, of all nations, the great tourist nation in China, on a per capita basis. An Australian is five times as likely as an American to visit China, and I would think - but figures are incomplete - an Australian is twenty times as likely as a European to visit China. Of course you may say that tourism from here to China is cheap but in fact it is rather expensive. Nonetheless, those Australians who tour China return, impressed, deeply impressed, even if they are pleased in part by things they would not like in their own society: automatic preference for foreigners in trains, theatres and cafes.

Chinese tourism in Australia, on the other hand, is on a small scale, and will remain insignificant. And yet Chinese culture in all its richness is here: witness the astonishing success of Chinese cultural exhibitions and the Chinese cafe. There are now far more Chinese cafes than English cafes in Australia: Victoria alone has 1,400 Chinese cafes. In Australia many of the daily newspapers bring us a flow of Chinese news, an analysis of Chinese events, which, in the course of some weeks, exceeds the news they bring from the British Isles.

It could well be that the goodwill of Australians towards China is close to its peak, at least for the twentieth century. The increase in sympathy towards China in the last ten years is remarkable, but it would be unwise to think that it will necessarily continue to increase.

I see in China at least four events or changes which could impair or weaken the present cordial relations.

Firstly, increasing concord between Russia and China. I would think there is only a one in four chance of that happening in the next 25 years; but my guess could be very wrong. After all, who in the 1950s would have confidently predicted that tensions between Russia and China would become so acute and be so prolonged? If, in the near future, Russia and China begin to smile at each other, many Australians will probably feel uneasy towards China and that new coalition of world power.

Secondly, if China were to become economically more powerful in the next quarter century - and its military potential were thereby increased substantially - many Australians would be less sympathetic towards China. One of the reasons why we are less enthusiastic towards Japan than towards China is that Japan, economically, has become a giant. Japan is almost too successful. Of course it deserves its success but we don't always admire success in others. Now it could be that China will go through an economic revolution in the next 25 years. In the last five years its economic performance has been excellent - its growth rate is far above our own. The injection of incentives and the end of the era of the dunce - otherwise known as the cultural revolution - have given new energy and purpose to the Chinese economy, and China might well shorten the gap between its standard of living and ours.

Thirdly, we employ double vision in looking at Russia and China. At present we close our eyes to China's suppression of civil liberties and its iron hand whereas we denounce similar events within the Soviet Union. The day will come when many Australians - that minority intensely interested in civil liberties and freedom of ideas - will be outspoken about events which they at present ignore in China. It is likely that the tolerance we now show towards suppression in China comes not only from the realisation that she is, in one sense, a relatively new nation, a nation reborn. More important, it comes from the hope that before long there will be an increase in civil liberties and in the right to express unorthodox views.

I doubt whether, in the near future, freedom of expression will be tolerated in China. If such freedom does come, it will be more in the economic sphere, in business enterprise, than in the cultural sphere. In the new China of the year 2000 a Rod Carnegie - a Chinese Rod Carnegie - is more likely to be tolerated than a Chinese Patrick White. If China continues to be a tightly-ordered society, a regimented society, then many influential Australians are likely to withdraw some of their sympathy.

A fourth potential for a disturbed relationship is Hong Kong. If the prosperity of Hong Kong ebbs before or after China re-occupies the colony, China's reputation will suffer. Hong Kong is one of the great economic successes of the modern world, a dynamo of a place, a triumph of the human spirit. If that dynamo runs down, and if civil liberties as well as economic enterprise in Hong Kong are weakened, then China will lose a lot of respect. Moreover if refugees leave Hong Kong in the years before the takeover, and leave by the hundreds of thousands, Australia is likely to be their main goal.

We coped with the unplanned coming of Vietnamese immigrants, the 'boat people', but that was no way to run a migration program. There are now very serious tensions in some suburbs where Vietnamese have settled in large numbers. The arrival of boat people from Hong Kong on ten times the Vietnamese scale could well create widespread tensions here and ill-will towards China.

If several of these events happen in the next quarter century, our relations with China will deteriorate - unless there are counteracting events moving in the opposite direction. I see little likelihood that China and Russia will shake hands, some likelihood that China will become economically strong, a great likelihood that her regime will necessarily remain regimented, and some risk that the repossession of Hong Kong will create tensions. Therefore I will be surprised if, during the next 25 years, our relations with China are always as relaxed as they are today. But so long as we are not taken by surprise by temporary disagreements, and so long as we continue to accept that we are very different societies and cultures, then we can cope with these difficulties. How sensibly nations cope with disagreements is the real test of their relations, not the flowery toasts drunk at state banquets.

For a few minutes I wish to examine our own country more closely. This is a placid period in our history. The seas to our north seem exceptionally calm, and we do not particularly see the threat of invasion. In the last hundred years there has been no period of ten years, I believe, in which we have - rightly or wrongly - felt so secure. A century ago we feared the Germans and the French and their designs on the south-west Pacific. We temporarily, in the 1880s, feared the Russians. We feared the Chinese, coming, unarmed, to the gold diggings, and then in about 1900 we began to fear the Japanese. After the defeat of the Japanese in 1945 there was a fear of what was called world communism. And when world communism split up, many Australians specially feared China. But since the early 1970s a calm has descended, a calm almost unique in our history, and our cordial relations with China are a crucial cause of that calm. What I am saying is so obvious that I don't think I have seen it expressed before.

So here we are, living in a freak phase of our history: no longer very worried (except those who live in the north) about our northern shores, possessing healthy relations with Japan and exceptionally friendly relations with China, having tetchy but manageable relations with Indonesia, and feeling uneasy about the Soviet Union but thinking Afghanistan is far away. It is not entirely a period of serenity because so many - especially the young - are perturbed by fears of nuclear war or some kind of technological disaster; but these are fears about the whole world, not particularly fears about Australia's vulnerability.

In this last decade we have felt unusually secure in our possession of this continent: we have come to feel almost too secure. Even our surveillance is inadequate. We are not very capable of preventing the illegal importing of drugs or exporting of gold; and we are not sufficiently capable of exercising the quarantine - human and animal and plant - which this isolated continent especially requires and which any self-respecting nation exercises. We are not even very capable of directing and regulating our immigration policies. Unless we have sensible attitudes to defence and surveillance we cannot even exercise the normal sovereignty of a banana republic or a sheepskin republic. Even to control our own internal destiny, even to be masters of our own society, we need far more control over our coast than we at present possess.

We were pretty proud when our yacht won the America's Cup, and the delight was compounded because victory was won in foreign waters. It will be ironical if, in the next quarter century, we are unable sufficiently to control our own coastal waters even to regulate the arrival, the peaceful arrival, of Asian refugees or wanderers. We should continue to welcome a variety of Asian immigrants, but they should come on our terms, through our choosing, and in numbers with which our society can cope.

I am not saying we are in danger. We are not, in my view. I am not saying we need very heavy defence expenditure, though experts tend to say we need more intelligent defence expenditure. But if large sections of Australians continue to see surveillance and defence as irrelevant or immoral, then the day might well come when our society - a relatively prosperous and free society - ceases to exist.

Nor am I saying that China in the near or medium future is in any way a danger to our independence. We cried 'wolf' about China in the 1960s; we enormously exaggerated its military power and we probably misread its leaders' intentions in Vietnam. And that is another reason why, amongst youngish Australians, the whole military world, defensive as well as offensive, has become unsavory.

I myself have difficulty in accepting the following ideas which are at present widely held in Australia and which limit our ability, in the long term, to maintain our independence as a nation.

I do not accept the widespread idea that we need only token defence forces if we resolve that henceforth we will be neutral in any war. Countries which successfully have proclaimed their neutrality have always been capable, in a crisis, of defending themselves to some degree. Moreover a nation can only be neutral by consent. Sweden and Switzerland were neutral in World War II because Germany permitted them to be neutral.

It is equally difficult to accept the widespread idea that if we have a strong ally we do not need reasonable defence forces. Sometimes the strong ally cannot help quickly enough. The greatest trauma in our history came because we relied too much on an ally, Great Britain, who in the end could not help us. Fortunately, early in 1942 the United States came to our aid but it would not necessarily have come to our aid if the strategy of the American war effort had not made Australia a vital place.

Likewise there is at present, in Australia as elsewhere, the widespread idea that it is wrong even to possess conventional weapons on any scale. This argument maintains that to fight a conventional war is dangerous because it might soon lead to a nuclear war. But hundreds of conventional wars have been fought since the invention of nuclear weapons, and so far not one of those wars has escalated into a nuclear war.

Finally, guilt is widely felt at present, especially by idealists. Many Australians imply that we have no moral right to defend this continent because we seized it from the Aboriginals, and because we do not open our ports, open them freely, to any Asian who wishes to enter. I have some sympathy with this view. And yet the fact remains that just as the Aboriginals, in their long reign over this land, had many triumphs, so we too since 1788 have had our triumphs.

We forget the greatest of our triumphs. Today this land supports some forty times as many people as it supported in Aboriginal times. This land, today, not only supplies the 15 million Australians with nearly all their needs but supplies food to tens of millions in other lands - stretching from China and the Soviet Union to Egypt - and supplies fibres to tens of millions of other lands, and supplies minerals to hundreds of millions in other lands. Our occupation of this continent, tragic for the Aboriginals, has been a gain to mankind as a whole.

If the founders of the Commonwealth could see Australia today, they would be proud and they would also be puzzled. They would be proud to see a nation possessing almost five times as many people as it did in 1901, possessing much greater prosperity, and exercising some influence in the intellectual and scientific world. But they would also be puzzled that Australia probably had no more ability to patrol the vulnerable parts of its coast, nor to defend itself, than was possessed in say 1911. As defence fears and hopes had been one of the main reasons for creating the Commonwealth, their puzzlement, today, would be acute.

Address to the National Press Club, Canberra,
22 November 1983

5

The Dilemma of Asian Immigration

I do not accept the view, widely held in the Federal Cabinet, that some kind of slow Asian takeover of Australia is inevitable. I do not believe that we are powerless. I do believe that we can, with good will and good sense, control our destiny.

Mr West, our Immigration Minister, sees our "Asianisation" as inevitable. Who knows what he means? There are fifty different Asias: there is a China Asia and a Pakistan Asia; there is a peasant Asia and a big-city Asia; there is a democratic Asia and a hierarchical Asia. Each Asia has its merits and defects.

If Mr West believes that our country is bound to be Asianised, it is vital for him to indicate which Asia we should as a nation prefer, and which Asia his department prefers.

For in that matter we do have a choice. And we should exercise that choice intelligently.

As a people, we seem to move from extreme to extreme. In the past thirty years the Government has moved from the extreme of wanting a white Australia to the extreme of saying that we will have an Asian Australia and that the quicker we move towards it the better.

Both arguments, old and new, stress the inevitable. The old white-Australia policy saw the 'yellow peril' as inevitable - unless Australia refused admission to every single Chinese, Japanese and other Asian. The argument was extremist and unbalanced - like the white-Australia policy which it buttressed.

The new policy of an Asian Australia suffers from the same fault. It sees us as powerless unless we adopt extreme policies.

One flaw in the old white-Australia policy was its extreme arrogance and its insensitivity to the opinions of many nations outside Australia. The flaw in this new Asian Australia policy is perhaps its arrogance and its insensitivity towards a large section of Australian opinion.

I detect a strong strand of guilt in the present policy towards immigrants from Asia, especially South-East Asia. Some guilt is understandable because Australian forces fought in Vietnam and therefore had some part in the dislocation of that region. But Australia's part in that war was tiny compared to that of France, the United States, the arms suppliers of Eastern Europe and the West, and some nations and peoples of eastern Asia.

We belong to the world, and we have to show compassion and share responsibility. But if the present inflow of immigrants from South-East Asia is a measure of the size of our guilt, various other nations, on the basis of their population, should take a hundred times as many South-East Asian refugees as we take.

As a people and as a Government, Australia is too fearful of international criticism, especially of uninformed criticism. Every nation in eastern Asia has stronger immigration restrictions and expresses its racial and cultural preferences even more positively than we express ours.

We are also the prisoners of our map as well as our past. Many Asians and Australians believe that because we hold a large area we should accept more immigrants from the crowded lands of eastern Asia. But the real Australia, where we live and where the soil and water are adequate, is not large. It consists of two coastal strips, one in the south-west and the other in the east and south-east.

The Australian Government should stress, in its overseas publicity, that much of Australia is more like the Gobi Desert or the Sahara than the banks of the Yarra or the Hunter. Such publicity will not be an easy task.

I have visited China annually in the past six years. Educated Chinese usually blink when I explain, in lectures or interviews, that much of Australia is uninhabited simply because nobody can exist there. Facts are facts, and we should tell them to the world.

The fact that we are one of the world's seven biggest lands does not give us an obligation to take in a disproportionate number of refugees. It is the cities which determine our ability to absorb migrants and give them a contented way of life. And our cities and our urban economy have serious unemployment.

The unemployment in many Australian cities, more than any other factor, causes the present unease about the increasing rate of Asian immigration. These are the suburbs where the Asians are most likely to settle. These are the suburbs where they are most likely to work. But these are the suburbs where the rates of unemployment tend to be the highest.

It is easy for me in my secure job to say that I welcome Asian immigrants. I do welcome them, but they don't compete with me for work, and they don't alter the way of life where I live. I am not sure, however, that I would be so welcoming if I was out of work.

Nor would I cheer if I was in work but paying more taxes than I could afford to pay, and seeing these taxes paying the dole to Asians flocking into my neighborhood.

I support the idea, disseminated from Canberra, of a multicultural Australia. But many of the Ministers, backbenchers and civil servants who preach the merits of that society still, in their private life and much of their public life, prefer a one-culture Australia. Multi-culturalism is often what is good for other people.

The poorer people in the cities are the real sufferers, and see themselves as such, in the fact of increasing Asian immigration. They are generally the least educated section of society, and rightly or wrongly are more wary of large scale Asian immigration. They are the silent ones upon whom Canberra, perhaps unthinkingly, is now trampling.

Ultimately it is not the politicians, it is not Canberra, which decides whether an immigration program will succeed. They shape the program, they finance it, they give it an ideology. It is public opinion which ultimately decides whether an immigration program will succeed. At present, the Government is shunning a vital section of public opinion.

It is in the interests of those Asian immigrants already here, and especially those who have contributed so much to this country, that the pace of Asian immigration should be slower. Many Asian immigrants, now naturalised and proud to be Australian, sense that the welcome to them is not as friendly as it was a few years ago.

A multicultural society has great merits, if it really functions. But when it fails to function it can be a sad story, as the history of South Africa and parts of the United States make clear.

Australia, to be a nation worth living in, must be monocultural as well as multicultural. It must possess shared values as well as different values. The Hawke Government, far more than the Fraser Government, has been unwittingly undermining these shared values when it insists that an immigration policy does not require a large-degree of public consent or tolerance.

Our tolerance as a nation has come a long way since 1950. We have begun to come to terms with the Aborigines, we have come to realise that they too had a civilisation. We are coming to realise that they have rights to this land.

Likewise we are far more tolerant than we were to those who are not of British descent. And we are far more tolerant than we were to those not of European descent. All these are welcome advances. As a nation, as a people, we have gained perspective: we have gained some sense of proportion. We should not undermine our gains.

<u>The Age,</u> 20 March 1984

6

The Man Who Struck it Rich

He would have been 100 last year but I forgot to celebrate his birthday.

At first sight he was the most ordinary of men. He was so everyday, so casual, so low-key, so poker-faced that he made the average Australian look like a swashbuckler. But he did so much for his country that to put him on a new postage stamp would merely pay lip service to him.

His name was Campbell Miles and I guess only two in a thousand Australians have heard of him. And yet every one of us has probably received, in pay packet or pension or superannuation, something from his life.

When I first met him he must have been in his early 70s.

We yarned for a while and then he delved into his right pocket. It was a sort of old-time general store, holding a bit of everything. He came up with a thin iron nail, a horseshoe nail, that seemed to remind him of a phase of his life in the bush.

In a slow, husky voice he began to talk about the workhorses he had owned and, inch by inch, a little about his own life. It all had to be plucked from his memory - like the nail in his pocket. "Who'd be interested in my life?" he said.

He had worked in Melbourne before going bush where he eventually became a carter and ploughman, driving a team of Clydesdales in the wheat paddocks of the Wimmera.

His found his way to Broken Hill, a kind of Gold Coast for the itinerants of that era - so long as they could work hard. There, in 1908, he heard that gold had been found near the Gulf of Carpentaria. Buying a pushbike and packing his swag he set out from Broken Hill to ride across the vast plains.

I think the gold rush was later called Kidston, after the Queensland premier of the day. It was not attractive for a latecomer. The gold was scarce, and even a drink of cool water was a luxury.

"Cam" Miles sold his bike - he needed the money. In the end he made a wheelbarrow to carry his possessions to the nearest railway.

Fifteen years later, still an optimist, he decided to be a prospector again. He had gone up in the world; not for him the bicycle and home-made wheelbarrow.

He set out from Muttaburra in central Queensland towards the Northern Territory with one gelding, two mares and three packhorses. He travelled in easy stages, usually halting for the day as soon as the sun began to sting.

He was leisurely, and he would stop in one place for a week because the feed for his horses was lush, or he would halt because somebody camping nearby was a fine storyteller, or he would stop to read a book - one of those railway-bookstall paperbacks which a passerby had "lent" him.

Banjo Paterson or Henry Lawson were his favorites, but even a month-old newspaper blown by the wind against the trunk of a gum tree would make him halt and read.

Drought was setting in and he became cautious before venturing on to the next waterhole. After a year on the track, a whole year, he had not even reached the western border of Queensland.

Early in 1923 he passed beyond the most westerly railway station and followed the mail-coach route from Duchess towards Camooweal and the NT border. He himself, years later, showed me some of his camping places, down by the dry riverbeds, away from the dust of the road.

One morning after making camp and fastening the bells to his grazing horses, he walked towards the red-brown hills nearby. He carried a blacksmith's hammer, the kind used for shoeing horses.

And that's how he found the first silver-lead at Mount Isa - simply by chipping the rock with his hammer, inspecting the fragments and observing how heavy they were.

Ultimately the mining engineers and company promoters arrived, and he vanished from the field that he had found and prospected.

For thirty years he lived humbly, almost anonymously, in Victoria, before returning to what was now one of the world's great base-metal fields.

He made his last visit to Mount Isa in 1962, about three years before his death. I went with him, by train, and he was fun to travel with.

Day after day he would peer out of the train window to inspect the countryside. "Poor mining country, that", he would say. He would ask in vain at the railway refreshment rooms for an obscure brand of pipe tobacco or a bag of boiled lollies, and be content with two slices of toasted raisin bread ("Not too much of that there butter, thanks").

He was the best of Australians, and nothing gave him more pleasure than the fact that the field he had discovered was giving work to thousands of people.

Everyone said he was lucky, but he also had stamina, alertness, intense curiosity and patience. If luck came his way he was likely to grasp it.

I sometimes think that we are inclined, more than other nations, to give too much emphasis to luck.

Perhaps the first hundred years of our history did resemble a lottery for many people. The convict years and their rewards and punishments were in part a lottery. The gold rushes seemed to be a lottery.

The fate of the sheep farmer and the cocky farmer sometimes depended on the turning of the capricious wheel that we call drought.

People like Campbell Miles were important because they shaped luck much more than it shaped them. Perhaps that's why I should have remembered his 100th birthday.

<u>Melbourne Herald</u>, 13 September 1984

7

A Brown Christmas

It seems remarkable that Christmas crossed the world so easily.

Coming from the land of snow and holly it set itself down, beneath our blue sky and hot wind, and eventually flourished even more than in Europe. But few settlers at Sydney Cove in 1788, or at Perth and Brisbane in the 1830s, imagined that Christmas would take root so strongly.

Facing their first Christmas here, most Europeans felt bewildered. "A strange Christmas day," lamented a visitor in Melbourne in 1860, "being intolerably hot." How he missed his English fireside, the icy air outside, and the relatives gathered together.

Women probably did more than men to carry Christmas to this new land. On Christmas Eve they gathered green boughs to decorate veranda and kitchen. They plucked any white-flowering bush and called it, nostalgically, the Christmas Bush.

In their enthusiasm they almost made the snow appear before the eyes of children who had never seen snow or sniffed roasting chestnuts.

In Western Australia by the 1860s one settler noted that excessive heat had come to seem normal for Christmas. The heat made for lethargy. But some of the Australian lethargy came from the bottle more than the sun. Especially in the men's camps, heavy drinking marked Christmas Day.

Far out in the bush, Christmas was a chancy affair. The German explorer, Ludwig Leichhardt, making his way in 1844 from Brisbane to northern Australia, noted in his diary that Christmas dinner was "suet pudding and steamed cockatoos."

Colonel Warburton, exploring in Western Australia a generation later, did not even have the suet. With an axe he cut into three bee-holes in search of native honey and found none. Sweltering and starving, he envied his friends in distant Adelaide, sitting down to Christmas dinner.

By 1882, Christmas in the main Australian towns was prolonged in a way unimaginable in Europe and North America. That year Christmas Day fell on a Monday, and most Australian offices and factories were closed from Friday night to Wednesday morning.

European visitors tut-tutted: "Whatever is the world coming to?" The long Australian Christmas was only just beginning.

Boxing Day here became widespread as a holiday long before it was common in Europe. Boxing Day was for picnics and race-meetings. Every two-horse town had a race meeting or a sports day on December 26.

When a bishop visited a small bush church and questioned the children about Christmas, he was surprised by the answer. As John O'Brien wrote in his popular poem "Tangmalangaloo", a gangling boy quickly told the bishop the significance of Christmas Day: "It's the day before the races at Tangmalangaloo."

My own memory of childhood Boxing Days is honeyed: picnics on the rug on the grass, other families joining us, the food so special because it was that other family's Christmas leftovers.

Just as Charles Dickens summoned magic in his story of "A Christmas Carol", so Henry Lawson caught the wonder of bush Christmases in a short story which will be read even more widely a century hence. He called it "Ghosts of many Christmases".

He told of his childhood on the goldfield of Gulgong (NSW) where Santa Claus came in many faces and spoke in many accents: perhaps an Irish Santa with his brogue or a Scandinavian Santa, blond beneath his red hood.

And there was certainly a Chinese Santa, a well-known storekeeper Sun Long Te, who gave Chinese dolls to the children of his customers and "strange, delicious sweets that melted in our mouths."

In the huts of the small farmers plum puddings were cooked weeks before Christmas and hung from the rafters with the same respect given to bacon. On Christmas Day the pudding was brought down and boiled again before it decorated the rough-made dinner table.

Henry Lawson wrote with some emotion about Joe the Drover - away for a year - and now riding his horse day after day in the hope of reaching his wife at Christmas. He came in sight at sunrise on Christmas morning, dusty and bedraggled.

He arrived in some triumph because his pay cheque was unbroken. In that era of easy spending, an uncashed cheque was the best gift a bushman could carry home.

Australians of those days still tended to remain puzzled by a Christmas which arrived at the height of summer. And yet the summer enabled Australians to celebrate Christmas more vigorously than they had celebrated it in their own cold homelands.

Summer was the sensible season for holidays here, and new holidays were increasingly added, forming a long break which was unknown in the northern hemisphere. Christmas eventually came to dominate our calendar of leisure.

There remains today, in our carols, paintings and Christmas cards, an insistence that the season belongs to snow. Large numbers of third-generation Australians going abroad for the first time long to find a white Christmas.

Curiously, the British Isles normally do not have a white Christmas. Dickens' stories did much to make snow seem normal at Christmas. Recent studies of British weather show his own childhood Christmases were marked by exceptional falls of snow.

Thus it was a freak combination of events which made generations of Australians, sweltering on the front veranda, nostalgic for a white Christmas which their ancestors, in fact, had rarely seen.

Happy Christmas!

Melbourne Herald, 20 December 1984

8

Celebrating the Wrong Australia Day

Australia Day should be a special celebration but the day continues to be a long yawn.

The Americans remember the landing of the Pilgrim Fathers but we cannot find a fit way of celebrating an Australian voyage which makes the Pilgrim Fathers, in comparison, look like Sunday-afternoon yachtsmen.

One reason for the failure of Australia Day is simple. We have chosen the wrong day.

January 26 is not an important day in our history, and even the increasing publicity from Canberra will not shape it into an important day.

Australia Day should celebrate the end of one of the most notable voyages ever undertaken, anywhere. For eight and half months an English fleet had made its slow way across the globe, calling at the Canary Islands, at Rio, and finally Capetown, before sailing eastwards into the vast unknown of the wind-swept Indian Ocean.

Governor Phillip's eleven ships could well have been a bigger fleet than any which had previously crossed the world in time of peace.

It dwarfed the expeditions which first landed colonists in Canada and the United States.

Whereas the settlers who landed at New Plymouth, near Boston, numbered only about 120, more than 1,000 people were landed at Sydney in 1788.

Compared to those early settlers of North America, the Australians were far from help. The nearest place of help - the closest corner store - was Capetown in South Africa.

The governor, after the settlement at Sydney was nine months old, had to send his ship *Sirius* to buy flour and other supplies in Capetown; and in the course of collecting supplies the ship actually sailed around the globe, passing Cape Horn on the outward voyage and south of Cape Leeuwin (WA) on the homeward voyage.

It is strange that the saga of setting up such a remote settlement should not ignite the public imagination. It is odd that our present Australia Day fails to recapture the magic and sheer audacity of these events.

What has gone wrong? Why do we neglect an occasion tailored for television, an occasion which many other nations would seize as a national day?

January 26 marks the decision, after Botany Bay proved dry and unattractive, to move the settlement to Sydney Harbour. On that day a few men landed at Sydney Cove and erected a flagpole for the Union Jack.

That ceremony was simply an event for officials. It was a day for bureaucracy, and therefore is unlikely to catch fire as a national day.

When the flag was ceremonially raised, the convicts probably were in the ships, locked below. As far as we know, no woman was present at the flagpole at Sydney Cove that day. Nor was an Aboriginal present, unless watching in puzzlement from a distance.

This ceremony marked the beginning of Sydney but not the founding of New South Wales nor the founding of modern Australia. January 26 was really Sydney's birthday.

After the Commonwealth was formed in 1901, there was a case for selecting a new day of nation-wide significance.

An ideal choice would have been January 18 when the first of the ships entered Botany Bay, and Governor Phillip and a few of his men walked ashore, stepping on to dry grassland which they thought was like the moors of England. But

Botany Bay savoured of convicts, and it was still the fashion to sweep the convict past under the nation's carpet.

So by default as much as by decision, Sydney's day became Australia Day. The day meant little to four of the six states because they had initially been settled from England or other places rather than from Sydney.

The day did not even seem to mean much to Sydney and now is celebrated with only half a cheer.

The real Australia Day - if we are to continue to celebrate it in January - is January 3 when the First Fleet sighted the white rocky peaks of southern Tasmania or preferably January 18 when the first ship, the tiny *Supply*, entered Botany Bay, her voyage of eight months over at last.

To set foot in a new land and to begin making a nation. That is the day for people to celebrate.

Increasingly, however, critics are denigrating attempts to commemorate 1788. They argue, with some justice, that Aboriginals have little reason to celebrate that event.

The fact remains that the arrival of the First Fleet from England led to the shaping of a nation whose people soon had many advantages which down-trodden Europeans did not then possess.

It is true that the coming of Europeans was at first a tragedy for most Aboriginals, but we overlook the infinitely larger number of lives that were saved - and are still saved in the Third World - by the food and fibres grown by the new settlers in Australia.

We forget that the Aboriginals, not through their own fault, had sat on rich resources and been unable to use them.

In the past hundred years, tens of millions of lives have been made possible, and tens of millions of lives have been saved, by the more efficient use of those soils which the Aboriginals neglected.

The arrival of the First Fleet in 1788 is still an event to remember, with pride as well as humility. And it will be celebrated with success when at last the governments, federal and state, realise that January 26 should never be the national day.

Melbourne <u>Herald</u>, 17 January 1985

9

'Sorry Australia, That's Not Real Money'

This month will go down in memory as the month of the diving dollar.

The dive took us by surprise. No doubt a few canny money-men half-expected it and even expedited it, but they were simply giving a push to a dollar which was already going down.

John Stone, in his Shann Lecture last year, warned that this kind of event could happen, but in Canberra he was silenced by indignant replies of: "How dare you say that!" Now the international money market has repeated its version of John Stone's warning.

We are shocked by the dive of the dollar partly because we had been told, especially in the long election campaign last November, that the eyes of an admiring world were fixed upon our economy.

Mr. Keating, as Federal Treasurer, had recently received an international award in recognition of his willingness to tackle the grave economic problems he had inherited from the previous government.

The award was a special tribute to his decision to float the Australian dollar, to expose it to the full inspection of the whole world of money. The dive of our dollar in the past few weeks is the unpredicted result of that mean-eyed inspection.

We are also surprised by the dive of the dollar because, on the eve of the State election, an international organisation said we owned just about the fastest-growing economy in the world. I can't even find the name of that organisation in the newspapers of recent weeks. It is suddenly silent.

We have been emphatically told by the world of money that the Lucky Country is becoming a fool's paradise.

We went to pay our bills overseas and were politely informed by the officials who scrutinised our money: "We're sorry Australia, but that's not real money."

It has happened to us before, even though the financial system then operating was different. It happened to us on the eve of the depression of the early 1890s. It happened in milder form in the Menzies era.

The only close parallel to the events of the past few weeks was in the first stages of the world depression of the '30s. The English pound, rather than the U.S. dollar, was then our yardstick, and our own Australian pound was about to fall.

Between January 4, 1931 and the end of that month, the Australian pound dived by just on twenty per cent before recovering a little.

If my calculations are correct, the Australian dollar this month fell even more quickly, declining by 19 per cent, before some recovery began.

The fall of our currency in the depression of 1931 had created a slightly lower sense of shock because the fall was largely shaped by Australians, led by Alfred Davidson of the Bank of New South Wales.

In contrast our recent experience was more humiliating because the dive of the dollar had the appearance of being a decision made overseas and quite outside our control. It was also more unexpected.

Our position today is far more comfortable than it was in the '30s depression. The economy is healthier and unemployment is much lower - except for the young.

At the same time the shock created by our fallen dollar can be a useful shock. Compared to most advanced nations, our economy has performed poorly in the past fifteen years. The fall of our dollar is in effect an accusation by the world that we are not quite as good as we think we are.

A major reason for the fall is the plight of many of our mines and farms. Thus the world price of copper is so low, by historical standards, that an enterprise as huge as Mt Isa is more like a deep financial sink than a mine.

Australia's income from exports is much lower than we expected but we are still busily importing goods and their price has certainly not fallen.

It is sad to say so, but the evidence of the past week suggests that, even in the midst of this economic shock, a large body of influential opinion in Australia does not understand the rules of national solvency.

This week on radio state and federal politicians - not Cabinet Ministers - made it clear that if they had their way they would impede even more some of Australia's main export industries. Significantly, the interviewers did not even ask the politicians whether such a policy might aggravate the problem occupying the week's headlines.

I know it is easy to blame our economic performance as a nation. We blame politicians too much, probably because they claim credit for too much.

Our own ignorance is even more to blame. Most of us live in cities and have little contact with the traditional export industries because they are remote.

More and more of us work in the sheltered public sector, where we cannot lose our job and so are less sympathetic to the needs and problems of the more adventurous industries.

Above all, we don't realise that much of our traditional success as a country has come from our willingness to borrow or devise the latest technology. We are no longer so willing, and so inventive.

New technology often destroys a few hundred jobs in the short term but creates thousands in the medium term. Unfortunately we now think only of the short term.

The dive of our dollar is really the outside world telling us what we should have told ourselves: "Wake up, Australia!"

Melbourne Herald, 28 February 1985

10

Is the Australian Flag Out of Date?

If some Australian genius could design a new flag which simultaneously satisfied admirers and critics of the present flag, we would all be gainers.

A flag should be a symbol of national unity, but the present flag is not entirely successful because a vocal minority of Australians dislike it or are not at ease with it.

Certainly, the new flag unveiled this month by the Ausflag syndicate will not satisfy most Australians, and if the Hawke Government were ever to impose this new flag on us it would be provocatively divisive.

The Union Jack which sits in the corner of the Australian flag is at the heart of the controversy. Most of the flag reformers want to obliterate it, but the more I look at their arguments the more I wonder why they are taken so seriously.

Some of the flag reformers argue that the Union Jack is misleading because we are no longer primarily of British descent. Mr Grassby is one of the persistent purveyors of statistics which pretend to show that the ancestry of the typical Australian has been changed drastically since 1945.

It has changed, but not as drastically as we are led to believe. If the ancestry of today's Australians is calculated, and Dr Charles Price of the Australian National University has done the sums, then 75 per cent of the total population is, by descent, from the British Isles and 20 per cent is from continental Europe.

We should praise the contribution which Italians, Greeks and other post-war immigrants in their diversity have made to Australia, but the fact remains that British customs and institutions and people of British descent still characterise Australian life. The present flag is therefore not a distortion.

But even if no immigrants since 1945 had come from the British Isles, and even if the English language ceased to be spoken in our parliaments, the case for removing the Union Jack from the flag would not necessarily be powerful.

It is absurd to argue that national flags - like computers - must always be up to date.

Many Australians argue that it is misleading to display the Union Jack on our flag because nearly all our political links with Britain have been severed. On the strength of that misguided argument, the United States' flag should never have been designed.

It is a modification of the British red ensign which flew over Boston and New York until the revolution began in 1775. When the Americans revolted against the British, they overprinted the red background of the British ensign with alternate white stripes.

An Italian-born friend, while not unsympathetic to our flag, told me last week that the time had come to change it. "It's out-of-date," he said.

He withdrew his argument when reminded that Italy's naval flag is adorned with the emblems of four Italian maritime republics - Venice, Genoa, Amalfi and Pisa. That flag is hopelessly "out-of-date", not only because those republics disappeared long ago but also because Pisa today can barely float a gondola and Amalfi owns only little fishing boats, whereas Naples - absent from the flag - is one of Europe's great ports.

As for the green, white and red colors of the Italian flag, they are more outmoded than the Union Jack on our flag. Those colors, representing faith and hope and charity of the old Catholic Italy, no longer hold relevance for millions of atheists and agnostics in modern Italy.

If a nation's flag is to be pedantically envisaged as mainly an information sheet, then Britain herself would have to change her flag, for the cross of St. Patrick - one of the flag's three crosses - is far less appropriate than it was in 1802 when Britain ruled all of Ireland.

Likewise, France would have to change her handsome flag of red, white and blue. The white traditionally stood for the king, but the French monarchy has been dead for more than a century.

We should not be gullible when we hear the complaint that the Australian flag highlights a British link which no longer is so relevant. Most of the old and famous flags in the world are even more answerable to similar criticisms.

If the years should come when French citizens say that the French tricolor must be abandoned because it displays the white colors of the overthrown monarchy, and if the year comes when Americans call for the replacing of those flag strips which retain the British red, then we might take more seriously the parallel arguments that are daily directed against the Australian flag.

Melbourne Herald, 20 March 1986

11

They View Australia's History as a Saga of Shame

The present debate about the Australian Bicentennial Authority in part conceals the government's failure and our failure as a people to tackle the big question: how far has Australia come and where is it going?

Mr Hawke in Canberra has been unable to say positively what he is celebrating in 1988. If he believes in Australia - as surely he does - he should set out boldly what we are celebrating. So far, however, he seems to have been subservient to three minority interests and neglectful of the great majority of Australians and their special interest in 1988.

The first minority group is the Aborigines. I respect a government which tries to see eye to eye with Aboriginal viewpoints. Most Aborigines, understandably, are not excited by celebrations that recall 1788. They are conscious of what they have lost and what they believe they have to lose. At the same time, a sense of sympathy towards Aborigines should not prevent a celebration of all the gains that have come since 1788. Many celebrations take account of gains as well as losses: Anzac Day is a simple example, for it celebrates loss as well as gain.

Second, the Government in Canberra, and in most of the States, is now wary of offending the vocal, richly subsidised but small multicultural lobby. The power base of this lobby is in the advisory councils of the immigration department in Canberra, in the State agencies and ministries of ethnic affairs, and in some of the churches. Public opinion polls leave little doubt that most Australians do not support the present version of multiculturalism, or what they understand by that word. It is likely that most of the post-war immigrants from continental Europe and Asia do not support multiculturalism.

While they rightly believe that every language should be genuinely tolerated in Australia, I am not sure how far they believe that foreign languages and customs should be positively encouraged at the taxpayer's expense or that of their own children's educational future. The great majority of post-war immigrants, and the great majority of Australian-born citizens, believe we should be one nation, not a nation of many nations.

The multicultural industry is the creation of Mr Grassby in the Whitlam Government, and especially of Mr Fraser in the late 1970s. The Hawke Government and various State Governments carried it on - likewise for electoral gain. It is a legitimate point of view: people are entitled to hold it. But its viewpoint is often disdainful of the main period of Australian history which the Bicentennial Authority was set up to celebrate.

The multicultural lobby has little respect for the history of Australia between 1788 and 1950. In the eyes of multicultural supporters, Australia was a desert between 1788 and 1950 because it was populated largely by people from the British Isles and because it seemed to have a cultural unity, a homogeneity which is the very antithesis of multiculturalism.

In the true cultural sense, however, Australia before 1950 was a multicultural society because the cultural difference between Irish Catholics and Scottish Presbyterians and Cornish Methodists and many other groupings was intensely felt, at times too intensely. These differences permeated politics, culture, education, sport, business, the public service and every branch of national life. The cultural differences in today's so-called multicultural society are, so far, not acute. If they were as acute as the old conflicts in the 19th century, we would probably hear much less advocacy of multiculturalism.

It is normal to see multiculturalism today as simply the Italian cafe, the Latvian folk dance, the Croatian soccer club or the Balinese artist. Those activities, welcome and charming as they are, do not change a way of life. They are often the veneer, the froth. I am far from sure that, in the beliefs held by most people, we are as multicultural as we were in 1855. Serious multiculturalism is potentially divisive and can be explosive. That's a lesson from the Punjab, Sri Lanka, Malaysia, Indonesia, and a score of other countries.

Unfortunately, too many supporters of the multicultural industry dismiss Australian history - the history, that is, until they themselves arrived in this land - as hardly worth celebrating. To them Australian history, in the days of the convicts or gold rushes or Gallipoli, is pale compared with the full-blooded and long history of their own land. But to many of us, our history is valuable because it is our history and, for better or worse, distinctive. It does contain many events to be proud of as well as some to be sorry for.

Every Australian today, whether Chinese or English by ancestry or Greek by birth, becomes the heir to our history simply by being an Australian citizen. A recent immigrant has the right to disown the history of his new land, but it is surprising that an Australian Government should kow-tow to such a disowning and subsidise its dissemination in many ways.

Support for multiculturalism is a second strong reason for Mr Hawke's lack of enthusiasm about 1988. Here indeed is a strange irony - that this creation of the politicians is beginning to tower over the politicians. They are fearful of their own child.

There is a third minority towards which Mr Hawke seems uneasy: a certain form of socialism. Many socialists have a balanced attitude to 1988. They are proud of what the average Australian has achieved, and are especially proud of our democratic tradition and the strong role of trade unions and working people's movements in our history.

But there is an influential group of socialists - present in Parliament and on several newspapers, not unknown in some parts of the ABC, and busy in some classrooms and university departments - who rarely celebrate Australia's past. They have a deep sense of grievance about much of Australia's history - the past treatment of the Chinese, of Aborigines, of women, of shearers, of seamstresses, of Italians, of Irish, of factory workers, of miners, of trade unionists, of orphans - and maybe even the personal treatment of themselves, prosperous and independent as they are.

They see Australia's history as largely the story of violence, exploitation, repression, racism, sexism, capitalism, colonialism, and a few other 'isms'. Some of their books on Australian history appear now in thundering prose, delivered from a moral height.

These historians and critics have a point of view: we should take it seriously. But by the standards of almost any utopia they care to name, Australian history in the last 200 years, for all its failings, has been a fortunate history.

Mr Hawke seems nervous of these three minorities - Aborigines, the multicultural lobby, and a section of the left.

I would be surprised if they, together, form five per cent of the adult population of this country and certainly no more than ten per cent. They are vocal, they have influence, they have a point of view, and it would be wrong to deny them their voice. The dilemma is that, if they remain too influential in Canberra, the celebrations in 1988 will be a national farce. If these voices become the dominant voices, the great majority of Australians will, emotionally, have little part in the bicentennial.

You may ask why it is that three relatively small groups should have such power? The main answer is simple. They have stormed the moral heights, even maybe the spiritual heights and captured them. Many of their spokesmen are so certain that they are right that they often throw overboard that very toleration to which they selectively appeal. From their position of moral superiority they see any opposition to certain issues as immoral. That was very much their attitude to the immigration debate of 1984.

In the past 200 years Australia has had powerful achievements and every part of the nation has contributed to them - the bush and the city, the women and the men, the shearers and the miners, the labourers and the scientists, the Catholics and the Methodists and Lutherans.

There are at last three achievements which we should be celebrating in 1988.

A first achievement was to establish one of the early democracies in modern history. In the 1850s, in most of the Australian colonies, democratic government was courageously set up under difficulties, for illiteracy was high, many of the voters were birds of passage, and most parliamentarians and ministers had no experience of public life, let alone of governing.

Soon a vote for every man was normal, the secret ballot (called the Australian ballot in many parts of the world) was devised, elections were held at least every three years, and there was freedom to hold unpopular views. Democracy flourished in Australia ahead of almost any nation in modern Europe, modern Africa or Asia. Here, certainly, is something to celebrate.

Second, Australians have, despite their numerous mistakes, developed this continent so that some twenty or fifty times as many people live here today as lived here in 1788. We not only feed ourselves but each year we feed tens of millions of people in China, Egypt and other lands.

We also supply the wool needed by scores of millions of people who live overseas and a large part of the minerals needed by hundreds of millions in other lands. In a world where most of the people still have a low standard of living, ours is an achievement.

A third achievement is that this nation of relatively few people has contributed so much to the world's stock of valuable skills and ideas. Whether it is in the separating of minerals, or in the understanding of disease, Australians have been innovative on a wide front.

These three achievements are worth celebrating because if we cease to be aware of them and the sacrifices they required, they will be imperilled.

Our prosperity, our ability to aid the standard of living of other nations, and our democratic system shouldn't be taken for granted. Every new generation will have to apply effort and skill to maintain them.

It is easy to denigrate these successes by saying they were the result of luck, or rich natural resources, or cruel exploitation. But these successes were primarily the result of hard work, common sense, skill, and faith in the future.

My view is that we should be proud of much of the ancient Aboriginal history of this land; we should be proud of much of the British history of this land; and we should be proud - early as it is to judge - of much that has happened in the last third of a century, when immigration has come from diverse sources.

My view is that we should be proud that this is a democracy, and by world standards a very tolerant democracy. We should therefore be careful of very small groups who at present are allowed to dictate to the government how we should see our past and our future.

> Annual community lecture, sponsored by Mt Eliza
> Uniting Church, 4 October 1985

12

Mr Whitlam Loads the Dice

I first met Mr Whitlam at a small meeting of the Commonwealth Literary Fund in Canberra soon after he became leader of the opposition for the first time back in 1967. There is something rather majestic about him when he is in full verbal flight, and he was flying high on that sunny afternoon.

As Leader of the Opposition, along with a leading Liberal and a Country Party politician, Whitlam sat on the fund's political committee which had to approve the recommendations that came twice a year from the fund's advisory board, of which I was the newest member.

Whitlam accepted the fact that the other two politicians could outvote him on any name we put forward. They generously recognised, however, that he was the more interested in writers. He made the most of the stage they offered him - and at times he held forth.

It was wonderful to hear him: the irony, wit, cheek, classical allusions, precise memory, and the careful choice and enunciation of words. Although he hadn't read many recent books on Australian literature he made the most of those he had read. I can still see the shine and shadow moving across the dark polished table, as he leaned forward to make his points.

Five years later, when he became Prime Minister, he had the chance to implement his own policies for the arts: and now, in his new book (*The Whitlam Government*, Viking Press), he describes in rolling prose what he did.

"Of all the objectives of my Government," he writes on page 553, "none had a higher priority than the encouragement of the arts." For Whitlam they were the wine of life.

In reading his long account of innovations in the arts, I admire much of what he recounts, but in the end he weakens his case by loading the dice.

He has a tendency to paint life in the decade before Whitlam as a Pope would portray life in the decade before Christ. He sketches a devastating picture of the music, literature and other boards which administered Canberra's cultural policies before he came to power. They were "frequently without expert membership or representation by artists themselves", he wrote.

This is far from true. The list of distinguished artists on those boards was longer than those on the present boards of the Australia Council.

His book shows a desire to put down those who worked hard for the arts before he came to power. He is especially severe on old people. Thus he notes that on the advisory board of the Commonwealth Literary Fund, the best known of the government arts agencies, the chairman was seventy-five and another member was sixty-five. If it is wrong that somebody of those ages should hold a high cultural position, one might well expect Mr Whitlam, aged sixty nine, to resign his post at UNESCO, though he fills it with distinction.

Likewise, Mr Whitlam complains that the old members of Canberra's earlier cultural boards stayed there too long. He singles out two who had held office for thirteen years. I would have thought competence and fairness should be the main criteria for holding such posts: and some members may well deserve thirteen years, while, some may not deserve thirteen days.

Once you introduce quick turnover, with members staying on a board for only a year or two, you soon run out of experienced and talented people who are qualified and willing to serve.

Thus, in February 1973, Mr Whitlam announced the names of the members of the new Australia Council and its various boards, and he argues with some truth that they "constituted the cultural galaxy of the time". Before long - and his book does not mention this - the stars of this cultural galaxy had largely disappeared.

A few were pushed out because they were too independent, but most were not reappointed because Mr Whitlam believed, perhaps as a reaction from the long tenure of the old Liberal boards, that members should serve only for brief periods.

In Mr Whitlam's last year, and by then he had many
problems on his plate, too many of the Labor Party's faithful
followers were being appointed to the Australia Council
and its boards. The dangers of political bias, which he rightly
points out did exclude Frank Hardy from a literary grant in
1968, appeared in different guise.

Of course, the Australia Council and its boards did great
work in the Whitlam era. They had more money than ever
before, there was a willingness to experiment, and there was
a new mix of people and ideas. I was proud to serve on that
first Australia Council and Literature Board, and a variety
of other new cultural committees. I am, therefore, slightly
puzzled to read, in the witty aside, that I resisted "the whole
idea of a literature board".

Mr Fraser, in his handling of the arts, receives a walloping.
We are told that at the Prime Minister's Lodge, his
preference in music was country and western and that he
"converted the music room into a spare toilet".

We are told of Fraser's frugal refusals: his refusal to buy a
stunning statue found in the Mediterranean sea, his refusal
to sign this or that convention or agreement, and above all
his "restrictive and niggardly policies".

What this book omits to say is that the "niggardly policies"
began in Mr Whitlam's final year. In his last budget in 1975,
Mr Whitlam neglected the Australia Council. While his
book maintains that he actually increased the council's
budget for the financial year, the fast inflation over which
he presided soon cut the arts budget in real terms. It fell by
twelve per cent. If my sums are correct, this was a larger cut
in real terms than the cut in any of the following seven years
of Mr Fraser's rule.

I happened to be chairman of the Australia Council in four
of those seven years and I wished that Mr Fraser would
grant more money. But his support for the arts was better
than that predicted by the great majority of artists when he
first came to power, and superior to that depicted scornfully
in this book.

Mr Whitlam's long account does not really need the bursts of high partisanship, the loaded figures, and the inaccurate tilts at those politicians who came before and after him. His record in the arts largely speaks for itself, and his willingness to promote the arts, both with eloquence and money, will be remembered long after most of his failures and his other successes are forgotten.

The Australian, 29 November 1985

13

In Praise of John Quick

John Quick should be a hero of Australian history but he is almost forgotten.

It is sad that he is in eclipse because the political lesson he taught our great-grandfathers would have prevented the Hawke government, last week, from muddling a matter of national importance.

In setting up a commission of 39 citizens to make a "fundamental review" of our Constitution, the government has turned its back on one of the brainwaves of our history: the idea that in making the Constitution the people should be masters not only of the last step but of the first step.

The decision to entrust the rewriting of the Constitution to a hand-picked team of citizens would have astonished the men who originally drafted the federal Constitution. They believed that the task was too important, too delicate and explosive, to be given to a non-elected body.

They believed, and rightly, that the people alone should decide who should write the Constitution. They accepted the plan largely devised by John Quick of Bendigo, a plan so open and so democratic that it makes the Hawke government's scheme look a little like the device of a benevolent African dictator.

Quick had come to Australia from Cornwall as a child during the gold rushes and at a tender age had worked in a noisy stamp mill and foundry. By sheer drive he had educated himself, studying law in his spare time, and eventually becoming a solicitor in Bendigo when it was the fifth largest city in Australia.

He sat in the Victorian Parliament in the 1880s, but he was in the political wilderness when he did his great work to promote the federation of the six Australian colonies.

In 1893 he went by train to a conference of federal enthusiasts at Corowa, just inside NSW, and there he masterminded the simple proposal that the people as well as the politicians should take charge of the struggling movement that was trying to create a Commonwealth.

He proposed that in each colony the people would elect ten delegates, and the assembled delegates would debate a new Constitution which in turn would be referred back to the people at special referenda. It was through that ultra-democratic process, attempted in no other country in the world, that we eventually achieved a federation.

Quick himself was elected to the Victorian delegation, played a crucial role in shaping the Constitution, and as a mark of public honor he was not opposed when he stood for Bendigo, potentially a marginal seat, at the first federal election in 1901.

He was a great Australian but he did not parade the fact. His manner and his mode of speech were plain rather than flamboyant.

It is said that his head was so large that in court his barrister's wig seemed to perch itself like a party hat. He had commonsense, patriotism and such stamina and dedication that his Sydney friend Robert Garran once called him "a steam-roller".

It sounds almost silly to say so, but his surname has been, historically, a heavy liability. Quick's formula for achieving the federation of the six colonies was not even given his name. They could hardly call it the Quick Formula because it was not a quick solution and was not intended to be.

Unfortunately no electorate honors his name, nor a suburb in Canberra. You do have to admit that it could be confusing, when asked your destination by a Canberra taxi driver, to reply "Quick". He might take you at your word.

The combination of Quick's surname, his modesty, and his failure to gold a place in a federal Cabinet for more than a year - these have eroded the public's memory of him. And yet the evidence is strong that if his unique formula had not been devised at Corowa and had not been accepted by political leaders and the public, federation would have been a hope rather than a fact in 1901.

In our long history we have few political heroes who are admired by most people, irrespective of party. Of those heroes who belong to the safe or long-dead past, only Curtin and perhaps Deakin and Lalor qualify.

Sir John Quick should be added to that list. If his achievements were better known, and if his distinctive Corowa formula were widely remembered, Mr. Hawke would have shown more hesitation in asking Cabinet rather than the Australian people to choose those who are to rewrite our Constitution.

Of course the 39 names which form the new Constitutional Commission and its various committees do command respect. Zelman Cowen, Whitlam, Hamer, Horne, Killen, McGarvie, the impressive list goes on and on. And yet too many of the 39 names have been chosen because they are sympathetic to Labor's view of what a reformed Constitution should say.

It is strange to see the Labor Party, having lamented what it sees as the breaking of our constitutional traditions, now discarding the basic tradition, that in making or remaking a Constitution, the people must always have the decisive say.

But in the end the people will have their say. And it is unlikely that they will think kindly of a Constitution rewritten by such an unrepresentative body.

Melbourne Herald, 2 January 1986

14

This Country is too Good to Ruin

Australia Day is not only an occasion for thinking of those who have gone before us but also for thinking about the present. My text for today is simple: "This country is too good to ruin".

As a nation we are running into difficulties, economic and social and political, partly because of the scarcely-noticed change in our way of thinking. I was reminded of this change when in a secondhand shop I picked up a book, written by the late Walter Murdoch in 1912 and called simply *The Australian Citizen.* The subtitle of this small blue-covered book is "An Elementary Account of Civic Rights and Duties", indicating that he saw rights and duties as linked.

In recent decades, we have moved from an emphasis on duties to an absurd emphasis on rights alone. Thirty years ago we possibly gave too much weight to the duties demanded of Australians as citizens. Now we give too much weight to all those minorities who are interested only in their rights. It is legitimate to emphasise the question "What does Australia owe me?; but it must not outweigh the question, "What do I owe Australia?"

Rights has become perhaps the commonest word in the contemporary political vocabulary. There is a Human

Rights Commission in Canberra, and very powerful it will become unless we are alert. There are Aboriginal Land Rights in federal territories and most States. And at present before federal parliament is a bill with the grand, all-pervading title of the Bill of Rights.

Other rights are insisted upon by the Human Rights Commission set up in 1981. It has affirmed the rights of disabled persons and the mentally retarded, rights with which we could hardly disagree. It also affirms the rights of young people. According to the latest *Year Book Australia* the federal government supports "the right of all young people to develop to their highest potential, which might include involvement with local institutions where they could develop their personal skills needed to create their future."

I don't know what that mouthful of words really means. It means almost nothing. We should be suspicious of a manifesto that confidently asserts the right of young people when, as a group, they have relatively less right to employment than at any previous time in our history. Compared to other age groups the young are the victims. The brunt of the present recession - unlike the depression of the 1930s - is being carried by the recent school-leavers.

A variety of rules and regulations, all sanctioned by the government, make it especially difficult for the young to obtain work. Isn't it strange for a government to assert the special rights of the young at the very time when the government ignores one of their traditional rights, the right to have a paid job. By asserting again and again that the young have special rights it disguises the fact that they now have special burdens.

The federal Family Law Act of 1975 asserts the rights of the child. And yet that law, irrespective of its other benefits, might well have done more than any other law in our entire history to undermine the welfare of those children whose rights it gravely upholds. To grant special rights to parents is very often to take away rights from children. Double-talk or woolly talk often conceals the reality of rights.

The granting of these new rights seems to be based on the idea that there is a huge national reservoir from which everyone can tap new rights - a reservoir which nobody has the obligation to refill. So many of the new rights depend on hoodwinking those who are in the process of losing their old rights.

This emphasis on special rights is visible in ethnic affairs and what is called multiculturalism. I hesitate to touch this subject but for the fact that the leading letters in *The Age* this morning attacked me for "views" I do not hold.

Our current emphasis on granting special rights to all kinds of minorities especially ethnic minorities, is threatening to disperse this nation into many tribes. An element of social cohesion is essential if a nation is to survive. A nation is ultimately bound together by a sense of shared obligations and duties. Ultimately it can be pulled apart and even shattered by an emphasis on the rights of each minority and on the virtues of divisiveness.

Another national problem - and it is also linked to the question of rights - is our economic decline. It is difficult to tell at present how fragile is our balance of payments, how vulnerable our standard of living, and how strong the chances of unemployment increasing rather than decreasing. Certainly, our economic situation, compared to other western countries, has deteriorated strongly in the last ten years and indeed the last 25 years. By world standards our place on the ladder has slipped.

Obviously we will not improve our position if we continue to plead for rights. At the end of last year, the editor of the *Far Eastern Economic Review* said that it was about time that Australia recognised the fact that the possession of rich natural resources did not automatically make a country prosperous. Some countries with few resources but with driving, energetic people were pushing far ahead of us. He warned that Australia could no longer "go on kidding itself that someone is going to give it a special teat to suck at". Our country is no longer so lucky, largely because very large numbers of us within Australia have emphasised our economic rights more than our economic duties.

In economics, as in politics, no national reservoir can stand the strain when everyone is turning on the taps and few are bothering to see that the catchments to the reservoir are working.

Previous generations of Australians created a successful democracy with a high level of freedom, a high standard of living, social cohesion to a valuable degree, and an ability to help other countries when they were in need. We are now in danger of taking these advantages for granted by an undue emphasis on rights and a neglect of duties. This country is too good to ruin.

Address to Australia Day luncheon,
Southern Cross Hotel, Melbourne, 24 January 1986

15

Tragedy for the Astronauts: A Lesson from the Titanic

The death of the seven astronauts aboard the space shuttle Challenger last week was one of those dramatic events which left us all groping for comparisons.

Commentators, made numb by the explosion and the way it was televised, searched for a way of explaining it and fitting it into history. It just didn't seem to fit.

I had gone for a walk before breakfast on the morning of the tragedy, and when I got back and turned on the radio, I heard the disaster announced on the news. I felt - I am groping for a word - bamboozled.

It was utterly unexpected, partly because so much had been accomplished so skilfully in exploring space. Moreover, we had seen the superb competence of the space program on TV at launching and after launching, whether it was a Russian dog in space or man treading on the moon.

Anything televised frequently becomes safe, at least safe for us. We are sitting on the couch or in the armchair, comfortably watching, and that compounds the feeling of security.

Events regularly taking place before us - no matter how risky - have the habit of becoming like a carton of homogenised milk, safe for another fortnight. Since the first man went into space in 1961, a journey of a mere two minutes, more than one hundred launchings had been made and only three astronauts and four cosmonauts had actually died, either on the launching pad or in space, before Challenger exploded.

This remarkable record of safety made the loss of seven lives all the more shocking, and in Washington the politicians grappled for a way of both comforting the relatives and stressing the significance of space exploration.

President Reagan likened the hazards of venturing into space to the exploring of the oceans more than four centuries ago. He spoke of Sir Francis Drake, not normally a top hero of American textbooks, a man who lived and died on the sea.

"In Drake's lifetime", said the President, "the great frontiers were the oceans.". We felt sympathy for the way in which President Reagan and his speechwriters tried to fit the sad event into the pattern of world history; yet it did not fit the pattern.

Exploration by sea has devoured infinitely more lives than exploration by space. The floors of the Atlantic, Indian and Pacific Oceans are littered with the bones and brass buttons of the crews of the early exploring ships of Spain, Portugal, Holland, France and England.

Some sea routes to the new world continued to be exploratory and dangerous because there were often no charts beyond a certain point and a captain had no sure way of knowing his own ship's longitude in very windy or foggy weather.

I have just read the story, now published in English for the first time, of the voyage by Dutchman Willem de Vlamingh, who found the Swan River in Western Australia and sent his men marching inland - one of our boldest explorers.

His original aim was to find survivors from the ship *Ridderschap van Holland*, which in 1694 set out from Capetown towards the West Australian coast and thence north to Java. Carrying 352 people, that ship was never seen again. Such disasters make the loss of the Challenger last week seem like a car accident by comparison.

Explorers in the three centuries after Vasco da Gama and Columbus died of scurvy, tropical diseases, drownings, shipwrecks and clashes with native peoples.

For the native peoples the new era of exploration was even more of a calamity, for they had no immunity to those European diseases from which they had long been isolated.

I have never seen the calculation attempted, but I would estimate that at least 9,000 European sailors must have died in voyages that could be called "exploration" in the 300 years from 1492 to 1792. That makes the lives lost in space exploration seem small indeed. The loss of Challenger was really a sign of the astonishingly high confidence, even complacency, which had begun to surround space travel.

Much of the sense of tragedy came from the presence of the New Hampshire teacher making a voyage, if you like, on behalf of all America's children. That the children of her school were all in the assembly hall, cheering her, wearing party hats and blowing whistles was a sign of super-confidence.

The space flight last week was not like the voyage of Drake or Captain Cook. It was more like the voyage of the *Titanic*.

The largest ship afloat and said to be unsinkable, she struck an iceberg on her maiden voyage in 1912 and 1,500 people were drowned.

Commentators then were astonished that a masterpiece of man's technology could prove so vulnerable. And that's probably what we were trying to say, without knowing how to say it, last week.

The Melbourne Herald, 6 February 1986

16

The Bombing of Police Headquarters - an End to an "Age of Innocence"?

The bombing of Russell St raises vital questions. Firstly, who did it? Secondly, will it inaugurate an era of violence?

We don't know who did it but many have certainly argued that the ruthless era dawned on Easter Thursday.

Mr Cain suggested that "this incident does add a terrifying dimension of violence new to Melbourne." His Police Minister, Race Mathews, said that we have now "come on the world stage for this sort of outrage."

A senior policeman - and the police response has been impressive - called it a new venture in terrorism, while the spokesman of the Victorian Council of Civil Liberties regretted that now "we have lost our innocence."

These high representatives had to assess the bombing on the spur of the moment, and yet thousands of people must have shared their feeling that the exploding bomb was not only outrageous but a sensational break from the past. But has our nation's past been so peaceful?

In the 19th century numerous Aboriginals, including women and babes in arms, were killed by European settlers in episodes which were possibly as unexpected and callous as the blast outside Melbourne's police headquarters.

Likewise it is worth recalling in this opening week of the football season that Tom Wills, whom many adjudge as the founder of Australian Rules, was lucky to have been two days riding distance from the family's sheep station in Queensland when his father and 18 other Europeans were killed by Aboriginals in 1861.

Several men now hailed as national legends endangered the life of innocent women, children and other bystanders.

Ned Kelly more than ever is a national hero, and yet the same Ned - if living today - could well behave like the thug who placed the bomb outside the police headquarters last week.

Kelly set out to derail a police train at Glenrowan: and if he had succeeded, and if the train had been travelling rapidly, the locomotive driver, fireman, guard and a party of pressmen might well have ben among the victims.

A blend of the heroic and the contemptible, Kelly virtually held as hostage many of the Glenrowan townsfolk, and knowingly or unknowingly he placed their lives at risk. Two of the innocent - a man and a boy - actually died in the shoot-out which led to the capture of Ned Kelly.

Kelly-lovers will take offence at what I say, but the Victorian Premier of 1880 could have fairly denounced Ned Kelly with the sentence rightly spoken by Mr Cain last Thursday: "It is just chopping down innocent people."

Shock is an appropriate response to the blast last Thursday, but we can hardly argue that such violence is new.

Even bombing is not as modern or as rare in Australia as we like to think. In the last decade, various cars were maliciously blown up in Melbourne, and the Hilton Hotel was bombed in Sydney, and somewhat earlier in Brisbane the Whisky A Go Go Club was blown up.

In Melbourne the ruthless bombing of police goes back
further than we care to remember. Exactly 80 years ago, in
January 1906, a bomb was thrown into the residence of Det.
Sgt. D.G. O'Donnell, in the long three-storey Royal Terrace
which still stands opposite the front of the Exhibition
Building in Nicholson St.

The bomb "cut to pieces" the couch where the detective's
daughter usually slept. The public indignation, not unlike
that of last Thursday, was mirrored in the headlines:
FIENDISH OUTRAGE AT FITZROY.

Without doubt Australia's history has been more peaceful
than that of the great majority of nations in the last two
centuries, and probably the streets and public places of
Australia are still safer than those in most countries.

And yet violence, and especially the endangering of the
innocent, has been sufficiently common in past decades in
Australia for us to think twice about suggesting that on
Easter Thursday "an age of innocence" came to an end.

The recent public investigations into the power of organised
crime in Australia should warn us that the age of innocence,
if it ever existed, is no longer with us.

Irrespective of whether a gang or a lone individual parked
the bomb outside the police headquarters, the evidence is
strong that the organisation of crime in Australia is now so
sophisticated that it makes Ned Kelly, for all his organising
skills, seem like a pale pickpocket by comparison.

Much of the first response to last Thursday's bombing was
in effect the reaction - "In Melbourne, of all places!"

This suggests that politicians have not yet digested the
warning clearly made in the Costigan report and other
ominous reports.

Melbourne Herald, 3 April 1986

17

Ah, Those Were the Days, Mr Mac!

The funeral for "Mr Mac" was yesterday. He had had a good innings, having just turned 94.

You could hardly say that he died before his time and yet in an odd way he did. He personified the adventurous, battling spirit which this country needs, but at present discourages.

He made his name by making Mac's cider, but long before he became a label on a bottle he was putting his head down and butting at the opposition.

His real name was George McGowan, he was a Manchester boy, and in 1918 he won the Military Cross on the Western Front.

The war over, he thought of migrating. Paying the large deposit of 200 pounds to a promoter of Tasmania with the formidable name of "Mr E.H. Peppercorn, AIF" he left London in 1919 in the *Ormond* as a third-class passenger, jammed like an apple in a packing case.

He always remembered his first sight of this land: "We had a full day in Perth, and were thrilled with the bright sunshine and clear atmosphere, and quite fascinated by the sight and sound of the high-stepping trotting horses harnessed to smart rubber-tyred jinkers, as they sped along the clean city streets."

Near Scottsdale he and an English mate bought a Tasmanian orchard with the absurd total of 42 different varieties of apples and pears.

I have seen Mr Mac's picture of the first load of apples, and there he is, tall and soil-stained, standing beside the flat-topped wagon with a fine draught horse between the shafts.

His first shipment to England failed. The fruit earned such a small amount he ended up paying for the privilege of exporting it. His comment on the orchard was pithy: "What a pup we had been sold."

As the market was fickle, he tried to turn unsaleable apples into cider. He managed to produce a few gallons by crushing apples with "a sharp spade and an old letterpress."

Mr Mac was learning our noble tradition of scavenging, and when he and his wife moved to Lilydale in Victoria during the 30s world depression he began to plan a cider-making business.

Buying a neglected orchard, he bought a capstan screw wine press at Yering, old brandy casks from a wine and spirit merchant in Melbourne, and oak vats at de Pury's cellars.

And of course he went to the glorious junkyard of Ma Dalley, where he found a machine for filtering the juice of apples and a second-hand bottling machine for his cider. He was in business.

In those days few people drank cider, and so it was a red-letter day when in July, 1938, *The Herald* praised his orchard and cider.

Soon he installed bigger equipment in a basement in William St in Melbourne and tried to enter the big time, he himself delivering cider in a panel van to the war-time army camps, the refreshment rooms of railway stations and, of course, the Glaciarium and the Tivoli Theatre. For his effort he actually lost money, but the time came when he made profits and employed more people.

To his delight he overheard old-timers say that his non-alcoholic cider was even tastier than Kitz's cider which, as everyone knew, "gives good complexions and prevents rheumatism". Ah, those were the days, Mr Mac!

I have no wish to advertise his business - it has long since been taken over - but many will take pleasure in his simple life story which, called 'The Core of the Apple', can still be bought at the Melbourne University's archives ($10 a copy, post free).

Two or three times I met him, his jaw jutting in defiance, his spirit forceful. The meeting over, this man of 90 would set out briskly down the street and one would notice that after so many paces the spirit was stronger than the legs and he would falter a little.

He died last Saturday, while the Labor Party was holding its state conference, and insisting there is no economic crisis.

One can support their desire to protect the unemployed, the sick and the old, but it will soon be difficult to protect anybody unless we foster those Mr Macs who provide jobs and create wealth for Australia.

And never before in our history have there been so many bureaucratic obstacles to the emergence of a new generation of Mr Macs.

Melbourne Herald, 26 June 1986

18

Don't Move House!

We have just moved house after 28 years. Don't you try it.

It's astonishing what one accumulates. We had moved into our old house the night before Collingwood won its last premiership - we actually saw it on that wet Saturday - and lo and behold I find in the corner of a cupboard the *Football Record* of the game of 1958.

The first day devoted to packing I found, under the house, a hoard of old letters that I couldn't believe existed. As a lad I worked for a Ballarat greengrocer, delivering fruit and vegetables each Saturday, and here is a black-banded envelope with a letter telling me of his death long ago.

I have read most of the arguments for and against the Australia Card but I had no idea that Australia actually issued such cards during the World War 2 - until I found under the house an Identity Card setting out my name and address and giving my tender age.

I'm lucky to have found that card because I was about to write an indignant article about Canberra's "unprecedented plan to introduce an ID card for a proud people who have never in all their history been thus enchained".

During 'the big clean-out' I took piles of old papers to the incinerator where I spent so much time reading them that the fire went out. I kept most of what I intended burning. Who knows, the day might come when I will want more than anything on earth - a clipping from the *Kalgoorlie Miner* of the 1950s and an old packet of Boomerang cigarette papers.

We seem to own thousands of books and it is hard to pack books without dipping into them. It's remarkable how one can remember the act of buying a particular book and first reading it. Some books were bought from a secondhand bookshop run by Mrs Bird at the top of Bourke St, where she tempted student-customers with shilling bundles consisting of six or seven books tied with string. Oliver Wendell Holmes's *Autocrat of the Breakfast Table* was present in most of her bargain bundles, and here was one of her copies.

When you rummage and pack, you realise how fickle your memory can be. Events you had completely forgotten, events you could swear had never happened are there, undeniable, in an old letter or postcard or book inscription.

And what do you do with 47 golf balls found under the house? I don't play golf - never have - and yet there they are, sitting in a big honey tin, collected long ago when I took Sunday afternoon walks past the greens and fairways where the Eastern Freeway now runs.

Some things you'd like to take away but fortunately can't. My one construction project was to build a sloping driveway out of 900 bluestone pitchers. I take pride in that driveway, even though that doyen of engineers, Walter Bassett, setting foot on its rough surface, sternly asked who was responsible for "that shoddy job".

Amidst the dislocation you wonder whether you should be moving at all. When the auction signboard is erected, announcing your imminent departure, you feel almost homeless.

And what about the cat? The vet said the cat would be so bewildered she would have to be nursed for the first fortnight in the new house. "A fortnight?", my wife asked with dismay.

The cat, sweet-natured, is the last survivor of the strays that have arrived over the years. Coming as a kitten, one of three, Tattie is now 107 according to the way they measure the age of cats.

"That poor centenarian cat", people said with their eyes. "How ever will she cope in the new house?"

On the day we moved - or 'the day and night' to use the phrase of the four removalists - the cat was foremost in my wife's thoughts. Taken to the new house, Tattie was kept in a quiet room, her basket shut, for some hours before she was allowed to explore. At first she heard the roar of wild beasts or the flapping of giant wings up every chimney but within a day she conveyed the distinct impressions that she owned the house and that we were merely her tenants.

She feels at home. "So she should", my wife says, "given the mountain of junk you've brought from the old house."

Melbourne Herald, 10 July 1986

19

The Day that Snow Fell

It's an exquisite sight, the snow falling in a city that rarely sees snow.

And when last Friday the snowflakes were whirled about by a gusty wind in Collins St, children clapped their hands as though some magician had appeared.

The last time snow fell on the heart of Melbourne was September 11, 1969, and the previous time was in the winter of 1951 when on three separate days it fell. The preceding snowy day was August 23, 1929 when, to be strictly true, it did not reach the city street though it landed on the rooftops of middle-distance suburbs. If this pattern continues we will be lucky to see snow again in the city this century.

They say that as a city becomes larger and its cars and heaters multiply, its chance of feeling intense cold is reduced a little, and so in my ignorance I was inclined to think that the prospect of snow reaching the City Square was gradually diminishing. But I am reliably informed that our snow usually comes in a thrusting wedge of cold air from the south, and it crosses the cold Bay and pushes straight into the city without much interference from the cocoon of warmth which the suburbs have created.

Indeed, wedges of icy air penetrated far into south-eastern Australia on several days in 1900 and 1901, laying a carpet of snow that half-buried trains in the high country of New South Wales, pushed down verandas in Bathurst and formed a white corridor stretching much of the way from Melbourne to Brisbane.

Melbourne seems to have escaped that snow, and its only record of snow around those years was on August 7, 1899, when Fitzroy Gardens resembled sugar and the boys from

Scotch College, which in those days overlooked the gardens, were said to be throwing balls of snow and hail.

Melbourne's most severe snowstorm was in August, 1849, when the town had barely 20,000 people and green paddocks lay within a mile or two of Princes Bridge. According to the *Argus* newspaper, the residents awaking that morning were "astonished to see the streets and housetops covered with snow to the depth of several inches".

Melbourne did not have another fall of snow for 33 years. Such long gaps between snowfalls took me by surprise when I looked up the official record, for I had not realised that last Friday was such a special event in the history of our town.

The typical Australian-born child did not see snow, even one certified flake of it, in the course of childhood. I first saw snow when I was 11, but that was at Ballarat where a light fall of snow was not rare. I was riding a pushbike around the lake and could hardly believe that the flakes were snow.

In the past few days. I have been wondering whether snow has found a place in our nation's imagination. To a Tasmanian or someone brought up on the higher goldfields of Victoria, or the uplands of New South Wales, snow is not an abnormal sight but it has left little trace on our paintings, literature and films. It is seen as too European, and untypical of Australia.

I imagined that the 'Man from Snowy River' would at least convey the magic and silence of snow, but even in the full version the only spasm of cold comes in the 13th and last verse:

> *Where the air is clear as crystal, and the white stars fairly blaze*
> *At midnight in the cold and frosty sky.*

That fine Sydney poet and playwright, Douglas Stewart, who died two years ago, brought snow most frequently into his work. He loved trout fishing in the high, cold Monaro and he also wrote a well-known radio play of the 1940s which he set in the Antarctic and named "The Fire on the Snow".

But then Stewart was by upbringing a New Zealander, and that's perhaps the sharpest difference in how New Zealanders and Australians imagine themselves - snow and fast water mean to them what the plains and heat mean to us.

Melbourne Herald, 31 July 1986

20

Padded Arguments from Padded Trade Unions

When, seven weeks ago, I was asked whether I would launch this book I had no idea of what I was consenting to. I guess I have spoken at more book launchings than almost anyone in Australia, but I can recall no other book of recent years whose launching has been so widely and excitedly discussed. Certainly no book of mine has been so awaited. Even more curious, the publicity has come from the very politicians who hope that the book will not be read. In the last year Canberra has set in motion various million-dollar advertising campaigns but not one of those propaganda campaigns has been as newsworthy as that directed by the Labor ministry against this book.

The book (*Arbitration in Contempt,* Melbourne, 1986) is a critique of industrial relations in Australia, of the role of governments and their arbitration tribunals, the role of unions and employers, and the poor performance of the economy as a whole. These are legitimate subjects for criticism. Mr Hawke actually made his reputation, when working for the ACTU, by making criticisms - many of them outspoken - on such topics.

Members of the federal cabinet, in recent weeks, have expressed alarm that members of the H.R. Nicholls Society should be trying to change the present system of industrial relations. But my understanding, from this book, is that the H.R. Nicholls Society was founded only because Mr. Hawke's government foreshadowed that later this year it would implement some of the revolutionary proposals contained in the Hancock report on industrial relations. The government has therefore been unwise to pour hysteria on a vital topic which the government itself had placed on its political agenda.

Some critics see this book - before they have read it - as simply an adventure in union-bashing. *The Age,* on 16 September, gave the top position in its column of "letters to the editor" to a writer who said that the main aim of this Society was to abolish unions. He produced no evidence for his sensational assertion. You will find none in this book. I would think every one of the twelve contributors to this book sees a role for unions. I certainly do. Hence two years ago I agreed (because no union would agree) to help underwrite the first big Australian exhibition of those ornate banners which once led the trade unions' processions.

I view trade unions as important institution in the nation, but they are not more important than the nation and at times they harm the nation and not least the trade unionists and their families. As many chapters in this book suggest, trade unions at key times have tended to become independent nations defying the wider nation.

Trade unions are extremely powerful in Australia mainly for two reasons:

1. Public opinion tolerates unions even when their power is excessive and their actions are unjustifiably dislocating.

2. A favoured position has been granted to unions by the law or captured by unions in defiance of the law. This topic is discussed again and again in this book, and is prominent in the chapters by Hugh Morgan on trade union power, by Wayne Gilbert on the S.E. Queensland power dispute of 1985, by Ian McLachlan on farmers and Paul Houlihan on Mudginberri, and by Peter Costello, John Hyde, Ian Spry, Gerard Henderson and G.O. Gutman.

Why did trade unions gain such power and why, on those occasions when their use of power is excessive, do they receive public tolerance? My answer is that in the depressed years 1890-1905, big business and employers generally were seen as too powerful in Australia. As a result a popular manifesto of political and economic measures strengthened the trade union movement, making it possibly the world's strongest. Even by 1911, as the dispute between Mr Nicholls and Mr Justice Higgins indicates, there was, in the new Arbitration Court, an inkling of a doctrine called the divine right of Labour.

You can read of the episode here. In 1911 the turbulent topic of labour relations at Broken Hill was before the Arbitration Court, and Mr Starke the barrister informed Mr Justice Higgins that at Broken Hill the trade unions broke agreements with impunity and in so doing "were encouraged by the Government of this country." The government then was Andrew Fisher's Labor government. Higgins, on hearing this imputation, and it was not made against him as a judge, erupted: "I will not allow you to speak of the Government of this country in that way...You have no right to speak in that way." This was a strange outburst. Higgins, in high emotion, went on to say twice that the barrister had no right to speak in that way about "those above us". Here was an independent judge, seemingly saying how beholden he was to the government, or how much he admired the government.

It so happened that H.R. Nicholls, the octogenarian editor of the *Hobart Mercury*, repeated in an editorial his belief that Mr Justice Higgins was very much beholden to the federal government. He was charged with contempt of court. It's an important case in the history of freedom of the press, for Nicholls was acquitted.

Mr Justice Higgins did more than anybody to create the halo around that arbitration system which is scrutinised in this book. Over time, new laws and rulings, many of which were justified at the time, pushed the pendulum too far in the other direction. Today, in aggregate, trade unions can be far too powerful. After reading the twelve essays in this book I see little to weaken this conclusion and much to strengthen it.

A persuasive ideology justified the practices of trade unions. Sympathy for the under-dog was the most potent argument. It remains a powerful argument but not in those situations when the under-dog becomes the over-dog. If we realized how outdated are some of the trade unions' arguments, we would think twice about accepting some of the practices based on those arguments.

I offer three examples of padded or blind arguments. First, the trade unionist is said to require special rights because he - unlike many other people - has only his labour and skill to sell. But at least 94 per cent of the working population now primarily exist by selling their labour. How can 94 per cent of the population possess, at certain times, a right to special immunity from the law?

Another padded arguments of unions is that they are busily fighting monopolies. But Australia has changed, and monopoly is now more a mark of trade unions than of big business in Australia. Indeed the opinion of John Hyde is that today, "We outlaw restrictive trade practices in all activities but employment".

Here is a third padded argument. In the 1890s, in a simpler world, it was possible to say that labour was fighting capital. In many disputes a victory for the unions was a symbolic victory for the average Australian. Today, capital has changed, and the big rich owner is not so typical, and many large companies consist of tens of thousands of shareholders representing every section of society, including the superannuation funds catering for hundreds of thousands of average Australians. Not only has capital changed but the public sector of the economy has become massive. A victory for a union in a dispute with the public sector is in no way a defeat of capital, as the term was once understood. And if an excessive claim by unions succeeds in the Commonwealth Public Service, the gain for say 5,000 unionists must come from the pockets of all taxpayers, including 3 million trade unionists. Thus the union movement, in addition to its numerous legitimate victories, has become a specialist in self-inflicted wounds.

There can be little doubt that the typical trade unionists in Queensland have so far gained far more than they lost through the defeat, last year, of the unions associated with the South East Queensland Electricity Board. According to this book, about $30 million a year has thereby been saved, the productivity in that electrical network has increased by an astonishing 30 per cent, and some 600,000 Queensland customers receive cheaper and more certain electricity than they would otherwise receive. The defeated unions have a case: the victorious customers have, in my eyes, a much stronger case. We need to look afresh at the myths - facts in 1900 but myths today - that are invoked to justify support for extreme union power.

This book surveys a wider range of issues. It examines the arbitration system and doubts whether its advantages exceed the disadvantages. Readers may or may not accept the case against our hallowed arbitration system, but the case is powerful and deserves attention.

The book also examines important economic decisions made by governments and tribunals. Sir John Kerr, who was a leading barrister in industrial law in the early 1960s, examines the Northern Territory Cattle Industry Case of 1965, which Sir Richard Kirby, president of the Arbitration Commission, sensed was his Commission's "greatest contribution" to Australian society. By raising the wages of Aboriginal pastoral workers, the Commission evicted large numbers of them from that industry which was their only stronghold in the outback. The Commission had predicted that there would be "welfare problems" amongst unemployed Aboriginals but noted that those problems "will be dealt with by those most competent to deal with them". Unfortunately we have not proved competent to deal with them. Citizens might well ask how the massive unemployment in many Aboriginal districts could possibly come from an arbitration system that wished them well. The evidence is in this book.

The young in the cities, like Aboriginals in the bush, have also suffered from new policies on wages. Many job-creation schemes for the young are really job-destruction schemes. The schemes knowingly destroy nearly all the jobs they have created. The dead-end job, at one time a derided concept, is now deliberately created in huge numbers by the Hawke government and several state Labor governments and acclaimed as work experience or evidence of economic recovery.

Why are so many young Australians unemployed? Does our arbitration system help to condemn them to unemployment? The burden of our serious unemployment is shouldered mainly by the young, but this was not so during the world depression. It is not so in Japan today. In this book Michael Porter informs us that Japan's unemployment rate in 1983 would have come close to ours if she had had our proportion of juvenile unemployment. The percentage of unemployment amongst our young is three times as high as in Japan. One reason is that youth wages are much lower in Japan, and so employers are more willing to employ young people. G.F. Carmody notes, in his chapter on the retail industry in NSW, how arbitration decisions to pay high wages to the young are actually depriving other single young people of employment opportunities. And yet the retail trade, potentially, is the largest employer of those aged from 15 to 19.

This book centres on our attitudes and theories. It simply asks, in the light of a wealth of experience, are we being sensible? Are we the victims of our own misguided theories?

Isn't it ironic that in the very name of equality and fairness, our employment policies have singled out for penalties the outback Aboriginal and the town teenager?

This book is about values and priorities, and about rewards and penalties that no longer make adequate sense. I conclude with my own example. We have gained kudos, deservedly, through the victory in the America's Cup. But it would be even more beneficial if Mr Hawke along with the arbitration authorities gave thought to our bigger ships. It so happens that our nation, of all the world's nations, has the second longest, navigable coastline. How we cope with that coastline is vital not only for our defence but also our standard of living. And yet what we achieved at Newport, Rhode Island, we cannot achieve in Australia. Our coastal shipping is far from efficient. We are a world leader in the alumina industry, but it costs more to ship alumina from central Queensland to the smelter in Tasmania than from Europe to Tasmania. It is better to operate efficient cargo ships than one fast racing yacht. If, as a nation, we gather our wits about us we can do both.

Australia is now entering a stormy strait. The course we navigate in the next year will possibly determine our future well into the next century.

Address at a dinner held by H.R. Nicholls Society, Southern Cross Hotel, Melbourne, 30 September 1986

21

Let the Poppies Grow Tall

Australia is in serious trouble, and we are unwise in blaming the outside world. Much of the blame lies with ourselves. Some of our attitudes and institutions belong to the era of the pencil and slate and dunce's hat.

One damaging attitude is our reluctance to foster talent. We are not alone among nations in cutting down the tall poppies, and a certain amount of pruning is harmless and even healthy, but we now stand out in our reluctance even to cultivate poppies which show promise of growing tall.

Our schools and even universities reflect this dilemma. There is an enormous difference between the abilities of students of the same age, and we are not sure how far we should even recognise those differences, let alone harness them.

The differences between students in the same classroom are startling. At high schools in suburban Melbourne in 1983, tests of students' ability to use words and number - those two essential skills - show that the most forward and backward student in a class of 12-year-olds were so far apart that one had the skills of a 17-year-old and the other those of a 9-year-old. And yet there they were, in the same classroom.

Other tests in suburban high schools in Melbourne showed that in learning a simple poem the fastest child in a class was often twelve times as fast as the slowest. You may reply that at one end was an infant Barry Jones with a freak memory, and at the other end was a child who, while capable, was deliberately dawdling. But those same tests also compared the fastest 25 per cent in the class with the slowest twenty-five per cent in the class, and even there the average student in the fast group was more than twice as fast as those in the slow group. That's a big difference in the useful learning skills.

Tests in England on children in grade 6 showed a remarkable range in their vital ability to read and understand. Selecting a large representative sample of grade 6 children from all over England, the test compared the reading skill of the top 10 per cent and the bottom 10 per cent. The top group was the equivalent of 7 years ahead in reading ability.

The contrasting competence among students in the same classroom can be seen in the individual ability to handle figures and words, in memory, speed in sorting out information, width of interests and the capacity to store knowledge.

Some Australian teachers and schools are coping effectively with gifted children; but in a teacher's education, little time is given to studying the gifted. In 1983-84 our teachers colleges and university departments of education were surveyed to see how much time was spent instructing would-be teachers on how to cope with "excess talent". Such courses occupied only one sixteenth as many hours as those devoted to the understanding of handicapped children. Of course the needs of the handicapped child are vital. So are the needs of the talented child.

One reason why our ability to help the needy, whether in schools or houses or hospitals, has diminished in the past few years is that as a nation we are performing poorly in the economic field. And one reason why we are not as competitive as we should be is that we waste too much talent.

Now some would promptly protest that by paying more attention to the education of the gifted child we would deprive the physically handicapped child or the slow learner. But only countries which fully use their pool of talent can achieve that high standard of living on which all remedial and disadvantaged programs depend.

It is talent, it is ingenuity and forethought and skill, and not rich resources, that have lifted up Hong Kong and Singapore in recent years. We should ask ourselves whether we are squandering our own ultimate asset, the talent of our children. To cultivate the talent in each child, as the retired federal minister, Kim Beazley, once said, is also to confer "the courtesy and grace due to every child".

There is a levelling attitude among a minority of teachers, especially those under 40, and they are suspicious of excellence and enamoured with the kind of equality that sometimes limits children's opportunities and sometimes fosters sheer mediocrity. Some of these levelling teachers belong to the far Left. They don't understand that Russia, Czechoslovakia and nearly all communist countries make a positive effort to cultivate tall poppies in their schools.

Of course, intellect is only one of the talents a nation needs. A Rhodes Scholar does not necessarily make a better prime minister than an engine driver, and yet a nation in so many sophisticated fields - ranging from medicine to geology and computers - needs a great weight of intellectual firepower if it is to be competitive.

There is merit in the recent plea by Professor K.B. Start, a leading Australian educationalist: "Among deprived groups in Australia, gifted and talented children are unique. They alone face concerted action to prevent their full development by the very agencies in our society to whom the development of the nation's youth is entrusted."

Many others believe, like him, that the time has come to introduce urgently, in the typical government school, programs to help the more gifted and talented children. This would not be in defiance of the principle of equality of opportunity, but in pursuit of it.

The fact is inescapable. If we thwart the development of gifted youngsters, we thwart the development of a nation which is already stumbling.

<u>The Australian</u>, 3 October 1986

22

Australia Holds Many Australias

Australia is many countries and regions but we are reluctant to accept this fact.

Brisbane and Melbourne, Tasmania and Western Australia have much in common but they also have differences and there is little sign the differences are fading.

To many Australians these regional or State differences are either annoying or trivial and not to be seriously discussed, let along encouraged. In my view they should be taken seriously rather than stubbed on the ashtray of history. Over a period the regional differences and loyalties will alter but they will not go away, much as the centralists would like them to vanish.

I was stirred to hear the 91-year-old painter, Lloyd Rees, reminiscing on radio recently about the Australia in which he grew up and pointing out how conscious he was, even as a young man, of those regional differences which persist but are currently dismissed by some intellectuals as aberrations which stand in the way of new reforms and visions.

Speaking as a painter, he pointed to landscape but hinted that landscape was only one of the ways in which each of our cities and regions were different. Reared in a large Brisbane family, he recalled that when he was six or seven an older brother, a bank clerk, had been sent to the Darling Downs and had written home a letter with the dramatic message: "The whole place is red."

Lloyd Rees explained that paved streets in Toowoomba were rare, and the wind whipped up the dry topsoil from the streets and surrounding farmlands, and a redness often pervaded the town.

At his home in Brisbane, he took his big brother's word-picture seriously and set out to draw the red bank standing, as banks did, on the street corner, with a vista of streets stretching away, all red. "It's a little episode that lingers," recalled Rees.

I listened, fascinated, to his well-chosen sentences, spoken enthusiastically in a slightly husky voice. There was no show-off or posturing in him - just a deep knowledge of Australia and a desire to share it with us.

How powerfully he conveyed the sense that every part of Australia was different to the eye and how every city was different in pulse and feel even in those distant days. It is still true, but that was not the main point of his reminiscences.

He first saw Sydney in 1916, and as his coastal ship came through The Heads in the early sunlight, he thought " it was miraculous". As there was no colour film worthy of the name in those days he had not been forewarned of the shape and texture of the harbour and city and was taken by surprise at the sculptured sandstone of the harbour shores and the city.

Walking from Sydney Cove towards the city he had the sensation of being enclosed by buildings mostly of sandstone. The impression was vivid, and Sydney Harbour still conveys it uniquely. "I've never seen such sculptured foreshores anywhere", said Lloyd Rees.

He also sensed the light was different and knew he had to find a way of capturing it. "Sydney was a blue and gold city", he said, summing up the landscape with the exactness one might devote to the colours of a football guernsey.

There can be no doubt that painters, writers, and lately the film makers, have been vital in giving Australians eyes to see with. The process of instruction is continuing, and in fifty years time the average Australian will probably have more affection for the immense variety of Australian landscapes, seascapes and light than is held today. It will be some centuries, however, before that affinity and power to see similarities and differences equals that of the tribal Aborigines of 1788.

Through Lawson and Streeton and Lloyd Rees and Fred Williams and dozens of others, we have begun to be on nodding terms with the environment, and to have some sense of place, but there is a current said to be moving in the opposite direction.

Many observers see Australia as marked by an increasing sameness. They argue that the accents of native-born Australians differ little from Charters Towers to Subiaco; they see a dull conformity over the way of life almost everywhere - an Americanisation, modified a little by new ethnic customs. They see television and jet planes as promoting uniformity; they see political attitudes as differing only a little from one end of the country to the other.

For my part I see no sign that regional differences and loyalties are diminishing. If anything they have increased in the past 10 or 15 years, and they have increased the more you move away from the Hume Highway. Queensland, WA and the Northern Territory especially have this sense of being different, almost irrespective of which party is in the electoral saddle, and one of the key questions in Australian politics and economic life in the next half century is whether those big warm States become more and more populous and powerful and challenge the dominance of the older cities of the south-east corner.

Most regions and States in Australia are proud to be different, and if they can't be different in the old way they will find a new way of being different. We should not be surprised that the desire to be different remains powerful. In a huge country, the sense of place, of belonging to one region or State rather than another, is stronger than we admit.

Some politicians lament that Australians are utterly conservative and rarely support constitutional change. I doubt whether Australians are more conservative than Italians, French or English. They are reluctant - as Mr Hawke will probable learn if he tries to change radically the Constitution - to abandon State loyalties and interests when an imagined rather than a real unity of interest is at stake.

That sense of regionalism is neither radical nor a conservative posture. It is simply affirming what Lloyd Rees the painter felt seven decades ago; that there is a chain of landscapes and societies, each the same but different, and each commanding a loyalty and sense of local unity.

The Australian, 31 October 1986

23

The Pope is Meddling in Our Politics

The Pope's visit was marked by an act of political meddling that has few parallels in Australian history.

The fact that his visit in so many ways was a triumph has helped his conduct to escape censure. For there can be no doubt that his own charm and grace, the skilled organising of his tour, and the enthusiasm of the crowds made his visit as successful as perhaps any royal tour of the last decade.

Long before the Pope reached Australia there was speculation on whether he would comment publicly on the thorny issue of Aboriginal land rights. Much of the publicity preceding his visit predicted that he would speak on this issue. And yet for him to speak too positively would amount to an act of political interference.

It seems clear that the Australian Bishops' Conference advised him to speak on this hot topic and indeed to take a specific viewpoint. It could even be that the Australian Government, before the Pope spoke at Alice Springs, vaguely sanctioned his speech, though this is very unlikely for it would convert the Pope into a travelling ambassador of the Australian Labor Party.

Whatever the background events might be, the Pope did meddle. At Alice Springs he adopted a clear-cut position on one of the most contentious issues of Australian politics.

It does not matter whether he was right or wrong in his views. In calling for "the recognition of Aboriginal rights to land", he was specifically telling the Australian people what to do on a topic which could become a crucial election issue in 1988.

There would be astonishment in Italy if an Australian Governor-General, visiting the Vatican, publicly called on it to widen the franchise for the papal election. There would be a roar of outrage from those now condoning the Pope's conduct at Alice Springs if the Queen, speaking in London or Canberra, made a partisan comment on Australian politics.

The Pope has every right, even a duty, to speak on the plight of the Aboriginals. If he had simply paid tribute to all Aboriginal peoples, drawn attention to their problems, and called on all other Australians to remember their Christian obligations, nobody could have fairly complained.

But to call specifically for the granting of more land to Aboriginals is to play party politics. It is emphasising one political proposal at the expense of alternative political proposals.

The Pope's comment on land rights was far more interfering than his earlier praise of our industrial relations system, and that was partisan enough.

It would be unfair to criticise too strongly a compassionate man, a distinguished visitor to our country, when he was possibly reading largely from a script written for him by Catholic officials who seized this opportunity to influence Australian politics.

The Pope, however, allowed himself to be a puppet at Alice Springs. He became the political marionette of Australian bishops. He violated the first rule of international hospitality - that a visiting head of state does not interfere in the affairs of a country in which he is an honored guest.

Meanwhile, nothing is more intriguing than the silence of the Federal Government, indeed its seeming acquiescence, at the Pope's meddling in Australian politics.

Are we really an independent nation or are we, under our present government, merely a mouse?

Melbourne Herald, 4 December 1986

24

The Death of the Saturday Herald

The death of the Saturday *Herald* is a sign of the impact of television and also an obituary for that special occasion, the old-time Saturday night.

In the first years of this century, when most wage-earners worked fifty or sixty hours a week, Saturday night was the busiest shopping time.

The pavements of Bourke Street in Melbourne, Smith Street in Collingwood, and Hannan Street in Kalgoorlie were so jammed that people spilled on to the road, where roaming paper-boys did much of their selling.

In thousands of households, Saturday was the evening when the water was slowly heated in the big wash-house copper, and one by one the children and adults had their weekly bath.

Saturday night was also the bumper night for the hotels, and Melbourne had far more hotels then than today, and their doors were open until close to midnight. Pay day for nearly everyone came at the end of the week, and hotels thrived on pay days.

Saturday night was really a last fling, a few hours of mardi gras, before the Sabbath arrived and closed virtually all shops and hotels, theatres and sports grounds.

In devout households the Saturday evening was spent in preparing for the next day, with toys and frivolous books put away and the Sunday clothes starched and ironed.

In such homes no work was done on the Sunday, not even cooking. The idea of buying anything on a Sunday was abhorrent. That was one reason why there was such busy shopping on Saturday night.

Finally, after shop assistants had clamoured, the big shops were compelled to close at 1 p.m. on Saturday, and Melbourne moved its late-night shopping from Saturday to Friday in 1909.

During World War I, 6 p.m. closing was imposed on the hotels, and that remained the rule for half a century. Henceforth those streets which on Saturday nights had been jammed with shoppers were almost deserted.

Saturday night still remained special, and from the 1920s onwards it became the night for the cinema.

For three hours on Saturday night people sat in the new palatial theatre with its succession of 'God Save the King' newsreels, supporting film, advertising slides, coming attractions and main black-and-white film. And when at last they filed out, the crackle of chocolate boxes and Columbine Caramel papers and ice-cream Dixies could be heard at their feet.

The coming of television in 1956 shook that pattern of Saturday entertainment, and within a decade a suburban cinema could hardly fill a fraction of its seats. Instead, people stayed home and many ceased to read an evening paper, for Saturday at first was the big night for TV.

The heyday of the Saturday night papers had been the era before the coming of radio, television and loudspeakers. In that simpler way of life the human voice was a vital way of advertising and dozens of boys hawked newspapers in every busy street, jumping on to trams, elbowing their way along the crowded pavement, thrusting newspapers into customers' faces, and shouting, always shouting, their news.

Their cry of "Her-ald" - so familiar on a Saturday night - always sounded like two distinct words. I suppose I shouted them that way when I had a *Herald* round at the age of 10.

For many people the repeated cry of "Her-ald", heard down the street in the darkness of winter, will remain one of the clearest memories of those old-time Saturdays when the printed word was still supreme.

> Written for the last Saturday edition of the
> Melbourne Herald, 20 December 1986

Part II

1987 - 1988

25

Dick Reynolds Goes North

The news that Dick Reynolds is leaving Victoria would have inspired the biggest headlines imaginable 40 years ago. Even today, long after he put away his Essendon jumper, his departure for the Gold Coast is a nostalgic event.

There used to be a phrase conferred by journalists on the fairer champions. They were called "an ornament to the game". Dick Reynolds was probably the ornament of ornaments.

No surviving footballer of the pre-war era holds a more secure place in the record books, for Dick won the Brownlow Medal in 1934, 1937 and 1938. But even if his roving had not won a medal he would be remembered as the playing coach who turned the unsuccessful Essendon of the 1930s into the glamorous side of the 1940s.

Dick Reynolds was brought up in Moonee Ponds but the family barracked for Carlton, and they walked from Flemington Bridge right across the windy expanse of Royal Park to the Carlton ground. All the way, Dick would be kicking a football made from a rolled-up newspaper or stuffed cigarette box. As he reminisced, he reminded me of the young Bradman: that intense practising, that obsession with perfection.

The thrill of his childhood was the day Horrie Clover shook his hand. Now those of you who squandered away your youth by reciting the names of the kings and queens of England rather than those of footballers both great and small will scarcely know that Horrie Clover was the Carlton forward.

His handshake was almost as magical as that of royalty. "After that I didn't want to wash my hands", Dick told me.

Dick Reynolds played his first senior game for Essendon when he was only 17. Today it is easy for a rising footballer to study his opponents by watching them on TV and then watching them again on video cassette, but in 1933 Dick had to find a simpler way of studying his opponent.

As Haydn Bunton of Fitzroy had won the last two Brownlow Medals, and as Fitzroy were about to play Essendon, Dick went with his "young lady" into the city on Friday night to study the man he would be playing against next day.

It was well known that Haydn Bunton was a floor-walker at Foy and Gibson, and so Dick went into that busy store and from a distance looked at the Fitzroy star, the way he walked, the way he used his arms and shoulders, and his physical balance and even his personality.

The anecdote vividly illustrates the contrast between our era of television football and that Depression era of ingenious but poorly-paid footballers.

I first saw Dick play at the old Corio Oval in 1938 or 1939 and I remember him especially because a mascot wearing his number ran onto the field with him.

These days, half of the small boys in Victoria wear a league jumper with a neat number on the back, but in those poorer days a child who could dress like a real footballer was a rarity and was looked upon with some astonishment and envy.

Reynolds had a distinctive way of running, and his long stride was almost a lope. I seem to remember him in his last game, the 1951 Grand Final against Geelong, when, in the hope of snatching victory in the last quarter, he ran onto the arena as 19th man. There was something dramatic even then in the way he thrust forward his ageing legs.

Few footballers have held the respect of residents in their suburb to such an extent. Indeed his fairness, modesty and sense of proportion have won him the esteem of people for whom football itself means nothing.

He will be 72 in June but he feels - in his own words - "on top of the world". In the eyes of Essendon I think he will remain on top of the world.

Melbourne Herald, 2 April 1987

26

The Voters Are Not Less Worthy Than the Politicians

There is now a campaign to give governments a longer term of office in Canberra, and the mainspring of this campaign is the belief that our present economic mess is partly the result of the short-term vision of short-term politicians.

In March the Democrats actually introduced a Bill to provide four-year parliaments in place of the present three-year term, and Mr Hawke is toying with the idea and *The Age* is enthusiastic.

Strong support also comes from the Business Council, the lobby of big business, which has produced a 20-page booklet skilfully arguing that a longer term of office would encourage a government "to plan effectively and tackle the major economic problems facing Australia today".

There is some truth in the claim of *The Age* and the Business Council that politicians should be positively encouraged to have a longer vision, and not think simply in terms of the next election. But why change the electoral system? In recent years the leaders, not the electoral system, have given us frequent elections.

Mr Fraser in 1983 and Mr Hawke in 1984 called for elections long before an election was due. Mr Hawke this autumn was again tempted to seek a premature election, offering the feeble excuse that the divided Opposition was now impeding economic recovery.

The evidence suggests that even if Mr Hawke did not have to face another election until December 1988 he would be no bolder in facing the economic mess. Lack of time is not the bugbear of the Hawke Government: its weakness has been a refusal to see the grave economic problems long after they were visible.

The present argument for longer parliaments also implies that there is something irresponsible about the Australian electors. It implies that electors must be pandered to, that electors think only in the short term, and that if they are called upon to make sacrifices they will refuse.

I see no evidence that in the past five years the public has been more short-sighted than the leading politicians. I see no evidence that Australia has been less willing than Canberra to face unpleasing facts. Indeed, most of the swinging voters were probably ahead of Mr Hawke and Mr Keating in knowing that the economy was in a mess.

Accordingly, I am not impressed by the arguments that with the present three-year parliaments a government can only "begin taking tough and far-sighted decisions" in its second year, and that by the third year those tough decisions must be deferred because of the approaching election.

The advocates of the four-year parliament insist that we have too many elections. *The Age* regrets that since 1901 the average federal parliament has sat for only three quarters of its allotted term. The Business Council regrets that since 1960 the diligent electors of NSW have been required to vote in federal or state elections in every year but four.

Are these frequent polls to be deplored? Those who have little time for democracy will regret having sacrificed half an hour every year in order to go to the polling booth: but that fiddling sacrifice is not too much to ask of a citizen. If the frequency of voting is an unbearable burden for some citizens, why not solve that particular grievance by eliminating compulsory voting?

The Business Council also points out that elections are costly in taxpayers' money. True, they are very costly, and the $40 million spent at the last federal election is an eye-opener. But a dictatorship, all in all, would be even more costly, though its election expenses would be nil.

We are told, too, that in most democracies a three-year parliament is now abnormal and that the Commonwealth should come into line with the "rest of the world". But today there would be no democracy anywhere if it had been thought vital to keep in step with the great majority of nations.

The Business Council's booklet is not entirely enthusiastic that a four-year House of Representatives will have to be accompanied by an eight-year Senate. But they accept this as the price to be paid for a useful reform. For my part, I don't accept that price. In several key phases of Australia's history even a six-year term for half of the senators has proved to be too long.

The main argument for now changing the federal Constitution and introducing a four-year parliament is economic: the belief that short parliaments are partly responsible for our economic decline. And yet Australia enjoyed economic prosperity when "burdened" by parliaments that were just as short-lived.

There is no clear link between the duration of the parliament and the well-being of the economy. Thus, in recent years the States have moved towards longer parliaments, but the evidence so far reveals no visible improvements in the economic performance of those States.

One of the glories of our short national history is that in the helter-skelter 1850s, men with little experience of governing or voting set up new democracies and made them work. Few facets of these young democracies were bolder than the three-year term for parliament, first adopted in South Australia in 1856 and Victoria in 1859.

The parliament of short duration was favoured because our pioneers emphasised the need for parliament to be answerable to the voters. The people are the ultimate repository of common sense. That is the essence of democracy, and the past twenty years of Commonwealth history do not give the impression that the electors have proved less worthy than the politicians. Indeed, by some definitions, the electors have proved the more worthy.

The Australian, 1 May 1987

27

The Pacific Rim: A Slippery Concept

You are nearly all, as architects, specialists in enclosing space. I wish to say something about a space that encloses you: the vast space of the Pacific Ocean. The fashionable concept of the Pacific Rim raises questions about the future of each of our nations as well as the broad shape of the architectural profession in the next fifty years.

To emphasise the Pacific is to note the relative decline of Europe. In 1900 all the prime industrial nations were European, with the exception of the United States, which was an ethnic satellite of Europe. In 1900 the great inventions came from European peoples. In 1900 the map of the world was largely a map of European empires, the notable exceptions being Japan, Thailand, China's interior, and the Ottoman empire: even the headquarters of the Ottoman empire were in Europe.

Today, Europe's colonies in the Pacific and along the Pacific Rim have nearly all vanished, except for Portugese Macao, British Hong Kong and the French territories in Polynesia. There is another big exception. The Eastern Soviet Union can in one sense still be called a Russian colony, for Vladivostok and its vast hinterland were acquired by the Russians in the colonial era, in the 19th century. While the Soviet Union would be a world power even if it did not extend east of Lake Baikal, its possession of a Pacific outlet increases its global importance. The Soviet Union's nuclear strategy depends heavily on its nuclear submarines in the land-ringed Sea of Okhotsk in the far north-west Pacific.

The importance of the Pacific also comes from the dramatic growth of heavy industry. The rise of Japan has been spectacular, Taiwan has become a powerful industrial nation, South Korea is now a large exporter of electronics and automobiles, while Hong Kong is one of the success stories of the modern world. China, after walking around in circles during the decade of the cultural revolution, has resumed economic progress, especially in agricultural and coal-mining: it is now the world's largest coal producer. East Asia in the last quarter century has undergone an industrial transformation which has closed competing factories from Detroit to Sheffield.

A scanning of the statistics in the international year books reveals a startling set of conclusions enthroning the importance of the Pacific Rim. Five of the six most populous countries in the world border the Pacific Ocean: the exception is India. Of the world's six largest countries, five border the Pacific, though two - namely the Soviet Union and the USA - see the Pacific more as their backdoor. The Pacific is the only ocean in which all the great economic and military powers possess territory and major interests.

The Pacific Rim is a valuable guide to the future. It is also a corrective to trusted old ideas, not least the belief that Europe and North America remain the undisputed hub of the capitalist and even the socialist world. But the Pacific, in several contexts, is almost too large to be a useful concept. The Pacific Ocean itself occupies one third of the globe. It is over seventeen times as large as Europe's landmass. If we also add the lands within 500 miles of the Pacific shores we have an area so enormous it is difficult even to contemplate.

Moreover, unlike Europe, the Pacific Rim lacks ethnic unity, cultural unity and economic unity. The concept of the North Pacific Rim would be more useful but it is now unlikely to supplant such an established, grand phrase as Pacific Rim.

Is the Pacific a physical barrier, or is it more an accelerator of contact between remote nations? We traditionally see a huge ocean as an impediment to the movement of peoples but it is much less an impediment today. Big ships and jumbo jets can cross the ocean with ease. Indeed, the advantage of the Pacific is that is has no big islands and archipelagoes, and no big reefs and shallow sand banks in its middle, and so as a general rule a ship can follow the shortest possible route when sailing from one Pacific port to another.

One effect of this huge open ocean is that two Pacific ports which are 5,000 miles apart can be closer to each other in travelling time than say two European ports which are only half that distance apart on the map. It is easy to give examples of ports which, relatively close on the atlas, are remote by the sea routes: thus Libya and Nigeria are not far apart on the map but are distant by ship. Istanbul and Leningrad, Canton and Calcutta, Montreal and Los Angeles, Adelaide and Darwin are other such pairs which are far more distant by sea than by land. Such anomalies rarely affect pairs of Pacific ports. With the relative absence of land obstructions, the Pacific in this sense is more compact than it seems. Of course the Pacific remains enormous. Many of the important Pacific ports are closer to ports on remote oceans than to some of the other big Pacific ports. Thus Melbourne, a Pacific port, is almost as close to the Red Sea as it is to San Francisco.

Let me think aloud about this vast region, especially in the next thirty years. My comments relate to the distribution of ideas, power, and people.

The Flow of Ideas

So long as international peace prevails over the Pacific nations, or the great majority of them, the flow of ideas - whether in architecture, engineering, cooking or the fine arts - will be quicker and smoother than ever before. The flow of ideas will be aided by ease of travel, by television and satellites, and by the new international tendencies in banking, insurance, manufacturing and other industries. New fashions and fads, new trends in design, will move quickly from country to country. A major new architectural movement, originating in say Japan or California, will probably spread with remarkable speed. At the same time, while communications will tend to unify the Pacific, the speed of communicating will also foster a reaction, thereby fostering regionalism, nationalism and tradition in architecture and many of the arts of daily life.

New communications obviously unite, but we are not so quick to notice that they also segregate. Not long ago the sense of neighbourhood, the sense of place, and the longing to keep what is traditional were often seen as the hallmark of the peasant: now they are often a hallmark of the educated city-dweller and the practitioner of the professions. The quicker that the world changes and the more that its daily life changes, the greater is the determination of some groups and regions to preserve part of what is endangered. The very desire for diversity, which fosters so many new ideas, can also help to preserve and revive old ideas.

The Movement of Power

Will the Pacific become more important? The future of China and Japan is a vital part of this question. After all, their increasing prominence helps to make the concept of the Pacific Rim so illuminating.

I doubt whether, on the basis of existing trends, China will be much more important in 2017 than it is at present. It has enormous population and area, but these two facts are liabilities as well as assets. China for long has been seen as an half-awake giant, and one day - far in the future - it might become, by certain criteria, the most powerful nation in the world. Many predictions made about the rise of China, however, have been too optimistic. Since 1949 the great majority of Chinese people have become better-off. And yet compared to Japan, China's economic performance has been mediocre: it is indeed pathetic if we compare the relative energy and drive of the overseas Chinese - small in number - with the efforts of the homeland Chinese, astronomical in number.

Conceivably the People's Republic of China may find a way of liberating the latent energy and ambition in its billion people, but its ruling ideology makes it wary of really releasing such an uncontrollable force. The socialist rulers of China virtually walk a tight rope, and they will probably continue to walk it in the near future. On the one hand they want urgently the latest and most appropriate technology from capitalist nations. On the other hand that entails increasing contact with those nations, which in turn allows the infiltration of an unwanted culture and the individualism which is common in capitalist, democratic lands. Hence China's rulers are like the organisers of a gigantic trade fair. Periodically they open the fairground to outsiders and their products and their ideas and then suddenly shut it again when the fair seems too successful.

It is a great pity that Britain has agreed to allow Hong Kong to return to the arms of Beijing. Hong Kong - much more than China - represents an economic triumph. After 1997, however, Hong Kong will find it difficult to maintain its zest and enterprise, in the grip of the long arms of the northern bureaucracy. True, China will lose face if Hong Kong slowly becomes a commercial backwater of the Pacific. Therefore it is conceivable that for at least one decade after 1997 the individualism of Hong Kong will permeate Canton and the most southerly region of China and so lead to a sharper division between the attitude and ethos of China's south and north. Hong Kong could thus serve as a Trojan horse. The more influential that horse becomes, however, the greater the chance that there will be yet another clamp down on disruptive ideas. All in all, in the next thirty years, China seems more likely to grow as a political than as an economic power.

Will Japan continue to rise or is it now close to its economic peak? It is easier for a nation to rise to the top rung of the international ladder than to remain on top. On the top, a pride and complacency set in, and so success quietly diminishes. My impression is that amongst big businessmen in Japan the belief is strong that it is more difficult for a nation to remain successful than to attain success. If this is true, then Japan might initially cope with the rust and erosion inevitably caused by success. Each new generation of leaders and public opinion, however, has to face afresh the insidious flattery of success as well as the higher competitive cost of continuous success. Ten years from now, Japan will possibly be more endangered than at present by its own stunning success.

Some observers see the rise of Japan, and also of West Germany, as partly the windfall accrueing to nations which lose a major war. If this view is largely correct, we would expect Japan by now to have lost such advantages and therefor to be losing its competitive edge. But, contrary to a widespread view, Japan and Germany did not receive U.S. economic aid on the massive scale. Between 1948 and 1961 the United Kingdom and France received, in total and for each inhabitant, more aid than did Germany and Japan. While Japan had the more rapid economic recovery it received less US aid than did Germany, much less than Italy, and substantially less economic aid than the U.K. and France. On the other hand it is true that Japan received an indirect form of economic aid - a post-war constitution preventing its government from spending large sums on defence. Nonetheless it is unwise to interpret Japan's economic ascent as largely an unexpected bonus for defeat in the Second World War.

Will Japan eventually become a great military as well as economic power? While certain factors inhibit its defence-spending, Japan in the next thirty years will probably become a front-rank military power. I say this not as an alarmist: such an event might be more advantageous than disadvantageous to the Pacific. At present Japan is number 2 or 3 in the world in economic power but only number 8 in military spending, and that is an unusual contrast. Moreover it is rare for a major economic power to be unable to defend itself adequately nor be able to defend the long sea lanes on which its economy, as a massive importer of fuels and raw materials, utterly depends. Ultimately, the United States, especially if it moves towards a balanced budget, might even urge Japan to share a large part of certain defence burdens, including the semi-military field of space research. Japan is unlikely to need such an invitation. But political controversy conducted at a high temperature will precede a Japanese re-armament.

While a re-armed Japan will not necessarily threaten the international peace any more than an armed France or India endangers the peace today, a re-armed Japan could ignite China's fears. A strongly armed Japan could do what no other event of the last quarter century has effected: push China towards an alliance with the Soviet Union.

People in Search of the Sun

The Pacific will see shifts in population as well as national power. Since the Second World War at least three Pacific nations have experienced a strong international migration from colder to hotter regions. New Zealand was perhaps the first to show this trend, and the cold South Island has declined steadily at the expense of the warm North Island. Similarly the United States now has its booming Sun Belt stretching from Florida through to California, while Australia has its Sun Hat - consisting of Queensland, the Northern Territory and Western Australia. This part of Australia has been growing at a more rapid pace than the other states lying towards the southeast corner. In these three Pacific lands, citizens can express their climatic preference by simply moving to a warmer region: they need no passport or permit and not even a new language.

If these movements of population to a warmer climate or to a more spacious living environment are to continue, they will have profound consequences. Thus the more rapidly California grows, and the more it becomes a powerbase rivalling the Old East, the more intently the United States will focus on the Pacific. Similarly there will be far-reaching consequences if older Japanese increasingly wish to move to retirement resorts across the seas, and are willing to pay for the privilege, or if in China a generation hence some freedom of internal movement is granted, enabling millions of Chinese to move from the cold north.

The migration to warm climates within these three Pacific nations also reflects the fact that in the last forty years the advanced world has transformed its economic base. Traditionally the workforce in primary industry and much of secondary industry was tied residentially to the site of the raw materials or those ports to which the materials could easily be transported. Now the demand for labour in manufacturing and in resource-based industries is falling, the tertiary sector is dominant, and there is a new mobility for industries, occupations and people within the more advanced economies of the western world. The migration to the sun, the coast and the new spaces is part of that freedom; and in the next fifty years even the Third World economies will experience it.

Chaotic Migration

In the last fifteen years, unplanned, illegal migration from one country to another has been more characteristic of the Pacific than of perhaps any other large zone in the world. This is not an east-west migration, for the Pacific ocean is so wide that small convoys of refugee boats are unlikely to cross it. Rather it is unauthorized migration along the west coast of the Pacific or along the east coast. It includes the strong migration from Central America and Mexico to the United States. On the other shore of the Pacific it includes the massive flow of emigrants or refugees from South China to Hong Kong, from Cambodia to Thailand, from Vietnam to Malaysia and even to places as remote as northern

Australia, from East Timor to Australia, from Irian Jaya to
Papua New Guinea, and by some definitions the large-scale
Indonesian plan whereby Javanese are being settled in Irian
Jaya without the blessing of the people of Irian Jaya. In
aggregate, more people have probably taken part in these
international migrations along the Pacific than in the trek
of refugees across Europe's international borders in the
post-war years 1945-1960.

These short-distance Pacific migrations have been spurred
by war and civil war but to an unusual degree they have been
spurred by a disunity, a patchwork quality, along the Pacific
Rim. Neighbouring nations of the Pacific, more than in
Europe, often show a stark contrast in ideology and religion
and especially in economic well-being. Thus the standard of
living of China is very different to that of Japan and even
Hong Kong; and California and Mexico contrast sharply in
wealth. Without this mosaic of sharp contrasts, there would
be little incentive for migrants to move illegally from one
coastal country to another. If Mexico were even half as
prosperous as the neighbouring United States, its
emigration today would be trivial rather than massive. If
Vietnam were prosperous or it provided civil liberties, the
exodus of its people since the fall of Saigon in 1975 would
have been small.

It is true that similar ideological and economic contrasts
distinguish Communist eastern Europe from capitalist
western Europe, but the greater efficiency of the
Communist security forces and surveillance in eastern
Europe has largely halted the outflow of discontented
people. Moreover the economic contrasts are not as sharp
- and therefore not as enticing to potential refugees - within
Europe as along the North Pacific coasts.

Illegal, unplanned migration - with its gains and losses - will
probably remain an awkward issue. It is of special concern
to Australia with its long, unguarded, northern coastline,
and of concern to most nations in South-East Asia. It will
become of special interest to Hong Kong residents in the
1990s. Incidentally, Hong Kong has been a refuge for people

fleeing from Vietnam, but after 1997 few Vietnamese will presumably seek refuge in Hong Kong.

The migrations can lead to the peaceful meeting of very different cultures. Sometimes these cultures clash. It is foolish to ignore Fiji, Sri Lanka, Malaysia, Indonesia, and other lands. Such cultural, ethnic clashes are more easily prevented by an authoritarian society, but refugees prefer to take refuge, if they have the choice, in a democracy, especially a wealthy democracy. In a democracy the refugees deservedly possess the right to live in the suburb of their choice and often they prefer to form a cultural ghetto with their own kinsfolk and, when necessary, to speak with one political voice. Likewise, in a democracy, the native-born citizens have a right to express a view about the extent of immigration which should be allowed. It is not surprising if, as a result, there are some disagreements and misunderstandings. The Pacific Rim, because of its characteristics, will continue to spur periodical, unpredictable migrations.

The way we see the land masses and the oceans of the world is based partly on the atlas. It is also based on our own perceptions and our own predictions, our own sense of past as well as future. To express it in another way, we like to see the world in terms of simple visual packages, and these visual packages are useful because they simplify what is complex. The Pacific Rim is a vital visual package, but it conceals a complexity of harmony and disharmony which we sometimes fail to observe.

Address to the Pacific Rim Architectural Conference,
Hong Kong, 10 June 1987

28

Four Years of Deft Footwork: The Hawke Government

The Hawke Government in its initial four years has been like a disciplined, well-dressed fire brigade. But it often arrives at the fires after the television cameras have arrived, and some of the fires that it so spectacularly fights are the unintended results of its own policies.

It was incredibly slow to realise that its overheated economy was in trouble. And yet, since Banana Republic Day - when at last it saw the flames - it has gained the maximum camera coverage and applause from its attempts to put out the fire.

Mr Hawke's ministers show an intense desire to stay in power. In pursuing that desire they even dropped such high Labor priorities as the obnoxious Bill of Rights and the wide-ranging Aboriginal Land Rights after public opposition to them grew loud.

It is a high political skill - the ability to decide when to abandon controversial policies and how to sell those policies which are still deemed crucial. Mr Hawke and his party organisation have exemplified such salesmanship - sometimes tricky, sometimes straight - to a degree which make the Opposition parties seem limp and lifeless at times. The Liberals kid themselves in arguing that if only they showed unity they would certainly have won this month's election.

This has been one of the most unpredictable governments in our history. It has little relationship to the Whitlam government in domestic policies or modes of implementing them and little to New Zealand's Labor in the wider realms of foreign policy.

In many ways Mr Hawke is more conservative than Mr Fraser. Whereas critics now say that the so-called New

Right has failed to capture the Liberal Party, the New Right has exerted a compensating influence on some of Mr Hawke's major policies in the last 12 months. His veering to the right was probably unmatched by a Labor leader since Mr John Scullin's rightwards move in the world depression in the early 1930s.

To a surprising degree, Mr Hawke has ignored the Labor Party's platform. His election speech at the Sydney Opera House in February 1983 resounded with promises from the official platform. Plank after plank from the platform have since been jettisoned or ignored.

His more radical supporters must now see his government as a failure or a very spotty success, but their protests are mild. Public opinion clearly prefers the flexible Hawke platform to the official Labor platform.

Perhaps Mr Hawke's skill, more than circumstances and luck, has prevented a serious split in the Labor Party. History suggests that the highest danger of a Labor split is when it holds office in most Australian parliaments, and that means the danger must now be high.

So far his party has suffered minor splits with the departure of the ardent nuclear disarmers in 1984 and the expulsion of Mr Bill Hartley in 1986, but it remains remarkably coherent. In the next three years the Left could well demand some of the radical legislation it has been patiently awaiting. That will at last rock Labor's skilfully-steered boat.

Curiously, Mr Hawke won this election largely on the economic debate, and yet the economic performance of his government can at best be called mediocre. By some definitions his economic record is feeble.

Admittedly in 1983 he had inherited an economy in difficulties. He then gained the twin boons of the breaking of the long Australian drought and the economic recovery in the northern hemisphere; but he partly wasted those windfalls by a process of job-creation (and tax creation) in the public sector that put a potential strain on the balance of payments. When export prices fell - and the government had been strongly warned of their likely fall - Australia was unable to pay its own way.

The economy is still unfit. The constant comparison of the weak Australian dollar with the weak American dollar is like comparing two rickety racehorses.

Our overseas debt is a disgrace to a nation which in at least two previous generations had learned the painful lessons of over-borrowing. Our inflation rate is three times that of European nations. Our interest rate looks like a final score in football.

The consolation is that the high unemployment of 1983 had been lowered from ten per cent to eight per cent, though by the standards of the last half century it is still high.

Many experienced businessmen who are not normally sympathetic to Labor argue that a Liberal government would have done no better in the past four years. Some of Labor's problems are simply old Liberal problems. Thus in 1983 the Liberals' taxation system had long ceased to be a system. At least Mr Hawke tried to reform taxation though with clumsy hands, hurting the outback exporters but shielding the public servants.

Supporters of Mr Hawke applaud him for giving a variety of grants to the unemployed, unmarried mothers, Aboriginals and other struggling groups which form the bottom twenty per cent of the income ladder. But in the last year and a half, those people have indirectly lost most of these gains. What Mr Hawke gave them in 1983-85, the weak economy now has mostly snatched back from their wallet and handbags.

Nobody expected Mr Hawke to stand up to the unions on many major issues. Then again nobody expected him to go so far in pleasing them that he would endanger his political career. Both expectations have proved correct.

He naturally claims credit for the decline in the number of days lost through industrial dispute in Australia but a similar decline has occurred in most advanced nations. Hard times have curbed the urge to strike.

It is a mark of his remarkable propaganda machine that the Australian public continue to believe that Mr Hawke is the same old last-minute fixer of ACTU days - the man who neatly solves industrial problems. What most Australians do not yet realise is that the sum total of production lost through strikes is small compared to the wastage that arises from sloppy, union-dictated methods and rules in the workplace.

Last year Mr Hawke belatedly made a gurgling sound of mild disapproval at the inefficient work practices that reduce the standard of living of Australians. He will have to gurgle more loudly. The present coal dispute in NSW is partly caused by the labour inefficiency which Bob Hawke sanctioned in his wilder days.

His relations with big business have been more cordial than those maintained by any previous Labor Prime Minister. Indeed he has pleased Big Business more than little business. It was his government which boldly brushed away the layers of cobwebbed curtains and the fading window-blinds which had protected the old financial system.

Mr Keating, in welcoming foreign banks, did more to change the banking system than had Mr Chifley, and Mr Keating did it in an instant whereas Chifley spent two years of emotional energy between 1947 and 1949 in order to change virtually nothing.

Those who observe Canberra closely and speak impartially about the Hawke ministry are strong in their praise of the cabinet as a group. Those who listen to parliament on radio are often impressed by the debating ability and command of detail of many members of the cabinet, whether Button, Walsh or Hayden, or Keating when he lays down his meat axe. Perhaps the two most muddled ministers were West and Hurford, both of whom were deservedly deposed as Ministers of Immigration.

Back in the 1950s it was often observed that Labor suffered because so many of its top men in Canberra were faithful but plodding career-politicians who had slowly come up through Labor branches and union meetings. Now that plodding point is more often made of the Liberals.

Apart from that political fox terrier, Mr John Howard, and a few other able politicians, the leading Liberals seem to make surprisingly little impact on the public when big issues are debated. In contrast, I doubt whether Australia since the birth of the Commonwealth has known a Labor government which is more skilled in political footwork than the present government.

Melbourne Herald, 7 August 1987

29

Can the World Avoid a Major Nuclear War?

I pose this question only in relation to the next fifty years: but even to look fifty years ahead is a perplexing task. To attempt to see a century ahead is even more hazardous because the most devastating military weapon in the year 2087 will not be a nuclear warhead but a military device which has not yet been invented and perfected.

Today it is a widespread assumption that the nuclear era will go on and on. It is highly probable, however, that the nuclear era, like every other era that has been dominated by a specific technology, will eventually give way to another era. I confine my comments to the nuclear era.

In the western world young people are especially fearful of nuclear weapons. Indeed, they tend to feel that the post-1945 generations are especially unlucky, being the first in mankind's long history to face an uncertain future. An uncertain future, however, has been more normal than we realize. Since the birth of Christ the imminent end of the world has been a common fear. In the sixteenth century, Martin Luther thought the world would probably end before 1600.

Some of today's scholars may dismiss Luther and other Christian prophets as the victims of outmoded superstitions, and insist that their own predictions of an ultimate nuclear holocaust are based not on superstition but on hard reason. In my view, however, superstition and dubious arguments underlie some of the nuclear fears that are widely held today. We should be very alert to the dangers of nuclear war: those danger are real. But several of the most frequent predictions about war in the nuclear era are risky. I detect at least three pessimistic myths.

1   It is widely said that an arms race inevitably leads to war, and that we are in the grip of such a race. This theory arose originally out of the events leading to the First World War in 1914. I examined the evidence while writing my book of 1973, *The Causes of War*, and was surprised to find that the theory did not match the facts. In that original arms race, which was said to make a Great War inevitable, some of Europe's big powers were actually spending a lower proportion of their budget on arms as the so-called arms race gathered momentum. An examination of Soviet and American spending in the years 1952 to 1976 by Organski and Kugler in *The War Ledger* has also cast doubt on the concept of an arms race in our era.

2   Gradual disarmament is therefore hailed often as the panacea for war. There is a powerful argument - on economic grounds - for arms control and for international disarmament, but the military grounds for such an argument are not as strong as they seem. Hitler's rise to international power in the 1930's was aided enormously by the arms reduction agreements signed amidst cheers a decade earlier by the victors of the First World War; and Hitler's Germany was powerful in Europe by 1939, partly because the big powers had reduced their expenditure on arms. I do not

wish to be dogmatic on this issue; I merely wish to warn that arms race theories are far from being as persuasive as they seem.

3 Some of the gloomy present-day theories about nuclear war are theories of inevitability which warn that a devastating nuclear war must eventually occur unless nations dramatically change their ways. I myself am not convinced that the next major war, if it occurs, will be essentially a nuclear war. It is widely assumed that a powerful weapon, once in existence, must be used, but I am not so sure. Perhaps the most devasting weapon at the end of the First World War was chemical warfare, and it was seen as one of the great weapons of the future. Gas is a devastating weapon, as the Italians showed against the Ethiopians in 1936, the Japanese against the Chinese on the Yangtze River in 1941, and as Iraq and Iran appear to have shown in the present Gulf War. But like germ warfare, gas has been used with remarkable restraint - presumably because of fear of retaliation. The same fear of retaliation, so far, has probably helped to control the use of nuclear weapons. I am not positively insisting that nuclear weapon will never again be used: rather I am challenging the assumption that they will be widely used, and will dominate the next major war. It is widely argued that if, in a crisis between the super-powers, one nuclear missile is fired, it will lead automatically to a clockwork succession of strikes. It is widely assumed that a nuclear war, once that first weapon is fired, will be unstoppable, will be incredibly devastating, and will be over in a few hours or days. This tragic scenario is possible. To me, however, it is not the most likely course of events.

Even in our computer era, warfare remains one of the least predictable of human activities. Wars rarely go according to plan. Rarely does the dominant weapon of an era - and in our era the nuclear missile is dominant - determine the course of the war in the way actually predicted. Nor is it true that a major war involving all-powerful weapons inevitably is a short war. One strong conclusion does emerge from a study of wars in the last 200 years. In Europe, in each generation, the big wars involving the major nations and their allies have tended to be longer than wars fought between a few minor nations. They are expected to be short, but they are invariably long. The present evidence inclines me to the view that a major general war, if it comes in the next fifty years, will not be dominated by nuclear weapons and will not necessarily be short.

I have challenged primarily those who, in my eye, are too pessimistic, but I should also touch on the optimists. There is a widely-held theory that nuclear weapons generally promote peace and that the present long period of relative peace amongst the technologically advanced nations arises mainly from the fact that all-out war is now self-defeating. The cost of war, it is said, now exceeds the likely prizes of victory. I myself think that, so far, nuclear weapons have probably promoted peace in the First and Second Worlds; but our present period of peace is not unique and so it does not require an unique explanation. Another long period of relative peace ran from the end of the Franco-Prussian War in 1871 to the outbreak of the World War in 1914; it lasted for 43 years. Our period of peace will not equal that period until 1988.

I offer one comment on the peace movement. Those who warn about the dangers of war usually carry out a valuable service. The peace movement also has a therapeutic quality, because it is partly an alternative religion which helps the young to confront the frightening prospect of nuclear war. But if a peace movement is based on dubious theories about the causes of war, it can actually promote war more than peace: it is as dangerous as a physician who knows nothing about medicine. I hope it is not unfair to quote Bishop Mandell Creighton's statement, delivered, I admit, rather too emphatically for a bishop: "No people do so much harm as those who go about doing good." Peace is too important an issue to depend partly on people whose heart might be in the right place but whose brain isn't. As we do not yet know enough about the causes of international peace, one of mankind's important options is to gather more knowledge.

It may sound cynical to say so (but it would be more cynical not to say so) but war has traditionally fulfilled an important function. International war has been the most acceptable way of solving serious disputes between independent nations. War is now less acceptable than in 1900 partly because of the brute power of modern military weapons, but it will remain somewhat acceptable until people realize that war has fulfilled a function and that they must find more effective ways of fulfilling that function. At present hardly a nation which values its independence is willing to entrust, unconditionally, the adjudication of a vital dispute to the United Nations or to an international court. You may say, "this is outrageous". But it is a fact; and one of the weaknesses of the international peace movement and indeed of all people is the reluctance to face this sober fact.

War will more easily be banned or regulated if there is another resort of final appeal. War, however, will remain the final court of appeal until we successfully ask: what is an alternative court of appeal which nations are likely to accept?

One solution to international war is a world government. Such a government was unthinkable even in 1900 but now, for the first time in world history, it is a possibility because of dramatic changes in communications and the swift flow of forces and ideas. In the next fifty years a world government - if it does arise - is more likely to emerge through conquest than through consent. Even if it initially comes through consent, it is unlikely to remain a democratic government. It is more likely to be authoritarian; and its success in keeping the peace - if it does succeed - is likely to stem partly from its suppression of liberty in many parts of the world.

In summary, I am not as pessimistic as the typical young person about the dangers of a nuclear holocaust in the next fifty years. To me a nuclear war involving hundreds of missiles and creating colossal death and devastation seems unlikely: I would place the odds as perhaps 5 to 1 against such a devasting event. I think there is a slightly larger likelihood of a major war which uses few or no nuclear weapons but is still devastating.

On the basis of the existing evidence, my inclination is to predict that eventually a world government will emerge and that it will not satisfy those who value freedom but will satisfy those who crave for freedom from international war.

An Address at the Centenary Symposium at Queen's College, University of Melbourne, 18 August 1987

A much-expanded version was published as Chapter 7 of the book, International Conflict Resolution, Westwood Press, Boulder, USA, 1988

30

Why We Know So Little About the Gulf War

They rightly called Vietnam "the living room war" because moving pictures of it entered each Australian and American home punctually at 6pm or 7pm, arousing intense passions.

In contrast, the Iraq-Iran war is a backshed war - it stays out of sight. It provokes few speeches of indignation in Canberra and not even one or two straggling peace marches.

We have been so brain-washed into viewing nuclear war as the main threat to human life that we don't grasp the devastation caused by other weapons near the shores of the Persian Gulf.

Given the mixture of secrecy and propaganda flowing from Iran and Iraq, we cannot know the exact death toll, but some calculations suggest that half a million men have been killed in seven years of fighting. In deaths on the battlefield, this war therefore could already rank fourth in the history of wars.

Iraq has fewer people than Australia, and yet since 1980 it has lost more servicemen than Australia lost in the sum total of the Maori wars, the Boer war, two world wars, and the Korean and Vietnam wars.

Not far from the head of the Persian Gulf these two war-crazed nations, month after month, are fighting their version of the battle of the Somme. Indeed this war has other characteristics of the bloody deadlock on the western front in World War I.

Though Iran is twice as big as NSW and Iraq is twice as big as Victoria, most of the blood has been spilled on a narrow stretch of frontline not far from the Persian Gulf. There the two armies have tried to regain lost territory by the sheer weight of numbers and fanaticism.

Both nations have broken one of the special taboos of modern warfare: they have used chemicals on the battlefield.

Gas had been a lethal weapon in France during World War I but was rarely used thereafter, except by the Italians against the helpless Ethiopians in the 1930s and briefly by the Japanese in central China. In March 1984, however, a United Nations team reported that gas was being used in the Gulf war, and on May 13 of this year the United Nations reported that Iraq had repeatedly used chemicals against the enemy.

If in this war the firing of one small nuclear missile had caused as many deaths and disfigurements as the chemical warfare had caused, the world outcry would have been loud.

The peace movement's fixation on nuclear weapons, while understandable, has tended to become a distorter of morality. It is also notable that the moral indignation of the

Western world has not turned towards the bombing of cities and civilians in Iran and Iraq.

Since March 1985 the aerial assault on those cities has been intense. Iraq's city of Basra, a little larger than Brisbane, is only a few kilometres from the enemy border, and half of its 1.5 million people are said to have fled.

Iranian cities also suffer. In January this year the Iraq air force, according to a recent report from the Foreign and Commonwealth Office in London, even dropped bombs close to the Ayatollah Khomeini's house in a Tehran suburb.

Both nations have also turned to the bombing of neutral ships which carry away oil from the enemy's refineries. Gargantuan oil tankers of 200,000 and 300,000 tonnes are easy targets for mines and missiles in the Persian Gulf.

As oil provides the sinews of war, each nation tries to thwart the other's exports. So the United States, British, Dutch and other naval vessels have now been forced to patrol the Persian Gulf. Since these are international waters, free from censorship, television in the last few weeks has captured the war and at last brought it to Canterbury and Glenelg at 6 each evening.

This Gulf war is in astonishing contrast to the Vietnam war which, day by day, mesmerised much of the world.

Admittedly, the super powers are not fighting in the Gulf war. It is also true that the Gulf war, unlike Vietnam, is not an ideological conflict between capitalism and communism or between East and West but rather a religious and nationalist conflict which a Westerner of the seventeenth century might more easily understand.

And yet the Gulf war is potentially as strategic as Vietnam. The Iranian capital, Tehran, is closer to that great Soviet inland waterway, the Caspian Sea, than is Canberra to Sydney. Above all, this war is being fought in the world's main oil region, and skirmishes in the Persian Gulf are now endangering a sea lane which carries more than half of the world's exports of oil.

In the last resort, our long ignorance of the Iran-Iraq war is indirectly a sign of the power of the free press and television. If, for seven years, independent war correspondents and cameramen had been risking their lives to report events on the battlefront, then Australia and the Western world would long ago have been closely watching that war, passing judgement on it, and imposing pressure on the two fighting nations.

But the two warring nations have applied strict censorship, thereby impairing the Western world's ability to judge.

It is one of the blind spots of the free world that it is easily blinkered by the censorship imposed by unfree nations. Hence the free world, ironically, is more willing to interfere in the affairs of nations which permit some flow of news and information than those nations which heavily censor it.

<u>The Weekend Australian</u>, 26-27 September 1987

31

Not Because they Are Aborigines, but Because they Are Australians

I have a deep respect for many facets of Aboriginal history and many Aboriginal achievements. I also support the case for reasonable grants of land to Aborigines, though I do not see it as a right.

But I do not accept the picture often painted by those Aborigines demanding vast areas of land as well as a signed compact, with its undertones or proclamations of guilt.

In their claim for compensation, the Aborigines depict themselves as one nation, living in peace and harmony until the British arrived. They portray themselves as a people declining largely through the newcomers' firearms and cruelty, rather than by infectious diseases.

They also claim that the Aborigines were unique among colonial or modern peoples in that they lost their sovereignty without even the recognition of a treaty. In my view that picture is mistaken.

The case for massive compensation also rests on the idea that any injustice committed far into the past can be publicly resurrected, with blame apportioned and reparations assessed. The history of the world, sadly, is laced with injustices. Many of the worst example in the past 150 years could be investigated.

Should we, for example, re-examine the plight of the 160,000 British convicts transported to Australia after 1788? Perhaps half of the convicts, especially the women and children, were sent into permanent exile for reasons that we would now see as unjust or even outrageous.

Should we now search for their descendants in Australia and pay them an annual compensation? For while the Aborigines sadly lost their lands, the convicts suffered a similar loss - the loss of a homeland.

Do we also go back to World War I and decide that the relatives of those Australians who lost their lives should be paid continuous compensation, generation after generation, for the serious losses they suffered?

And do we reopen the wounds of World War II and decide that Germany and Japan and Italy should pay massive compensation now that they are far wealthier than they were in 1945?

In international affairs, as in civil affairs, there normally has to be a kind of statute of limitations - a limiting of the time during which long-gone events can be revived and turned into litigation. Otherwise, countless wars of the past could well be fought again.

Some say that the Aborigines were victims of a unique injustice. Certainly it was devastating and tragic but not, perhaps, unique.

Some commentators argue that the Aboriginal tragedy was unique because it harmed "an entire race". But that does not make it unique either. In the persecution of racial minorities in China, Africa and Europe in the last seven centuries, infinitely larger numbers were killed or displaced than in Australia.

To be invaded and dispossessed of lands or culture has been a common experience in human history. It has been inflicted without a treaty, and even with a treaty, which the losers were forced to sign under protest.

I find it astonishing, therefore, that a constitutional committee set up by Canberra has now recommended that in 1988 we should proclaim to the whole world that Australia's right to this continent is dubious, and amend the Constitution to read: "Australia is an ancient land, previously owned and occupied by Aboriginal peoples who never ceded ownership".

On the other hand, a strong and compassionate case can be made that Aborigines, more than most other peoples, found it unusually painful and slow to adjust to the regime of their displacers or conquerors. Certainly, they suffered long and hard from the loss of their lands, culture and, above all, their self respect.

I accept the argument that large numbers of Aborigines still suffer to an unusual degree, partly because of the European occupation of their lands. The nation should certainly help and foster them, not because they are Aborigines, but because they are Australians.

Many Aborigines and their white supporters want a sweeping and permanent compensation for all Aborigines. But that argument rests more on racial criteria and a distorted view of history than on real need.

There is an irrefutable case, which is in the interests of all Australians, for a strong attempt to improve the daily life of Aborigines. In most facets of life, this will succeed only if the attempt is made primarily by Aborigines.

Their health will probably not be improved unless they themselves are determined that it should improve, and unless they have a powerful say in formulating the plans for that improvement.

The future of the Aborigines lies in looking to the 21st century, not to the 18th century.

Even if a minority of Aborigines succeed in keeping alive parts of their traditional culture, their future and success will be more as Australians than as Aborigines. I am sure that some Aboriginal leaders, especially women, accept this view of their future.

The argument by white and black Australians that the events of 1788 are primarily to blame for the plight of many Aborigines is far too negative.

The solutions which have been proposed - massive land rights, white confessions of guilt and the granting of hereditary privileges to Aborigines - essentially look backwards. Moreover, the solutions are based on a version of history which is much less valid than its exponents believe.

The Weekend Australian, 10-11 October 1987

32

A Love Affair With the Arid Heart

It is significant that in the television picture used most frequently to advertise the Bicentenary, a crowd of stars and lesser glitterati are trying to be happy in the red-brown sand near Ayers Rock.

That Central Australia should have been chosen as a main symbol of this nation would have been inconceivable when Australians celebrated their 150th anniversary.

I doubt whether Sir Robert Menzies, over a quarter-century ago, would have seen Ayers Rock as the symbolic face of Australia. Nor would most of his fellow-Australians, except perhaps the Chamber of Commerce in Alice Springs.

It has been a slow process, this coming to terms with the arid inland, and the process is far from complete. I believe that, in a quarter of a century hence, most Australians will be surprised at the way we now see Ayers Rock and all the arid land for hundreds of kilometres around.

How we view the dry interior is a mirror of how we view our nation and its goals and future.

At first, there had been no thought that great deserts existed in the interior. Thus, William Charles Wentworth summed up the hopes of so many Sydney men when in 1819 he wrote that surely Australia must be like every other continent, with one or more great rivers dissecting it.

Explorers set out in the hope of finding our Mississippi River or Caspian Sea, and came back puzzled. When eventually it was clear that deserts or lean grazing land occupied the site of the imagined inland sea, Australians were intensely disappointed.

Meanwhile, poets and painters depicted the desert, and rarely did they see magic in it.

One of the first to write of the dry inland with affection was the gifted journalist and mining promoter Randolph Bedford, and around 1900 he marvelled at Central Australia and the dry gold country of Western Australia, but even he preferred his desert after rain, especially when the salt lake became a plain "rippling away in waves of crimson to the horizon, a great garden filled with pink amaranth and native lilac".

Dorothea MacKellar, about 1904, also made a revolutionary statement when she said that "I love a sunburnt country". Most other Australians didn't.

It was still seen as a national duty to develop the uninhabited lands - otherwise another nation might snatch them - but this sense of duty is rarely voiced at present, and even those who call for huge immigration simply envisage the newcomers settling in coastal cities.

The dream of inland development was especially vivid in the 1920s. Then, the famous Sydney geographer Griffith Taylor made a host of enemies among Australian developers and outback mayors with his insistence that more than half of the continent would probably remain largely uninhabited.

He said it so persistently that in the Federal Parliament in 1924 a member called on him to "resist from his perpetual slander on Central Australia". Years later, Taylor, from the safety of Canada, reported that the honourable member had actually become lost for some days in that arid region, the existence of which he had virtually denied, and was eventually found semi-conscious "with his mouth choked with oil from his motorcycle".

Griffith Taylor also said that it was folly to build the long, expensive railway from Oodnadatta to Alice Springs in the late 1920s. Economically, although not militarily, he was correct, but the railway had one curious effect.

It enabled Hans Heysen and other artists to visit "The Alice" for the first time, to depict it in strong reds and ochres, and thus introduce the Australian public to a majestic landscape that belatedly has become one of our national symbols, as the Bicentennial advertisements show.

So the love affair with the Dry Centre is very recent. It has been helped by the slow rise of Australian nationalism, for nationalism often selects what is distinctive in its landscape, and the Dry Centre is certainly distinctive.

The love affair with the Centre has been helped since about 1970 by the conservation crusade, and probably by the new respect for Aboriginal culture.

Enthusiasm for what Professor J.W. Gregory used to call our "dead heart" has also come from the global accessibility of Alice Springs and Ayers Rock and the deluge of tourists arriving in air-conditioned planes and buses.

Ironically, half a century ago, when Australia tried to advertise itself in foreign lands, it featured places that would attract immigrants. But now it shows the places that will attract tourists. Thus, Martin Place, Burrinjuck Dam and the Adelaide Hills have been ousted by Ayers Rock, "Crocodile Creek" and remote places that few would-be immigrants of the 1930s dreamed of visiting, let alone living in.

Symbols change. No matter how pregnant and permanent they may seem, they can quickly be eclipsed as new nationalist emotions and priorities emerge and as new calls for economic development and new fears for the nation's security arise.

I will be surprised if, when we celebrate our 250th anniversary, the dry red heart will be such a prominent symbol.

<u>The Weekend Australian</u>, 28-29 November 1987

33

Where Australians Come from: The Myths of a Nation's Family Tree

The great flow of immigrants into this land since the end of World War II has caused enormous changes, many of them - perhaps most of them - very beneficial.

And yet it is still difficult to make a verdict on what we have gained and what we have lost as a nation. It is not even easy to agree on what actually has happened to Australia's population.

There is a strong tendency in Canberra to inflate some of the consequences of the inflow, and that tendency has given rise to slogans that serve as misleading formulae for the future.

We are often told that since 1945 Australia in its ethnic diversity has become unique amongst the nations of the world. And yet the figures used to support the idea don't add up.

The chairman of the Government's inquiry into immigration and population, Dr Stephen FitzGerald, emphasised another side of the same picture: "When our immigration policy was formulated in the 1940s we were predominantly an Anglo-Celtic people". Now, he said, with pleasure, this was no longer so.

Not often in the history of Australia has a major government inquiry begun with the chairman unconsciously revealing that he was astray in the major facts and even suggesting social changes which should follow from his erroneous facts.

I greatly respect Dr FitzGerald and I respect his skills, but he seems to have been handed government propaganda. For better or worse, Anglo-Celts form 75 per cent of our population, as Dr Charles Price of the Australian National University has demonstrated.

When I discussed (*The Australian*, November 14) the ancestry of Australians and noted that about 94 per cent of them were of European and British Isles ancestry, my statement caused disbelief; and some people wrote to express puzzlement that this ethnic myth should have gained such currency.

While some politicians and ethnic leaders have cultivated the myth to gain votes or public money, the myth is aided by the widely-quoted claim that 40 per cent of our population are either migrants or the children of one or more migrant parents.

Let me offer a parallel observation. It could well be that nearly 90 per cent of the present population consists of people who were born here, or have at least one parent who was born here or in the British Isles or New Zealand. That statement conveys a picture of similarity more than diversity.

The labels we fix on our nation can also mislead. The word multiculturalism has had a wonderful innings in the past ten years and is mostly used in such a way as to imply we are now a non-British people. The word helps to convey an impression of sweeping ethnic and cultural changes which have, in fact, not yet occurred on that scale.

I would be very surprised if the United States, Canada, England, West Germany and Sweden - to name just five nations - did not also have citizens drawn from as many nationalities and ethnic backgrounds as Australia.

Ethnically, we are even more European than the United Kingdom. With big pockets of West Indians and Indians and Pakistanis, it has a higher proportion than we have of non-Europeans.

Similarly, if we compare our ethnic mix with that of the United States we are not as diverse, by several crucial definitions. Their non-British component is higher, and they also have a higher proportion of non-Europeans than we possess.

Even compared with Fiji and Malaysia we are not very diverse, judged by one of the most important definitions of diversity; the vigour of the challenge offered by the minority cultures to the dominant culture.

It is therefore rather misleading for commentators to insist with pride that we have an ethnic diversity such as exists in no other lands. In fact we have a relative uniformity which at least 20 nations, now torn apart by multicultural strife, must wish that they could possess.

Here are our twelve largest ethnic groups, and their proportion of the total population as calculated by Dr Charles Price: English, 44 per cent; Irish, 17 per cent; Scots, 12 per cent; German, 3.8 per cent; Italian, 3.8 per cent; Greek, 1.9 per cent; Dutch, 1.5 per cent; Welsh, 1.4 per cent; Scandinavian, 1 per cent; Aboriginal, 1 per cent; Croatian, 1 per cent; and Polish, 0.9 per cent.

What is unusual - not unique - is that at least ten different ethnic groups each have one per cent or more of the population; in short they form noticeable minorities. In that sense we have diversity, though probably less diversity than the USA.

The Weekend Australian, 2-3 January 1988

34

Charles Perkins is a Brave Man

There is more humbug in the Federal Parliament's attitude to racial issues than in any other topic of importance; and this week Mr Charles Perkins was the target for the humbug.

The first charge is that as a senior civil servant he made controversial political statements. There is something in this charge, but, originating from the Labor Party, it can't be taken too seriously. Last September, Labor ministers defended Mr Perkins when he attacked Mr Howard as "irrelevant".

The second source of deep indignation against Charles Perkins has to be explained delicately. I think many politicians are indignant about his viewpoint because he is of Aboriginal descent. In the illogical mixmaster of opinions that often passes today for logic and compassion, it is widely believed that a coloured person should support other coloured people and that if he doesn't he is letting down the side.

Oddly, the same viewpoint also holds that while it is non-racist for one group of black people to support other black people, it is racist for a group of white people to support other white people.

Charles Perkins sensibly ignores this silly stereotype of how people should behave. He has directed against brown Asians the type of criticisms which he often directs against white Australians.

How ironic that Labor and Liberal politicians, while mounting the pulpit in order to castigate that stereotyped thinking of which "racism" is the main evil, should have unthinkingly demonstrated their own offensive form of stereotyping. They assume that a spokesman for Aborigines must automatically side with other coloured people. But why shouldn't an Aboriginal have independent opinions?

Mr Hawke wants his Aborigines to be cardboard people and predictable. Neither he nor his ministers offered a rebuke when on June 17 last year Mr Perkins made against white Australians an attack far punchier than he made this week against Asian Australians. Presumably, in the view of politicians, Mr Perkins was then behaving according to their own racial stereotype of him.

This week Mr Perkins has courageously defied this cult of double talk which, currently fashionable in the social sciences and politics and even Aboriginal matters, will ultimately be seen for what it is. Curiously, the organisations which were set up to curb ethnic discrimination have become the very agents for that form of prejudice.

In the name of the people they are quick to cry "racism" if any Australian-born citizen makes a legitimate comment on migration but silent when a newcomer makes a more loaded and patently disloyal comment. The Human Rights

Commission quickly but courteously denounced Mr Perkins this week but if he had used exactly the same words against Scottish or Irish immigrants it would have been silent.

The sharpest slander against the greatest number of Australians in the past year was made by an official and diplomat more senior than Charles Perkins. John Menadue, the chief executive of Qantas, had said that our nation suffered severely from "Anglo-Celtic arrogance". I assume he excluded himself from that stricture.

Mr Menadue's address to graduates at Griffith University was not contradicted by the Human Rights Commission. He was not sneered at by an ABC reporter - a fate reserved this week for Mr Perkins on the television program the ABC had the effrontery to call "the news".

Whether Mr Menadue was correct in labelling Anglo-Celts as especially arrogant does not matter. His remark was much more "racist" than Mr Perkins's but it was allowed to go unchallenged and was even given free publicity in China by the Hawke Government.

While "racist" is one of the most cutting taunts in the Federal Parliament I cannot remember hearing any minister define the word. It is safer not to define it: in that way the minister is not boomeranged by his own definition. It is surely hypocritical of Labor and Liberal politicians to lay such a strong charge against Mr Perkins but refuse to use a definition that allows him to defend himself against an allegation that could deprive him of his position.

The Acting Minister for Immigration, Senator Reynolds, also showed how double standards prevail in this delicate topic. Rebuking Mr Perkins, she announced that it "is dangerous to stereotype any cultural group, in whatever terms". But she herself was deafeningly silent during the election campaign when Mr Hawke often tried to make political capital out of those very stereotypes.

The Australian on January 13 ended a decisive editorial by arguing that the Government "could lose whatever credibility it has on Aboriginal and multicultural issues if it does not discipline Mr Perkins". I believe, however, that Canberra, on racial issues, is far stronger in hypocrisy than credibility.

Weekend Australian, 16-17 January 1988

35

They Will All Be There on Sydney's Shores

They will all be there, on Australia Day. Coming from unknown graves in the bush, coming from Gallipoli and the Burma railway, coming from suburban cemeteries and even the ocean floor, they will stand unseen on the shores of Sydney Harbour on January 26.

A nation is shaped by politicians and builders and inventors, but it is made by the millions of everyday people who bring in the harvest, bake the bread, give birth to children and hope that their children will live a fuller life. Those past Australians, now forgotten, will find their way to Sydney in the coming week.

Men who cut the first tracks into dense forest will come just for the day. "Philosopher" Smith, who, in 1871 carried his supplies on his back and found, far from the Tasmanian coast, the rich tin of Mt Bischoff, will surely come. "I cannot remember ever hearing him laugh," his son once said. Perhaps the philosopher will laugh this Australia Day.

A young nation wins a high standard of living only if tens of thousands of its people give, in effort and ingenuity, a little more than duty demands.

Chinese shepherd Yen Soon, minding his flock in Australia on the morning of Black Thursday 1851, stood with his sheep when a huge bushfire raced towards him. It is said that he "stayed too long amongst them and was suffocated by the dense smoke". He will breathe the Sydney sea air on Australia Day.

Thompson and McGregor set up their Times Bakery at Gulgong goldfield, NSW, in the early 1870s and arose in the darkness each morning to light the fires and knead the dough. They will visit every harbourside suburb on Australia Day because they stand together - perhaps more credit-worthy than in real life - on the top of our $10 note.

Long before the painters of the Heidelberg School began to paint bleached grass and blue ranges, people stood in the doorways of bush huts and learned to appreciate landscape, light and vegetation that at first could seem harsh and even bewildering. They will sit alone in the scrub on Sydney's headlands, away from the tiled suburbs, on Australia Day.

Followers of various codes of conduct will find a vantage point and not argue. No busybody will tell the lady who won "the married women's race" at the first Mt Isa picnic sports that she was not really married. The mayor of gold-rush Leonora in Western Australia will read the Koran without interruption. But the first mayor of Moonta in South Australia will pretend to be absent, just to reassert that wonderful dictum that "you have not travelled until you've been to Moonta".

Invisible, above the cliffs of North Head, the men of Gallipoli will see the sun rise again. Many had spent their last hour climbing steep slopes at sunrise. What will they say if they learn that their "war to end all wars" was followed, two decades later, by a more terrible war? Disillusion as well as triumph will walk on the water on Australia Day.

For 24 hours a host of Aboriginals will speak languages now dead. At nightfall their bark canoes will rock on the waves, but the fire traditionally glowing on a pad of clay on the bottom of each canoe will go out at midnight.

Around the harbour the nation's symbol-makers will find a place. John West will be there: congregational minister from Launceston, he was the first to place the Southern Cross on an important Australian flag - the banner of the proud alliance which in 1850 fought to end the transportation of convicts to Australia.

Young Evans, the Box Hill schoolboy who in 1901 was one of five who designed the new Australian flag, will sit near Mr West. At night they will assure themselves that their constellation - dearer to Australians of earlier generations - still sits low in the sky. Unlike most of today's Australians they will know where to look.

Among the millions who will come without an invitation to "the celebration of a nation" will be Simpson's donkey, the Colt from Old Regret, broken-down dray horses, Clydesdales, camels, Jersey cows, sheep dogs, australorps, a proud Camden ram, and even Mathew Flinders' cat, the charming Trim who will purr once it sniffs the salt air again.

We forget that working animals as well as people made this nation. On Australia Day we will faintly hear the clip-clop of Edward Dyson's old horse. We were taught to chant in school that "he's an old grey horse, with his head bowed sadly", but on this day his head will be high.

You will not recognise them when the camera zooms on the spectators but they will be there: Jack Dunn of Nevertire, Jack Howe with his sheep shears, the tent-hospital nurse, the lighthouse keeper's wife from Torres Strait, and the women who held the big teapots at Albury Station in the days of "all change here".

For half an instant you might almost glimpse the wheatbelt pastor who knew the Old Testament by heart, the stoker from the *SS Orungal*, the Aboriginal cricketers who toured England in 1868, Granny Smith who will dress herself in green, and the drover's wife with her four dried-up-looking children. One of those children, the youngest, could still be alive, her life encompassing exactly half of our nation's history.

They will all be there, somewhere around the harbour.

We should cup hand to ear, for that great cloud of witnesses will try to speak on behalf of earlier generations who probably were more successful than our own.

Weekend Australian, 23-24 January 1988

36

Sheer Energy Swamps a Visitor to the States

The feeling I have whenever I visit the United States is of the sheer energy of the nation.

That feeling is almost overwhelming when you walk from the aircraft, reach the street and see the rush of people and the purpose on their faces. America might not be sure where it is going, but it will arrive before we do.

For a long time to come, Australians will probably have a different mixture of values and priorities to those of the typical American; and our mixture is probably preferable. But it does have one disadvantage during an economic downturn. Our preference for leisure rather than work does not really aid our recovery as a nation.

This morning, in a cheap breakfast house on the corner of Second Ave and 44th St, New York, a man in his forties was presiding over a small black stove on which he grilled an array of eggs, sausages, bacon and mashed potato. The deftness of his movements, the speed with which he worked in his jammed space inspired awe. He told me, without looking around, that five people from his Greek village had gone to Australia. He could say little more: he was too busy listening for shouted orders while he turned eggs and meat.

No nation is uniformly a ball of energy, and the US has many regions that, in local parlance, are "laid back". Climate as well as culture affects the eagerness for work in Chicago as well as Darwin. This evening, flying from New York to Ohio, I found in the seat pocket a magazine discussing New Orleans and its appetite for leisure and fun. "Don't be fooled," it noted. "The American work ethic does not reach here."

To glory in work is, for better or worse, an American tradition. Thus Theodore Roosevelt, the American president who made the teddy bear famous and thereby did much to boost our own koala, said emphatically in 1903: "Far and away the best prize that life offers is the chance to work hard at work worth doing."

I am sure that similar affirmations in praise of work were made by various of our prime ministers, and were certainly made by the Labor leaders Curtin and Chifley in the difficult 1940s. Such statements have come from Canberra less often in the past twenty years.

For most of our history the tempo of work has been easier than in America. In the gold fields of both lands in the 1850s the energy spent in digging was probably similar, and on the small farms of Ohio and the back of Bathurst in the 1870s the pressure of hard work on every day except Sunday was equally strong. But in the typical Australian town the hours of work for most men and women were fewer than for their counterparts in Boston and San Francisco.

A century ago, a Bostonian visiting Melbourne and Sydney was quick to detect, sometimes wrongly but usually correctly, a certain slackening of tempo in dozens of occupations ranging from underground mining to building and blacksmithing. That many Australians already enjoyed an eight-hour day led to a fair deal of moralising and clicking of Yankee tongues. "What will become of this lazy lotusland?" they said.

They did not yet realise that while America in many ways was the mirror of the world's future, Australia was also a mirror. Eventually, America copied the shorter working hours in vogue in urban Australia in 1888. But it has never really "caught up", if that is the appropriate phrase. Moreover, in the typical New York deli, factory, bank and airport office, a little more energy and a lot more tension are spent in the typical working hour.

It is easy to attribute our national preference for leisure and a quieter tempo of work to the sway of trade unionism - and no doubt the unions have played a strong part - but a preference for leisure was already emerging when the unions were not yet a force in the land.

Moreover, Australia today has many unionised industries in which hours are short but the pace of work is impressive. Similarly, it is easy to blame the national attitude to work on the semi-skilled and those who work with their muscles when in fact it is just as easily seen in white-collar jobs and also in those professions that offer more stimulus and pleasure than many kinds of manual work or process work afford.

The whole nation - there are plenty of exceptions - has developed an easy attitude to work; and a wide variety of customs, habits, rituals and institutions reinforce that attitude. The attitude now forms one of the causes of the falling standard of living of the average Australian at a time when nations which work a little harder than we do are prospering.

All is not utterly lost. On the rushing freeway between Los Angeles and San Diego is a large neon sign advertising the energy in a certain brand of battery. The face on the neon sign is unmistakable: it is "Jacko", the former Geelong footballer who is now a stuntman.

It is curious that we, more than perhaps any people in the world, admire success in sport, and yet somehow we forget that professional sport is simply hard and highly-skilled work, disporting itself. We like our work to be disguised.

Weekend Australian, 27-28 February 1988

37

A Message from the Afghan War

The war in Afghanistan is nearly nine years old, but it has made no more impact on our imagination than a mere month of the Vietnam War.

It is curious that a war so similar to the one in Vietnam, a war that has caught one of the superpowers in a trap of its own setting, has aroused small interest in Australia. It has not even ignited the local peace movement. And yet the war has something to tell us.

Afghanistan shares long borders with the Soviet Union and Pakistan, a shorter border with Iran, and the narrowest of mountain borders with China. Thus it has two communist and two Islamic neighbours: and indeed its own tensions arising from a militantly secular and a militantly sacred culture are part of its dilemma. You could call Afghanistan an interesting specimen of multi-culturalism.

The wars that interest us these days are the television wars; and as the Soviet Union mostly succeeds in keeping television cameras out of Afghanistan, we don't see the fighting on the evening news. Moreover, Afghanistan is not on the transport routes to Australia. It is remote, being much closer to Dublin than to Canberra.

There is another reason for our lack of attention to the war in Afghanistan. The war is not high on the Labor Government's agenda of the world's woes, though it was so high on Mr Fraser's when he was prime minister that Australia's participation in the Olympic Games in Moscow in 1980 was in doubt.

Only twenty years ago, Afghanistan seemed relatively secure. In some ways, it was one of the most self-reliant nations of this century. Even more than Australia, Afghanistan had a tradition of fierce independence and an alertness to maintain that independence. Twice the Afghans pushed back British troops at a time when Britain was a mighty power, and they continued their suspicion of Britain by displaying a pro-German policy at crucial stages of the two world wars.

One of the few peoples of the world to remain unconquered during Europe's vigorous quest for colonies, the Afghans walked skilfully the same tightrope when communism became a zealous coloniser.

Back in 1967, the *Britannica Book of the Year* concluded that Afghanistan's relations with communist and non-communist nations were "equally cordial". Furthermore, its government was neatly walking that other tightrope between the old rural, Islamic way of life and the antibiotic world. In 1966, the government of the day even appointed a woman as minister for public health - a rare female feather in a Muslim cap.

In the past quarter of a century, various new or weak nations have slipped into danger, but Afghanistan did not seem vulnerable, so strong was its tradition of independence and fighting prowess.

In 1973, however, Afghanistan's monarchy was overthrown. The king's successor, his own cousin, was overthrown as president by a revolutionary council five years later. Then came personal struggles, assassinations, the rise and fall of leftist ethnic-political factions and the alleged invitation in 1979 for the Soviets to intervene. By the end of 1979, the Soviet troops controlled the capital, Kabul, and they still control it, although an Afghan puppet now gives Moscow's rule a certain credibility.

While tens of thousands of Afghans have waged a guerilla campaign against the 115,000 occupying Soviet troops, and have even carried the war into Kabul, a far larger number of Afghans decided to flee the ravaged countryside and move to the capital.

More Afghans took refuge in Pakistan and Iran. Today, some $5^1/_2$ million refugees are camped just outside

Afghanistan's borders. It is doubtful whether there is any similar record, even in our century of turbulence, of a moderate-sized nation losing more than a third of its population through a deliberate exodus.

The extent of the exodus is a sign not only of the oppression and hardship in Afghanistan, but of the willingness of two Islamic neighbours to receive Islamic refugees. We forget that "a refugee problem" is created on both sides of the border. For every refugee there is a pull as well as a push factor. Thus there is little sign of Afghan refugees entering China, nor would they enter Pakistan and Iran unless they were tolerated and fed there.

One of the world's perplexities in the next generation will be how to show sympathy towards refugees, but not such sympathy that the flow becomes fifty times larger than otherwise.

Australia so far has taken only a handful of the Afghan refugees. There is no international pressure on us to accept them, and clearly there is also an unspoken reluctance in Canberra to bring in Islamic refugees in large numbers, especially from an environment where Soviet occupation has heightened Islamic fervour.

In Australia, the Afghans represent one of the weakest of the dozens of busy ethnic lobbies. I guess they form just as tiny a proportion of our population as they formed in the era when Afghans and their camels were the noble carriers in much of the vast dry country between Coolgardie and Cloncurry.

It is reasonable to assume that if the Afghans here were as numerous as, say, the Greeks or even the Vietnamese, they would long ago have persuaded both Labor and Liberal parties to sanction a vigorous intake of Afghan refugees as well as the family reunions that inevitably follow. None the less, a strong flow of Afghan refugees might eventually be channelled here.

This week's news confirms that the Soviet Union is now eager to withdraw its troops and aircraft, but there is still no assurance that it will restore peace to Afghanistan.

The Soviets will retain their air bases, and they will be succeeded by a communist government. A large part of the Islamic population will then try to supplant communist rule, but even if they win there is no sure prospect that the rifts will be quickly healed.

Just as the Afghan communists are often divided on cultural, regional and ethnic grounds, so their opponents are split into regional and sectarian groups, including the Sunni and the Shia Muslims, the fervent and the moderate, the pro-Pakistans, those who long for a rousing Islamic republic, and those who see virtue in the old way of governing.

The lesson that well-informed observers glean from the war in Afghanistan is that the Soviets - like maybe all large imperial powers - are never reluctant to enlarge their empire. The lesson overlooked is that a fragmented nation, lacking an overriding loyalty, really invites outside attack.

<u>Weekend Australia</u>, 16-17 April 1988

38

The Death of a Lighthouse

Stephen Murray-Smith died suddenly last Sunday morning. To label his life with one phrase is impossible.

Some people have such enthusiasm and spend it in so many ways that when they die it is as if broken bridges suddenly appear along every road they used to travel.

His father was a horse trader in the era when Melbourne was a great shipper of horses for the cavalry in India. The son was also a trader, but mainly in ideas and words.

Stephen once said in an aside that the family was not really wealthy, but occasionally did their best to appear so. Born in 1922, he studied at Geelong Grammar and then, during the Japanese onslaught, went to New Guinea as a private in the 2/5th Independent (commando) Unit.

He was a communist for a dozen or so years after the war, and served in London and Prague before becoming an organiser of the peace movement in Australia.

It must have been soon after he fell out with the Communist Party that I first saw him, at a writers' committee that met each month at the suburban house of A.A. Phillips.

Stephen entered the room a little late with a briefcase so full of books and papers that opening it was a difficult task. Even then he was a walking filing cabinet (in the heyday of the quiz he represented Australia in international contests).

He was strong, with a face fit for sculpture. In later years, when his walk was slower, he sometimes looked like a galleon in full sail. That image makes him seem absurd, but he wasn't. Immense was his dignity.

He was an accumulator. Books, manifestos, news clippings and people - he gathered them all in. In the long train journey between his home in Mount Eliza and his place of work in Melbourne he would write short notes, often on foolscap, telling friends that he had just come across something that might interest them. He must have written thousands of these notes.

Stephen Murray-Smith also collected quotations, and in 1984 produced the first *Dictionary of Australian Quotations,* a huge and individualistic book, the compiling of which would have occupied the time of a whole secretariat in some countries.

He wrote with authority on several dozen subjects that had not much in common. He was among the top two or three authorities on the writings of Henry Lawson and on the history of technical education in Australia, and he was master of another two handfuls of diverse topics.

It puzzled him that educated Australians did not share his superhuman interest in everything. He once surmised that "no country is as incurious about itself as ours is". But to acquire knowledge was not enough. You had to pass it on, with enthusiasm.

Some of his special indignation - he used about six brands of indignation - he directed against those censors who prevented the flow of knowledge and those bureaucrats who mangled or concealed knowledge.

In his resonant voice, he called to order those academics who merely wrote for each other. In his magazine, *Overland,* he insisted that people should try to write with such lucidity and spirit that "the matron of the Port Hedland Hospital would read them with pleasure".

Remote islands and their people and lighthouses commanded his imagination in later years. Once we sat at a football final, his pipesmoke all around us, and he spoke about St Kilda for three sentences before it became apparent that the isolated Scottish island, not the football team, was on his mind.

Of course, he had visited it. In the early 1980s he went to Cape Town and took a berth on a tramp steamer that called at the River Congo. It was the only way of reaching the lonely island of Tristan da Cunha, far out in the South Atlantic.

Each summer he and friends would go into hiding on an uninhabited island at the eastern end of Bass Strait. By chance, a yachtsman told me that last summer he had sheltered in an anchorage there and, going ashore, he met a patriarch and his warm-hearted wife. Instantly, it was clear to me whose island he was on.

He loved Bass Strait, even on white-water days. The names of the lighthouses, islands and coves gave him delight: Tin Kettle Island; Pea Jacket Point; Guncarriage Island; and Thunder and Lightning Bay. How they rolled off his tongue.

In a Melbourne paper this week was a small death notice; a tribute to him as the founder of the Australian Lighthouse Association. It seemed just right, for he too was a lighthouse.

<u>Weekend Australian</u>, 6-7 August 1988

39

Who Holds the Key to the New Fort Knox: The Problem of the Universities

Australian universities have long been the scene of a tug-o'-war between the government which seeks more control and the university staff which seeks more money. The present crisis is not as unusual as we think it is.

The first two Australian universities were opened in ports which were essentially gateways to goldfields: today the federal government sees the universities themselves as gateways to new goldfields. Some critics complain that the federal government, under Mr John Dawkins, sees the universities as a kind of all-purpose lathe or machine-tool which can reshape the Australian economy. In the eyes of many lecturers in the social sciences, Mr Dawkins is the prime philistine in Australia's educational history.

It is appropriate to question Mr Dawkins' goal and his skill in approaching his goal, but it is not fair to see him as an ogre. In Australia, as in many other nations, the utilitarian approach to universities is hardly new. It tends to flourish during every major economic downturn.

Even in the 1850s, utilitarian arguments were recited. Thus the New South Wales Legislative Council, in formally legislating for a University of Sydney, said simply that a university was deemed expedient "for the better advancement of religion and morality, and the promotion of useful knowledge". In short, there was a Mr Dawkins, an exponent of *useful* knowledge, living in Sydney in 1850. A few years later the inscription in Latin on the foundation stone of Melbourne University also expressed a desire to extend "the bounds of science". In first place, however, was a desire to honour God by "establishing young men in philosophy, literature and piety". Today, piety can find no room on the foundation stone of a new university; and the adjective *pious* is almost derogatory.

Utilitarian goals later became more prominent in tertiary education. In the years 1904 to 1914 the University of Melbourne, out of favour with the state government and heavily in debt because of sustained embezzlements by its own accountant, invoked the Dawkins formula. Melbourne opened courses in veterinary science and agricultural science, though they attracted few students. It revitalised the school of mining engineering, launched mechanical and electrical engineering, and awarded the first degrees in dental science and the university's first certificates in the fields of education and architecture. Lest you think that this was a general period of expansion for every faculty, I must add that in 1886 the Arts Faculty had five chairs and fifty years later it still had five.

The federal government's first real support for universities was the generous financing of thousands of ex-service students in the first post-war years. It was largely the brain-child of Mr Ben Chifley, who in 1945 was to become the Prime Minister. His scheme carried a title which even Mr Dawkin would not dare to give to his plan for reshaping of universities. It was called the Commonwealth Reconstruction Training Scheme. In 1945, in the name of national reconstruction, it financed 12,000 of the 30,000 students in our universities. Just as the giving of a farm to a returned soldier was a hallmark of the 1920s, so the granting of a university place to a soldier symbolised the late 1940s.

We may not care to admit the fact, but utilitarianism has been a persistent strand in the educational philosophy of modern Australia. Mr Whitlam, Prime Minister from 1972 to 1975, placed the universities firmly in the Commonwealth's area of responsibility, partly on the grounds that national greatness and economic well-being required a high expenditure on education. He in 1974 could promise money in plenty. In 1988, Mr Hawke and Mr Dawkins cannot.

Mr Dawkins, if he spent more money, would not be depicted as an ogre. For universities, an increase in annual income has become almost as much a sign of prestige as of the pressing needs which the money fulfils. It was our undue absorption with money which made us welcome the centralism which is now the danger.

Mr Dawkins is arousing anxiety and excitement; and as his name is already prominent in this seminar, I state my own tentative position on his reforms:

1   It is legitimate to challenge the universities. Mr Dawkins, to his credit, has issued the strongest challenge seen in my lifetime.

2   It is not a heresy to make the users pay for part of their education. Consumers pay part of the cost of their public transport, public housing and public health, and they used to pay part of the cost of universities until the fee was abolished by the only prime minister in our history who was not interested in his government's revenue. At the same time the principle that the consumer should pay part of the cost has to be applied with skill.

3   The present Dawkins' plan represents the biggest venture in centralism in the history of higher education

in Australia. If it fails it will impose unprecedented losses, quickly.

4   In calling for a more utilitarian approach to university education, Mr Dawkins represents an old Australian tradition. My worry is that he defines national utility too narrowly. There will be great nations in the future just as there have been great nations in the past which do not lead in utilitarian research.

"The nations which have put mankind most in their debt have been small states - Israel, Athens, Florence, Elizabethan England", wrote Dean Inge. His affirmation of values is worth remembering. In the first half century of the university in Australia, most teachers - and through them the students - had a powerful sense of the value of the knowledge possessed by earlier generations. The vital place of Latin and Ancient Greek in the undergraduate syllabus was a tribute to classical civilizations. The university's respect for mainstream Christianity - even though theology was taboo as a specific university subject - was another testimony to the living past.

Today, in contrast, we over-value recent knowledge. A considerable proportion of university teachers in the humanities and social sciences would probably be condescending towards a university textbook of 1940, a doctoral thesis of 1940 (they were rare, then) and a lecture syllabus of 1940.

The post-war emphasis on specialisation and on its step-sister, research, has tended to advantage the staff at the expense of the students in many of the social sciences and humanities. I say tended to, knowing that the exceptions to this tendency are numerous. In big departments such as history and political science and English the practice is for the staff to lecture in the area of their research, or close to it. In many big departments the syllabus for undergraduates reflects more what is in the interests of the staff to teach rather than of the students to learn. In some departments the grandsweep courses have declined, and in others they have almost vanished.

I am unable to judge whether students receive an education inferior to that which their grandparents received: so many factors have to be considered. I am certain, however, that they do not receive as wide-ranging and as stimulating an education as they should receive from a staff which is now much larger and a library which is far larger.

Nor am I sure whether the staff themselves, even in their own research, are as productive as they might be. Working in the walled cities and streets of their own research discipline, they might extend knowledge more if they pushed down those walls of their own careful making. The research cult is useful. Carried too far, it does not even aid the advancement of knowledge. Additions to knowledge in many fields depend on some balance and perspective, both in the mind of the investigator and of those who receive and evaluate the new knowledge. If research is prized too highly, new knowledge becomes over-valued compared to the old. The intellectual industry has a street-front, plate-glass window where the new is given far too much space. It is almost as if learning is becoming a public-sector branch of the fashion industry. As a long-time beneficiary of this trend I cannot complain too loudly.

Today we emphasise not only new fields of research - nearly all of them worthy - but we also emphasise a way of communicating which itself has to be novel, and finds that novelty in obscure prose or the unreal precision of algebra and excessive decimal points.

A modern university seems to carry an inbuilt tension which we gladly ignore. The university tries to carry on the different tasks of teaching and examining and research without fully coming to grips with the conflicts between those tasks. After all, one aim of the university is to enthrone the undisputed, but another vital aim of the university is to dispute the enthroned. As a generalisation the Australian universities of a century ago were very successful in enthroning the undisputed and extending its influence, but in the last forty years the universities have been more successful in disputing the enthroned. The disputing role is now most vigorous in the social sciences and the arts; and yet that is the section which traditionally tried to uphold the main values of civilization.

An emphasis on research gives a strong premium to new evidence or statements of probability. It carried the assumption that knowledge is always advancing. That the universities greatly aid the advancement of knowledge is an axiom of those who defend the universities in the presence of the government. But do universities, outside certain sciences, advance knowledge as much as they claim?

If knowledge can advance it must, by definition, be capable of retreating. Knowledge in one macro sense is probably advancing but in the micro sense, in terms of the individual minds of our students, it might well be retreating. If, in the last forty years, knowledge has advanced on countless fronts, and tens of thousands of academic frontiersmen and women have made their discoveries, who possesses the new knowledge which they found? Much of it is in the stacks of libraries, undigested. Have we built a new vault, a new Fort Knox, to which nobody has the master key? If travel usually broadens the mind, why do so many Qantas stewards and Pan Am pilots miss out? Today the same observation could well be made of many of the educated.

> The concluding part of an address to the conference
> on "The Idea of a University" organised by the
> Seminar on the Sociology of Culture,
> La Trobe University, 8 October 1988

40

A Nation of Islanders, We Can Hardly See the Sea

When the Soviet Union suggested this week that perhaps it should close down its naval base in Vietnam in return for the United States abandoning its big naval base and airfield in the Philippines, there was no mighty upsurge of attention in Australia.

The removal or the retention of these naval bases of the world's greatest naval powers could, in 30 years' time, have profound effects on a confrontation, skirmish or war in Australia's seas. And yet the question of the continuation of these naval bases arouses little interest here.

A century ago, any rumour that the French might build a naval base in New Caledonia, or that the Germans might fortify their new harbour in Rabaul, would have aroused excitement in Brisbane and Adelaide. It almost goes without saying that in our shrinking world, the Soviet base in Vietnam and the US base at Subic Bay are, in sailing time, closer to Australian shores than was Rabaul a century ago.

Back in the 1930s, there was widespread Australian interest in what was happening to the British naval base in Singapore - an interest that was justified when the Japanese stormed the Singapore causeway in February 1942. And yet we only nod when we read that the future of two nuclear-age Singapores, with their nuclear ships and submarines and air fields, could be open to negotiation between Moscow and Washington.

Strong reasons have eroded Australia's interest in what seapower can do to protect us or harm us. There is a powerful view, especially among those in their teens and 20s, that in this era of nuclear weapons, navies are outmoded. But to all intents it is not yet the nuclear era and, of the hundreds of wars fought across the globe since 1945, not one has used a nuclear missile.

Admittedly, most wars in the last 40 years have been fought essentially on land, and this has turned attention away from naval power. In contrast, in the era of colonies, many wars were fought by European regiments and vessels far from home, and seapower was vital to protect their supply lines.

In Australian eyes, the value of seapower has also waned because it was not conspicuous in Vietnam. There is now, however, an informed view that it was a grave mistake for the US to spend enormous effort in bombing North Vietnam's land routes and oil depots when the same goal could have been achieved quickly by blockading the sea lanes to North Vietnam's ports.

The world's most powerful navy had little effect on the course of the war in Vietnam. It allowed a procession of oil tankers to pass within sight of its guns and safely enter North Vietnamese ports. This mistake - if mistake it was - indirectly did much to devalue naval power in the eyes of the intelligent layman in Australia, the US and many other Western lands.

The continuing value of a strong navy has also been concealed temporarily by the fact that, for perhaps the first time in history, the world's largest merchant fleets belong to nations owning at best a tinpot navy.

Liberia has 18 per cent of the world's merchant shipping; Panama has 13 per cent. Yet, did you see the might of the Liberian and Panamanian navies at the naval display on Sydney Harbour last weekend? I think not.

Add the merchant fleets of Greece and Japan, and we have a total of 50 per cent of the world's shipping belonging to nations which cannot offer adequate naval protection. This remarkable fact - a sign of a long period of relative peace on the world's oceans - disguises the importance of naval power.

We live in a phase of world history when naval power seems temporarily silent. Furthermore, we live in a nation where yacht, kayak, speedboat and the water ski capture the imagination more than big ships.

World War II taught a generation of Australians the importance of combined sea and air power. Australia in 1942 would have been close to disaster if the Japanese had won the battle of the Coral Sea and had pressed on to Port Moresby and captured it, thus enabling the repeated bombing of Queensland ports and railways and placing a mighty obstacle against Australia's recapture of New Guinea.

Even the battle of the Coral Sea has faded from the public imagination. More than half of the present population of Australia probably has not heard of it. If the Australian navy had been the main opponent of the Japanese fleet in the Coral Sea, the victory might have lived in folklore. But the Coral Sea, in public memory, could never become another Gallipoli, partly because Australian pride was quietly wounded by the fact that their nation was saved by Americans.

So here we are, a nation of islanders who de-value seapower. We should take more interest in it. The sea still counts.

<u>Weekend Australian,</u> 8-9 October 1988

41

Japan Rises - Australia Cringes

The rise of Japan is the remarkable event in the economic world since the end of World War II. No other nation has ever risen so swiftly.

Astonishing as was the rise of Germany late in the last century and the parallel rise of the United States to economic might, Japan's performance is eye-opening.

Whether she is number one or two in the world today is open to dispute, but it was sobering to hear the astute commentator, Alan Carroll, say in Sydney this week that 1988 might well go down as one of the landmarks of the 20th century - the year when Japan passed the US.

Most of what the Japanese have achieved has been the result of their own work and teamwork, but they did have one big advantage over Germany from 1945. Whereas Germany was divided by the victors of World War II, Japan was allowed to remain united.

The Japanese also had a huge home market, being one of the world's six most populous nations before Nigeria, Indonesia and other Third World nations began to multiply in population.

Another Japanese advantage is that her defence has largely been paid for by the US. Apart from that gain, there is little merit in the idea that Japan's post-war miracle was a result of her favoured position as a nation that lost a major war. Contrary to recent assertions, it does not pay to lose a war.

We still have difficulty in coming to terms with Japan's new power. For too long she was underrated in the Western world. Thus in the 1930s, Japan was simply seen as the maker of shoddy products. A Japanese toy given to an Australian child for Christmas was usually falling apart by Boxing Day.

And yet that same Japan was capable of making fighter aircraft which, to the surprise of Britain and Australia, quickly snatched control of the air during the lightning Japanese advance at the end of 1941.

The unexpected fall of Singapore in February 1942 and the threat to Australia's security stemmed from the tendency in Canberra, and even more in London, to undervalue Japanese skills.

After the war Japan recovered slowly. Rice was scarce and a worker in Yokohama ate only 1600 calories of food a day. In 1946 Japan's industrial production was a mere one-sixth of the 1940 tally.

In an era when the production of steel was seen as the index of industrial power, Japan ranked low. In 1956 Japan ranked sixth in output of steel, just behind France and well behind Britain. By 1961 Japan had outstripped them both and was about to pass West Germany to become number three in the world's hierarchy of steel producers.

Australians who visited Japan in 1961 could see her strength but sensed that, financially, she was just another Australia - prosperous but easily buffeted.

Both nations in 1961 had faced acute difficulties in their balance of payments. Ironically, Australia today stands in a more serious position than in 1961, while the yen, once a dicey currency, now rules the world.

Whereas Japan in 1955 built only half as many ships as the British shipyards, ten years later her shipbuilding industry was four times as large as Britain's. Japan was now building the largest ships the world had seen and she was also the world's second largest manufacturer of cars and buses.

By the early 1970s Japan's success was at last accepted. Teams arrived in Tokyo in search of the Japanese formula. Was it in industrial relations that her secret lay? Was her secret recipe an almost feudal loyalty? There were, however, still doubts about how far Japan could go in world competition. The oil crisis of 1973-74 hit hard. Perhaps Japan had reached her peak.

It became common to hear the argument, directed against Japan, that she was simply an imitator. It became normal to point out that Britain and West Germany and the United States had paved their road to economic success with a chain of wonderful inventions. Where, it was asked, were the Japanese Edisons, Stephensons and Benzs?

Where indeed? But still Japan grew. Japan mainly imitated, but she often improved and streamlined what she imitated.

Now that Japan is ascendant, and determined to remain so, we are inclined to cringe in the face of such a mighty power. The most conspicuous form of cringing comes from certain federal ministers and government corporations who uncomplainingly see Australia's future as tied firmly to Japan's and who believe that public discussion of the dangers as well as the merits of massive Japanese investment should be curbed. Mr Hawke deems it wise, electorally, to hush up this explosive topic.

For too long we have failed as a nation to grasp the extent of Japan's economic success and, at best, have accepted dubious explanations of that success. Now, however, we are leaping to the other extreme and regarding the Japanese penetration of Australia as inevitable and beyond sensible discussion.

The evidence suggests that the Japanese investment here is far more extensive than Tokyo is prepared to admit. How far is that investment in our interests? Should such an important matter be camouflaged? The Federal Parliament is reluctant to discuss this crucial, wide-ranging topic. Now, rather than later, is the time to discuss it.

One final comment is beyond dispute. If we were the economic giants and we began to take over many Japanese industries and suburbs, the Japanese would not be silent.

Weekend Australian, 22-23 October 1988

42

Kangaroo and Kiwi

I see a strong chance that Australia and New Zealand will merge or federate sometime in the 21st century. One vital but hazardous step towards that ultimate political merger is taking place right now.

That step, observed with intense interest in New Zealand but with hardly a yawn by the Australia public, could affect Australia's way of life in the long term. In essence, New Zealand and Australia will form a kind of common market, a trans-Tasman economic community on July 1, 1990. Thereafter, all commodities will cross the Tasman freely without paying import duties or enjoying special bounties and subsidies.

Thirty years ago, when ocean liners rather than jet planes were the main carriers of people across the Tasman, there was little thought that one day the two nations would seek ways of marrying their economies. Then, both Australia and New Zealand were prosperous and stood on a higher rung of the world's economic ladder than they occupy today.

Adversity, however, has now knocked their heads together. New Zealand, once one of the world's five most prosperous nations, had been bruised by Britain's entry into the European Economic Community in the early 1970s. It was also lacerated by the petroleum crisis of 1974, because it imported nearly all of its energy.

One of New Zealand's answers to these twin blows was to welcome the opportunity, which Mr Doug Anthony generously supported as a leader of the National Party, to tap the bigger Australian market. As the National Party could lose through strong New Zealand competition in butter, meat and other rural products, Mr Anthony's sympathy for closer economic relations with New Zealand was as vital as the trade unions' support for large-scale immigration just after World War II.

Australia's interest in tapping the market across the Tasman was further spurred in the early 1980s when our economy tasted the same bitter medicine New Zealand had swallowed some ten years earlier. Whereas 1995 was to be the year in which free trade in all commodities - whether potatoes or steel - was to be introduced, agreement was reached this winter to bring forward that date by five years.

Trade between the two nations is already large. With no duties and no bounties, this trade will probably multiply after 1990, and each nation will specialise in producing those commodities in which it can outsell its partner.

Cars and office machines are two of our three main exports to New Zealand while our main imports are paper, paperboard and live animals.

Mr David Lange, the New Zealand Prime Minister, insists that our two nations are on the way to an economic relationship unequalled by any other two sovereign nations. Perhaps he is walking on the Tasman, buoyed more by hope than reality, but there is some truth in his comment.

At the same time, we should not hail the trans-Tasman market as revolutionary. Without any of today's treaties and oratory, commodities and people flowed just as freely across the Tasman in the 1860s as they will in the 1990s.

At that time, the dominating South Island of New Zealand and its gold mines were economic satellites of Melbourne: many ships left Melbourne weekly for Bluff, Dunedin, and wild Hokitika, and the import duties did little to impede trans-Tasman trade, and cheap shipping did much to accelerate it.

Cheap shipping is vital for the forthcoming arrangement. The goodwill of politicians can marry two isolated economies but, unless ships are efficient, the marriage will be fragile.

No doubt all the high-value commodities will be carried efficiently by aircraft but steel, paperboard, pulp, cars, wood, petroleum products and most of the mainstays of Tasman commerce require cheap shipping.

There is little purpose in liberating tran-Tasman commerce if the seamen's and waterside unions, and the shipowners, refuse to be liberated. Since 1974, Australian and New

Zealand seamen have virtually monopolised the Tasman. This monopoly would not matter if the ships were efficient, but they are not.

No doubt the seamen have a case - and also a long list of historic grievances - but so do the nations whose interests they claim to serve. Even Australia is not truly a common market because transport on so many routes remains too inefficient and costly.

Trade with New Zealand does not have the compensating advantage of road and rail transport, thus making a cheap sea-link even more important. The test of whether Canberra and Wellington are serious will be their willingness to make shipping a satisfactory means of transport. That will not be easy.

One old axiom of Australian politics is that if we can only increase our population and the size of the home market, we will make economic progress. The roping together of Australia and New Zealand fits that axiom.

Conversely, an axiom of Australian economics is that, if coastal transport is expensive, Australia will remain a chain of isolated markets masquerading as one. In other words, an increased population may mean little. To bring New Zealand and Australia into a common market, separated by sea, is certainly more hazardous than linking Canada and the US, or Germany and France.

The economic marriage of two nations will be tricky. If it succeeds, the political marriage becomes a little more feasible. But, in my view, it will be defence fears, not economic fears, that promote the prospect of a political merger forty or sixty years into the future.

<u>Weekend Australian, 26-27 November 1988</u>

43

The Perils and Hazards of Selecting 200 Great Australians

The bicentennial honour roll of the 200 great Australians was no sooner published than the howls of outrage could be heard in every State and in every profession and sect.

Dismay or outrage is unavoidable, because any decision on who contributed most to this nation must be based partly on private values, guesswork and supposition, and on the patchy state of historical research.

At the same time, the committee which bravely took on this task of choosing the great 200 handed too much ammunition to its critics. To include many brave soldiers, but to exclude the first Australian field-marshal, Sir Thomas Blamey, was a little rash, especially as he led the Australian forces when the nation, for the first time in its history, was in peril.

Likewise, Barry Jones, whose knowledge of Australian biography is awe-inspiring, was correct to query the omission of several famous scientists, just as historians were entitled to ask why Peter Lalor, the hero of Eureka, did not appear under the Ls, even though that letter of the alphabet was stretched enough to accommodate a worthy but minor film star from the era of silent movies.

I did not hear the complaint actually laid, but many West Australians must have marvelled at the omission of Paddy Hannan, whose discovery of gold at Kalgoorlie in 1893 did more to boost the West than any other day's work, or even lifetime's work, by any one person.

If a West Australian had to be deleted to make way for Paddy, then Walter Murdoch, fine essayist as he was, could perhaps have been removed. But could he? Scholars, leaving aside a few celebrated scientists, are already represented meagrely in the list of 200.

The dilemma of the bold selectors of the famous 200 at once becomes clear when you think of all the categories of achievement that should not only be recognised but also receive more than two names.

Nobody could accuse the selectors of deliberately ignoring the claims of women. Thus, Joseph Lyons, the prime minister for seven difficult years, has no place, but his talented wife, Dame Enid, is here. Probably, both deserve to be honoured, not least because Tasmania is treated sternly by the selectors, at least in the eyes of Tasmanians.

The controversial issue of whether to include sportsmen has been answered courageously; and the Bradmans and Cuthberts and Haydn Buntons rightly run on to the great arena in all their glory.

Unfortunately, the sportsmen of the 19th century have been entirely overlooked. Bill Mandle, who has done so much to foster interest in sporting history in Australia, once wrote that the two initial sporting giants in this land were Trickett, the sculler, and the "demon" Spofforth, the fearsome fast bowler. World figures, their names are absent.

Meanwhile, one of our national leaders, scanning the list of 200, said with some indignation that the "ethnic community" had been shunned. As the community of that name was not large until at least the 1950s, his case would need to be argued carefully.

The more I look at the names and notice such remarkable Jews as John Monash, the soldier, and Issac Isaacs, the governor-general, and see the German-sounding surnames of Hinkler the aviator and Goldstein the feminist and Opperman the cyclist (whose admirers are still legion), and then observe such European names as Borovansky of the ballet and Delprat of BHP, I am not persuaded that the vital role of continental Europeans or their children has been neglected.

Catholics receive a visible priority among the chosen churchmen, but which Catholic do you omit? Before attending the funeral of the poet Vincent Buckley on Thursday, I read part of his book, *Cutting Green Hay*, and was moved by his pages on Daniel Mannix, for long the Catholic archbishop of Melbourne: "When I was a child, his portrait hung in my parents' house, in the front parlour, next to those of my grandparents." The same portrait sat above 200,000 Victorian fireplaces or nooks.

Whether the list of 200 **contains** Mannix for his politics or his religion does not matter. A giant, he rightly belongs to the 200.

The reluctance to recognise the powerful role of the Protestant churches, especially in the period from 1860 to 1960, seems to have retarded the search for notable names. But several of the names appear indirectly in the top 200, through a kind of laying on of hands.

Thus, "California" Taylor is said to have been the greatest evangelist of our history; and in the late 1860s, in a Wesleyan church at the Victorian gold town of Stawell, he converted a young boy named Fred Cato and shaped the course of his life. This week, nearly 120 years later, one of Cato's daughters, Dr Una Porter, must have felt pride and humility that she should have been honoured in the great 200.

At present, our great painters, novelists and poets are deservedly held in esteem in many circles. Indeed, they are the new high priests, but their great predominance over the old priests and pastors within the favour 200 is not easily justified.

There is a tendency in making any list of the notable to single out fashionable names of today and forget those whose influence in their era had been infinitely larger than any present-day hero. Clergymen, as well as a poet such as Adam Lindsay Gordon, suffer under this rule of selection.

There will always be a dash of the lottery in compiling lists of the great or mighty, for some are great because they were ordinary people standing in the right place at the right time, and some are great because they fought with astonishing skill and courage against a fierce tide and lost.

The losers are much less likely to appear in the list of the great, and yet often their personal influence on events, and even the nation's history, was the larger.

Come to think of it, that's what Ned Kelly said. His final words, apparently, were: "Such is life".

His name is not in this list, and that in itself will fire a thousand arguments.

Weekend Australian, 19-20 November 1988

44

The Strange Statistics of Suicide

I was astonished to see the statistics on suicide that came out this week.

If 30 years ago a commentator had predicted that the year would come in Australia when the number of suicides would be fast approaching the deaths in car accidents, the prediction would have been dismissed as ridiculous. But today the suicides are not far behind the car deaths.

The suicide rate made a leap in 1987, according to the Australian Bureau of Statistics. In Victoria alone, the rate jumped by 25 per cent to 15.5 per 100,000 people. And one gloomy fact tucked away in the official table was that nine of the suicides in Victoria were children who had not yet reached their 14th birthday.

Some commentators see suicide as the clear mirror of the state of tension and instability in a nation. Sweden has often been singled out for its high suicide rate, which has been variously attributed to the effects of too much prosperity, too many social services and too little religion.

And yet Sweden - so far as my scanning of yearbooks reveals - has rarely stood near the very top of the global list of suicides.

Even if Sweden did head the list, we should have to be sure that it was not partly a reflection of Sweden's more accurate statistics. If the social stigma against suicide is too severe, those who conduct inquests or give evidence will do their best to promote a verdict of accidental death rather than suicide.

The colder regions of Europe have long had a higher suicide rate than the milder or warmer regions, and there is evidence to suggest that even if statistics are imperfect, the Italians and Greeks have been less inclined to commit suicide over, say, the past hundred years than have the English, while the Swiss and Danes and Czechs - to name only three - tended to report a suicide rate that was up to eight times as high as that of the Irish.

A cold climate must be only one of the complicated ingredients in a national tendency to suicide. Early studies of suicide in Europe, especially in the lands of ice and snow, found that the common months for suicide were not in winter but in warm May and June.

Amidst the climatic extremes of Australia, suicide seems to have been affected less by climate than by masculinity. Thus, cold Tasmania a century ago had a much lower suicide rate than warm Queensland, and the main reason was probably that Queensland was still a man's world with a high male-female ratio.

Suicide is often interpreted as a signpost of the fragility of modern civilisation, and it is true that the suicide rate tends to be higher in the cities than the farmlands, and higher among those with time on their hands. The ACT at one time stood at the top of the Australian ladder of suicide by a startling margin.

The belief that suicide is somehow the bane of the sophisticated, lonely city helps to explain the sense of astonishment and high indignation towards the disclosures that in the 1980s, many Aborigines were "committing suicide" while in police custody.

In discussion among the concerned and the educated, it was often asserted that Aborigines do not commit suicide and that therefore foul play was the overwhelming cause of the deaths. Such an extreme assertion is unlikely to be vindicated by the royal commission at present studying Aboriginal deaths in custody.

Earlier this year, I spoke about Australia at Denison University in Ohio, and a pointed question came from the audience about Aboriginal deaths in custody. After the lecture, one of the professors showed me a graph revealing the unusual incidence of suicides by American Indians today. Clearly, suicide does not fit as neatly as we would like into the loose theories which most of us carry in our head.

Suicide is widely seen as a sign of acute individual stress. Even so, stress itself is not so easily measured. A war, for example, does not increase the suicide rate. In the tense years of World War II, the suicide rate in Australia slumped. In 1944, the number of deaths from suicide was only 7 for each 100,000 people. By 1948 it had climbed back to a more normal 10.

A suicide is a shattering event to a circle of relatives, friends and acquaintances, partly because it is unexpected and seemingly avoidable, yet it is not placed high on the list of avoidable casualties.

The statistician William Archer, trying to collect his statistics during the chaos of goldrush Victoria in 1854, made an alert observation. In a footnote in the tiniest of print he ventured to suggest that perhaps the deaths from suicide and the more numerous deaths from alcohol should be added together to form a new category called "self-destruction".

In our civilisation, "self-destruction" wears many labels. Suicide, for all its emotional impact, is still a minor label.

Weekend Australian, 17-18 December 1988

Part III

1989

45

Sydney and Melbourne Lag in the Population Race

The economic and political power of Sydney and Melbourne is far from assured in the long term.

Sydney now has 3 million people and Melbourne 2.7 million, but the 1980s have been one of their leanest decades in the past century.

Both cities are failing by a big margin to keep pace with the rate of population growth in Australia as a whole. While property values are soaring in the two big cities, one conclusion is simple: most Australians no longer wish to live in what once were the meccas for footloose Australians.

Melbourne, especially, is struggling, a fact which was strangely obscured in the Victorian election campaign last year. The Premier, Mr Cain, shrewdly made much of the statistics that Melbourne and Victoria had the lowest rate of unemployment in the Commonwealth.

His opponents did not highlight the parallel fact that one of the likely reasons for Victoria's excellent employment record is that unemployed Victorians are flocking interstate.

Are the latest counts of city populations reliable? It is not easy to define where a city ends in these days of commuter farms and satellite towns, but the Commonwealth Statisticians's definition of urban centres shows up Melbourne in an unfavourable light.

Of the eight capital cities, only Hobart performed more poorly than Melbourne in the five years leading up to the census of June 1986.

Adelaide and Sydney, neither of which has managed to grow as fast as Australia as a whole, occupied the middle of the ladder of population growth. That Adelaide should grow at the same slow pace as Sydney is hardly a pat on the back for Sydney.

As expected, the attractive metropolis of Canberra-Queanbeyan - "the paper city" - grew faster than any State capital. Darwin was even swifter in its growth.

Of the cities of any size, Perth and Brisbane remain the success stories of the 1980s. Both are growing at about the same pace and increased their population at a rate about four times faster than Melbourne's.

They are still so far behind Melbourne in actual population that even a continuation of their recent growth will not easily allow them to overtake Melbourne. But if present trends continue, in the lifetime of children now at school, Brisbane and Perth could begin to rival Melbourne.

Present trends, however, might not continue. It was in the 1950s that Melbourne was the racehorse of Australia and Perth the foal. Now the foal is clearly supreme.

Melbourne and Sydney are failing in what they prize most - their ability to grow rapidly. They attract between them the lion's share of the new immigrants to Australia, and yet they lose their existing population at a surprising rate.

For the six years ending in June 1987, NSW experienced a large exodus to other States every year. Victoria had the same experience. But Tasmania in two of those six years actually gained from the interstate movement.

People moving permanently from one State to another constitute one of the main ingredients of population change in Australia, and they are now pouring out of the old States in the south-east corner of the continent.

Melbourne grew in the years 1981-1986 at an annual rate of about 0.5 per cent. Brisbane can exceed that rate simply on the strength of the people poached from other States, without bothering to count the larger gains from its own birth rate and its own intake of migrants.

It is legitimate to argue about urban boundaries. It is legitimate to query why the Sydney "urban centre", for example, extends west to the Blue Mountains and even further north than Gosford.

But there can be no disputing the speed at which Brisbane and Perth, irrespective of boundary definitions, are growing. Nor can we doubt that Sydney, and especially Melbourne, are lagging.

Possibly it is in the interests of Australia, and the daily life of the average adult and child, that the big cities do not become super-cities.

And yet there can be no debate unless we realise what is happening. And if we live in Melbourne or Sydney, we have little idea of the movements of people to which the census of 1986 clearly points.

Weekend Australian, 4-5 February 1989

46

Outrage at the Gate to Yarralumla

There are strong reasons why Bill Hayden, as Governor-General, needs good luck. And the reasons were given inadequate thought in all the discussion that preceded his appointment.

The post of governor-general has become a vital symbol of national unity. But it is difficult for a politician, least of all one as controversial and individualistic as Mr Hayden, to be led from the political jungle and unveiled as free of claws and clawmarks.

That such politicians as Lord Casey and Sir Paul Hasluck have gone from Parliament House to Government House and done their duties with impartiality does not constitute a real precedent for Mr Hayden's appointment. Since the crisis of 1975, the post has become far more delicate. Moreover, Australia for a variety of reaons is less united and would therefore gain from a governor-general with the right blend of restraint and forthrightness.

It may well be that Mr Hayden will rise to the occasion, but he it was who once implied that the occasion was not worth rising to.

Mr Hayden's suitability for the post was also open to legitimate challenge because of the role of his wife. The leader of the National Party, Ian Sinclair, raised the issue. He did it obliquely; the cry of public outrage was astonishing.

Some of the outrage at the mention of Mrs Hayden's suitability was a smokescreen to divert discussion of a matter that should have been discussed, though discussed with delicacy. The outrage also arose from sympathy for a woman who had faithfully carried out all the thankless tasks of a wife of a leading politician, performing them with special charm when Mr Hayden was leader of the Opposition.

It would be interesting to count the number of television and radio commentaries that concluded that Mr Sinclair, merely by raising the matter, had unintentionally ended all discussion on the suitability of the Haydens. In short, he had confirmed an appointment previously in dispute.

The Liberals were timid during this carnival of indignation. They could have pursued the issue, after hinting, if they so wished, that they did not like the particular way Mr Sinclair had raised it. Or they could have said that they felt sympathy with Mrs Hayden but that the question of her fitness for the accompanying position was of prime relevance. Instead they made it clear, under the pressure of media indignation, that they now placed less importance on the very post that hitherto they had insisted was so crucial.

A tidal wave of indignation was thus allowed in the space of a few days to silence discussion. Overlooked was one fact of fundamental importance: the position of governor-general is the only high office in which the role of the spouse is officially deemed important. A prime minister can be a bachelor, the chief justice of the High Court can be a spinster; but the absence of a spouse will simply be a matter of social comment and not a major reason for questioning the candidate's suitability.

In contrast, the wife of the governor-general has been absolutely essential in the success of that office. We need read only the first report of the office of the official secretary to the governor-general, signed on September 30, 1985 and presented to the Prime Minister.

After referring to the governor-general's formal responsibilities, the report sets out the vital duties that have arisen largely through "the great growth in national awareness". In outlining the duties the incumbent performs as the symbol of national unity, it begins what in effect is a job specification with the striking phrase: "The governor-general and his wife."

No other high Commonwealth job could be described with such a phrase. It was therefore ignorance, more than reasoned indignation, which spurred the outcry last winter.

The denunciation of anyone who tried to pursue it was another episode in the increasing tendency to specify certain attitudes and topics as taboo. In a democracy, no tyranny is more dangerous than the arbitrary decision to exclude specific topics from the agenda for national discussion.

While there were strong precedents for challenging the appointment of Mr Hayden, his is a post for which precedent has not always been a sound guide. Widespread unease was expressed when in 1930 a Labor government recommended that for the first time a Briton should not be appointed governor-general. But Sir Isaac Isaacs, born in Australia of Jewish descent, disarmed most of his critics during his distinguished term.

In 1944, there was almost universal pleasure when a Labor government nominated King George VI's own brother, the Duke of Gloucester, as governor-general. Then in 1947, dismay spread amongst half the population when he was followed by the reigning Labor premier of NSW, William McKell, originally a metal worker by trade. Yet there can be little doubt that McKell proved a great success.

It is far from impossible that Mr Hayden will prove to be an excellent governor-general and that his wife will be the key to his success. Most Australians wish them luck.

Weekend Australian, 17 February 1989

47

Mourning the Death of Emperor Hirohito

Many Australians felt astonishment and anger when they saw the Australian flag flying at half-mast on federal government buildings yesterday.

It is honourable to pay respect to the dead. It is dishonourable if respect is paid in such a way that tens of thousands of others, now dead, are thereby dishonoured.

To wonder at the servility of Mr Hawke before the Japanese throne is not to give offence to the Japanese people or the Japanese nation. Japan deservedly has her self-respect and the right to the respect of others. But if Japan were in Australia's position, it would surely not go to the lengths to which Mr Hawke has gone in his grovelling.

Sending high Australian officials to Japan for the funeral ceremonies of emperor Hirohito is to carry out the normal civilities. But to fly the flag at half-mast throughout Australia (except at war memorials, gardens of remembrance and repatriation hospitals) is the action of a Prime Minister who increasingly fails to see the wide gap between shaking the hands and licking the boots of a powerful nation.

Australia conducts diplomatic relations with some 150 nations, and each year the head of State of at least one of those nations dies. But Australia usually take no steps to lower the national flag as a mark of respect.

If Mr Hawke deeply valued the Australian flag he would hesitate to use it in a way that inflicts pain on hundreds of thousands of loyal Australians.

So in Perth yesterday, the brother of an Australian prisoner of war who was stripped and then gunned to death by Japanese at the Malayan town of Parit Sulong in January, 1942, would have seen the Australian flag at half-mast and wondered why the leader of the men who killed his brother should be so honoured.

In Brisbane, the frail mother of an Australian prisoner of war who died in the Sandakan deathmarch would have felt bewilderment when told that the Australian flag was flying at half-mast in her own city in honour of the emperor whose loyal soldiers killed her son.

In small beach resorts and hot towns on the plains, children will have been flabbergasted at the flying of the Australian flag in a way that positively dishonoured the memory of grandfathers who were beheaded by the faithful Japanese servants of Hirohito.

I do not for one moment see emperor Hirohito as a war criminal of the same order as Hitler, Himmler and other German leaders. In wartime Japan his power, though real, was limited. And yet there can be no doubt that he was a major war criminal, as defined by the United Nations War Crimes Commission. The Australian leaders and jurists of the 1940s had no doubt Hirohito was a war criminal.

The Americans, especially General Douglas MacArthur, saved Hirohito from trial. Perhaps their decision in 1945 was sound, because it made the conquered Japan more amenable to American influence. In retrospect it was a pragmatic decision, a shrewd act of favouritism rather than an assertion that the emperor was not guilty.

The fact is unmistakable that the Australian flags, at Mr Hawke's directions, flew yesterday in memory not only of the post-war emperor of a remarkable, resurgent nation, but of a wartime leader who, by United Nations definition, was a war criminal.

The emperor's death patently called for delicacy and tact on the part of the Australian Government; it called for a divided response. Mr Hawke, however, has behaved like a loyal Japanese citizen.

The Prime Minister's response is even more astonishing when we recall his impassioned speeches announcing that every war criminal of 1939-45 still living in Australia should be brought to trial.

In the words of the new preamble of the War Crimes Act, assented to on January 25 this year: "Concern has arisen that a significant number of persons who committed serious war crimes in Europe during World War II may since have entered Australia and became Australian citizens or residents." The faulty grammar of the preamble is as conspicuous as the shoddy morality. A Japanese war criminal who becomes resident of Australia is exempt.

At times in the past it has been a legitimate criticism of Australian leaders that they were too servile to Britain and merely displayed "a colonial mentality". Now there is a new colonial mentality. Mr Hawke's stance proclaims that now we are a colony of Japan.

The Japanese are worthy people. They are fully entitled to honour their dead emperor. Australians are equally entitled to honour their own kith and kin, but to fly the Australian flag at half-mast throughout the land, dishonours generations of Australians, both living and dead.

Weekend Australian, 25-26 February 1989

48

Throwing Stones Across Torres Strait

Events in Papua New Guinea in the next twenty years could well affect our future as much as the events that will happen in Canberra. Papua New Guinea is probably as vital to Australia's long-term future as was the English Channel and Flanders to England's security in bygone centuries.

We have nearly forgotten that the Battle of the Coral Sea - one of the crucial events in our history - arose from the Japanese attempt in 1942 to capture Port Moresby and thereby threaten Australia. One reason why so many Australians are astonished at Mr Hawke's servility towards Japan at the time of the death of Hirohito is that they do remember the peril which faced Australia in 1942 and the fact that Papua New Guinea was the spearhead of the Japanese advance.

Even if we ignore Papua New Guinea's importance for Australia's national security, we should not forget its own right to an independent existence. It has been, so far, a remarkably successful democracy - a fact worth savouring at a time when Fiji and a host of African and Asian nations have not lived up to their earlier democratic goals.

Many Australian observers in the past few months have been hasty in condemning the Port Moresby Government. They see it as a nest of political instability, with politicians flapping their wings and waiting for a chance to swoop, while the nation's troubles multiply.

An over-critical assessment of the politics of Port Moresby is unfair. Moreover, it is hardly our privilege to throw the first stones. Should we really compare ourselves and our long history of continuous democracy with a nation which became independent only in 1975 and, as an independence gift, received roughly-tailored replicas of our own institutions?

Papua New Guinea, for all its present political troubles, has probably been more successful than the first democratic parliaments that were set up in Australia during the gold rushes of the 1850s. When the first freely elected parliaments met in the Australian cities, and for the first time controlled nearly everything except foreign policy and defence, they were hardly object lessons in political stability for the 109 members of parliament in Port Moresby, who have far greater responsibilities.

Early Victoria, with one of the most democratic parliaments the world had seen, initially changed its premiers as if they were cards in a much-shuffled pack. Victoria had ten different premiers in its first thirteen years. Papua New Guinea in the same timespan has had only four - Mr Somare, Sir Julius Chan, Mr Wingti, and now Mr Namaliu.

South Australia, which was viewed by European radicals as one of the cathedrals of world democracy, had a procession of seventeen premiers in just twelve years between 1856 and 1868. Compared to oldtime Adelaide, Port Moresby seems politically placid.

Admittedly, Papua New Guinea gained a little extra stability because its parliaments usually have sat for five years, whereas most of the early Australian parliaments were forced by law to go to the polls after a maximum of three years. Nonetheless, the contrast overall still favours Papua New Guinea.

In the present eagerness to extract light amusement from the long-awaited vote of no-confidence in the deadlocked parliament in Port Moresby, we forget that our first federal parliaments were even more adept at musical chairs.

In the Commonwealth Parliament's first thirteen years, there were no less than nine separate prime ministers and ministries. In the same timespan, Papua New Guinea has been content - well not completely content - with four. That almost makes it seem a serene capital city.

Jim Griffin, an Australian historian who has long taught in Papua New Guinea, recently observed that the young nation almost has an excess of participatory democracy. Such a comment cannot be made of some of the African autocracies which Mr Hawke helps to prop up with arbitrary gifts made by his globe-circling ministers.

In one sense, Papua New Guinea is a democracy on trial because from the outset it was one of the least cohesive of the multitude of nations created in the past 30 years. It speaks a babel of languages and dialects. A proud sense of regionalism, along with the isolating effects of mountain walls and sea straits, does not make for national unity.

The nation faces serious lapses of law and order in Bougainville, the Highlands, and Port Moresby itself. It also owns a troublesome border with Indonesia.

The nation faces formidable problems, but we undermine its ability to tackle those problems - and thereby we weaken our own national security - if we unfairly belittle its parliament. All in all, its parliament has probably been more successful than those first Australian democracies of which we are rightly proud.

<u>Weekend Australian</u>, 11-12 March 1989

49

Gold - A Lesson or Two?

The upsurge of gold production in the 1980s is, in many ways, the most remarkable of such booms experienced in Australia since 1851. It is especially remarkable because of a fact which is rarely remarked upon. The average Australian does not even know about this gold boom.

There have been four great leaps in gold production in Australia's history. The first came in the years 1851 to 1856 and centred on Victoria: it virtually trebled Australia's population in the space of a decade. The second leap in gold production came in the years 1887 to 1903 - generally remembered as the gold boom of the 1890s, it was centred on Western Australia. The third leap, not quite as dramatic, came in the 1930s, and again Western Australia was the main springboard. And now comes the gold upsurge of this present decade.

I doubt whether any modern nation, with the exception of South Africa, has been so influenced as Australia by the discoveries of gold. Gold rushes are one of the recurring threads of our history. Event after event in our history was shaped directly or indirectly by gold - the end of the transporting of convicts to Tasmania, the Eureka rebellion, the rise of Victoria and Melbourne to economic dominance in the second half of the 19th century, the inflow of Chinese in the 1850s, the protectionist ideology born in the late 1850s, the founding of a chain of isolated ports in tropical Australia, the easing of the depression of the 1890s, the awakening of Western Australia after its long sleep, the building of the first inland railways. I could go on and on, listing national landmarks which were shaped by gold. We could even add world events, such as finding the first oil in the Middle East which owed much to a fortune won at the Mount Morgan gold mine in Queensland in the 1880s.

What surely is remarkable is that in a nation so conscious of the historical role of gold, the present surge in gold output has made little mental impact. To the ears of the typical Australian the gold rush of this decade has been conducted in silence.

If we were to place a television crew outside Parliament House in Canberra and ask typical Australians what they thought of the present gold rush, the great majority would say: "What gold rush?". In Melbourne and Sydney the answer would be the same. Of course all stockbrokers and most share-buyers know about the leap in gold output in the 1980s, and most federal politicians know about it. A Western Australian, too, is more likely to know about it than a Victorian because more gold is mined there and because most Western Australians are conscious of minerals and their power to change economic life.

If we were to thrust a radio microphone in front of twenty Perth people and ask them in which year Australia produced the most gold, those game enough to answer would probably say a year in the 1850s, or perhaps the 1890s. Does even one in ten of Australia's adults - and most are interested today in the state of the economy - know that 1988 was the record year of gold production? If I were asked twenty years ago - will the gold record of 1903 ever be broken? - I would have been inclined to say 'no'. But it has come to pass. In a year when we need all the export revenue we can earn, gold is vital. A new gold record will be set again this year.

Why is the gold revival so little noticed by the Australian public? You may ask, does it matter if a fact is ignored? Yes, it does matter, because gold mining like every other industry depends not only on what happens in the mine but also on what people think is happening. Public opinion is vital to the gold mining industry: it always has been. In the last resort it is public opinion which sets the rules for the exploring for gold, the mining of gold, the area of ground allocated to each company, the environmental barriers, the taxes imposed, and the ultimate rewards and incentives.

Possibly the most powerful single reason why gold mining in Victoria is still so lethargic is that there the parliamentary opinion and public opinion are nervous of new gold mines. Victoria, the second greatest gold producer in the history of Australia, produced less gold last year than in the worst year of the fifty years from 1851 to 1900.

Why has the present gold rush - to use the familiar 19th century phrase - failed to capture Australia's notice, let alone its imagination? Why is it less glamorous than the gold rush of the 1890s? Two quantitative reasons must initially be given for the relatively small impact of this gold boom on the public mind.

Firstly, every ingot of new-mined gold had more impact on the Australia of three million people in the 1890s than it has on the Australia of 16 million today. The same stone makes greater ripples on a smaller pond. If a new Paddy Hannan were to find a twin sister of Kalgoorlie tomorrow, that new goldfield would not be as influential on the nation as was the old Kalgoorlie.

A second reason for gold's lesser impact today is that it is not our main export. It was the main export in the 1850s and 1860s and again at the start of this century, and that helped to give gold an importance in the eyes of all Australians. In the present upsurge, gold has not overtaken wool and coal; perhaps it won't.

There are other revealing reasons why gold in the 1980s has not attracted the favourable attention of the average Australian. One reason is that the gold mines, physically, are not visible. They operate far from the capital cities. In contrast the booming tourist industry is very visible in Melbourne and Sydney. The overwhelming majority of Australians will see a Japanese tourist this month but very few Australians will see anything connected with gold mining, even on television.

There is a more compelling reason. Gold mining in this latest boom has created no brand-new Australian town with a population of say 2,000 or more, whereas in the 1880s and 1890s a long list of new gold towns sprang up in the wilderness - Mt Morgan and Croydon in Queensland, Coolgardie and Kalgoorlie, Leonora, Menzies, Cue and many others in Western Australia. Every Australian was aware of these towns for countless reasons. Thus Coolgardie became famous for its safe. Even Menzies won fame because there, on Easter Monday in 1906, the world footrunning record for the premier professional distance of 130 yards was broken by Arthur Postle.

Today, the employment created directly by our new gold mines is surprisingly small in relation to the capital involved and the wealth produced. In Kalgoorlie or Charters Towers in 1900 an army of men was needed to mine 100,000 tons of rock. Now only a few men and a few heavy machines mine that same tonnage of ore.

We still mentally inhabit a world where we measure the dynamics of a new industry by the visible employment which it creates. Gold mining once gave wonderful service, by that measurement. Now the public service and the bureaucracy rate highly by that measurement. If job creation in the short-term is to remain the simple measure of economic worth, then Mr Whitlam was the greatest job creator of all time! Our debt burden, our balance-of-payments crisis, partly come from our failure as a nation to distinguish between job creation and wealth creation.

A diagnosis of our present economic mess must give weight to the following elementary fact. The jobs that are crucial to our well-being, to our standard of living and to our solvency as a nation are in those few industries where, through high efficiency, few people produce great wealth. The industries that win us export revenue are, by and large, those which are highly efficient and productive. And yet well-informed opinion has difficulty in appreciating the importance of these industries.

In essence, ninety years ago, all Australians recognised the importance of gold mining to the nation's well-being. It created work and prosperity. It planted towns where previously stood only rainforest, spinifex or mulga. Today, gold mining is more efficient than in past years, it is crucial for our balance of payments, and yet it receives inadequate recognition.

Gold mining is not only seen by the general public as less productive of wealth than a century ago. It is also seen by an influential minority, as more destructive of the environment than in the past. This is a curious change because there is not much doubt that most gold producers in Australia are far more sensitive to their environment than they were a century ago.

The old gold mining industry usually paid little attention to the environment. Victorians in the 1850s could tell when a new gold digging had opened forty miles upstream: the river water downstream quickly changed colour with the clays and gravels that had been overturned upstream. Soon after the gold rush broke out at Blackwood, the Victorian Railways, far down the Werribee River, observed that the water fed into the boilers of its locomotive was hardly fit for a steam-boiler. Just north of Bendigo about 1860 the tide of clay from the puddling machines, flowing along the creeks, slowly buried fences and bridges and roads and some of the most fertile farmland in the district.

Stawell, which, in the late 1870s, was the deepest goldfield in Australia, announced its presence to approaching travellers by the taste of sulphur from the kilns where the gold-bearing pyrite was roasted. People didn't see Stawell as they approached: they tasted it. Above all there was the voracious and huge wood-cutting industry which, in the vicinity of most goldfields, supplied wood for the engine house and, less often, props for the underground workings. To reach many goldfields you passed through a cemetery of stumps.

During most decades of busy gold mining, people accepted this devastation. They called it the price of progress. They saw it as unavoidable, and on most goldfields it could not be avoided. Today, after cheaply-transported oil has replaced local firewood, much of this devastation is avoided. But a section of public opinion has changed even more rapidly; and it tends to see every new mine as an enemy of the environment.

Concern for the environment is sensible. Equally sensible is the desire to mine gold, at a time when Australia's standard of living is falling and its long-term external debt is mounting.

Another deep change in public attitudes is now visible. The mineral discoverer is no longer a hero. Paddy Hannan, soon after finding the first surface gold at Kalgoorlie in the winter of 1893, became a folk hero. In a time of economic depression he found a goldfield that gave jobs to tens of thousands of Australians. Long after his death his grave in the Melbourne General Cemetery was the scene of pilgrimages.

In contrast the remarkable revival of gold mining in the 1980s has produced no folk hero, and a hero is unlikely to emerge. Mineral exploration is now more scientific and more complicated: it is also the work of a team of specialists rather than a Paddy Hannan with his hobnailed boots and canvas waterbag.

My own view is that the mining industry is in error in not publicising its greatest living prospectors. To discover and develop new deposits remains a difficult task: it will be increasingly difficult. And yet numerous educators and intellectuals think that mineral discovery and mineral development is easy. They believe - and Senator Richardson as Minister for the Environment mirrored that belief in a recent speech in the United States - that Australia's big problem is not how to find payable mines but how to prevent them from coming into production too rapidly.

There is a destructive side to mining, as to nearly all human activities. There is also a creative side: ingenuity is needed in the finding of buried mineral deposits. And the wealth produced has a creative effect which Australians, of all people in this Year of Our Debt, should recognise.

When a sizeable section of public opinion is suspicious of the major export industries and another section of opinion is indifferent, then the economy is in more serious trouble than we are willing to accept. Never before in our history have gold and the other main export earners been viewed with such suspicion and seen as offering so little, economically. That might not matter so much if the export industries were powerful within the electorate. But electorally they are weak; eighty per cent of our exports comes from about six per cent of the population.

My conclusion may seem a little strange but is supported by strong evidence. Our economic crisis - our increasing debt overseas and our falling living standards inside Australia - are as much as anything the result of the political and public delusion that we can survive without adequate exports. And one stronghold of that delusion seems to be Canberra, a city which virtually produces no exports.

Luncheon Address at the Australian Gold Conference, Burswood Convention Centre, Perth, 16 March 1989

50

Mr Hawke's True Confession

When the Prime Minister of Australia, Mr Bob Hawke, admitted on television last week that he had committed adultery, he aroused in his own nation a blend of hot curiosity and cool puzzlement.

Most viewers decided that Mr Hawke had said nothing newsworthy, while the curious seemed to think he had not yet said enough and that more revelations must surely follow.

In Australia the Labour Party's main asset is Mr Hawke. Its liability is the limp state of the economy. What if the party's main asset had drastically depreciated himself at the very time when the economy was so vulnerable?

The man who made the confession last week is not easily fathomed. Walking down the street, a few yards behind the television cameras, he radiates genuine warmth and a wonderful vitality. He has both the composure of someone who knows he leads a nation and the larrikin - "bovver boy" - streak which would assert itself far more if he were not leading a nation.

He often gives the impression, in interviews, of being completely in command of his nation, and he treats his more severe critics as if they were idiots or - his favourite word of abuse - "hypocrites"; and yet the standard of living of the average Australian has probably fallen during his six years of office. Australia's overseas debt has soared. In the face of the nation's economic decline he often appears complacent.

His personal popularity exceeds that of any Prime Minister of Australia in the last half-century with the possible exception of John Curtin, who, from 1941 to 1945, drew the nation together under the shadow of the Japanese advance. But Mr Hawke's prestige - and prestige is often a more dignified and remote form of popularity - is insecure. In the public eye, Sir Robert Menzies, PM from 1939 to 1941 and then from 1949 to 1966, possessed more prestige than Mr Hawke is likely to acquire even if his term should equal Sir Robert's and thus extend beyond the year 2000.

Mr Hawke's success since 1983 has depended on able colleagues who debate with skill; on division within the opposition parties; and on his willingness to occupy middle ground - even ground well to the right of Labour's normal frontier. His own skill as leader of rigid factions within his party and his public popularity have furthered Labour's chances.

The core of his popularity was probably not affected by the TV confession. Labour's own pollster defensively observed that Mr Hawke was actually dismantling the camouflage screen which is the hallmark of most politicians. Maybe five per cent of the Australian electorate was seriously perturbed, but many of those voters have never been his supporters.

Mr Hawke has built his career on the unexpected. He does not fit into neat categories. A Rhodes Scholar, he is less polished as a public speaker than all but a few of the past prime ministers. Initially making a spectacular career in the trade unions with support from the extreme Left, he is not the friend of some of the richest Australians.

By all outward signs an Australian nationalist, he now bows more readily to the Japanese than Australian politicians of the 1850s would have bowed to Queen Victoria. While he is a populist and quick to hear the applause of the crowd, he is an individualist who can until the last moment thumb his nose at sections of the crowd.

He was sometimes a heavy drinker ("drinking problem" is a frequent entry in the index of the biography of Hawke) until he set his ambitions on becoming Prime Minister: now he is so sober that some of his old drinking friends call him dull.

His sympathetic and astute biographer, Blanche d'Alpuget, once used the phrase "harem male" to depict his private life before 1980, when he resolved to make his run for Parliament. In such a context a slightly tearful confession by Mr Hawke about his sexual life years ago will neither surprise nor shock most Australians.

To outward appearances Australians are less likely than Britons and Americans to reject a leading politician because of his private life. When John Gorton was Prime Minister and gave the impression in 1968 of enjoying the company of pretty young women - and reportedly appeared at the US Embassy in Canberra for a private briefing on the war in Vietnam in company with a pretty 19-year-old journalist at 2.30 in the morning - there was more public amusement than indignation. Moreover, the indignation backfired, politically.

The public approach to the private morality of politicians is forgiving because of unusual factors. The federal capital, Canberra, is remote and seen by many as a yacht offshore. There also exists the tradition of the "fair go", of exempting the wife of a leading politician from the rough and tumble of political attack.

Above all, there is scant public awareness that in a crisis, the nation's security may well depend on the personal and private qualities of the Prime Minister. Australia for too long has been a political satellite, first of Britain and then of the USA, to recognise this fact. Personal qualities are at present widely seen as lying outside the legitimate political agenda.

Women last week were especially critical of him for doing what he likes - talking about himself in public - and doing it so thoughtlessly that he entangled his wife, for whom there is widespread respect and sympathy.

That the leader of the Opposition, Mr John Howard, refused to seek political gain from Mr Hawke's embarrassment was shrewdness itself, for the issue thus ceased to be discussed on party lines, and all kinds of citizens leaped in and gave their uninhibited views.

The main objection was not to what he had done in private but to what he had said in public. As an up-country woman observed in a pithy letter in *The Age*: "Mr Hawke should find himself a friendly priest and save us all this tripe."

Sunday Telegraph, London, 26 March 1989

51

Making a Farce of Australian Citizenship

Tens of thousands of migrants are flocking to become citizens in this Year of Citizenship. And yet some Australians are beginning to ask why Mr Hawke is extolling the importance of becoming a citizen when in practice his Government has so downgraded it.

The unintended value of this Year of Citizenship is that it could force us to see that citizenship is in disarray. No other nation places as little value on citizenship as Australia.

We are told again and again - and rightly so - that we should learn from Asia. Curiously I can find no nation in Asia which hands citizenship to newcomers like fast food. We have taught our former colony, Papua New Guinea, not to belittle citizenship but we have yet to teach ourselves.

A recent news release from the Department of Immigration announced in bold letters: "You may find it easier than you thought to become an Australian citizen." In fact, it is absurdly easy.

Those who now apply for citizenship do not even have to forswear allegiance to their previous nation. Until recently a new citizen, on taking the oath or making the affirmation, agreed to "renounce all other allegiance" but in 1986 the minister for immigration, Mr. Hurford, persuaded Parliament to weaken the oath.

He explained that many new citizens mistakenly thought that in renouncing allegiance to their previous nation, they were also renouncing "their cultural background and all other ties with their country of origin".

In other words he proceeded to debase Australian citizenship largely because some newcomers were ignorant, confused or did not understand the English language. The same paternalistic argument could be used to excuse us all from penalties when, in ignorance, we break a law.

Mr Hurford went further when he persuaded Parliament that new migrants should no longer have to announce their own name when they make the oath of allegiance. He explained that one became confused when one was asked to state his name, others did not understand what was being said to them, and "this confusion often detracts from the ceremony".

It shows the meagre requirements we make of new citizens when we baulk at asking them to declare their own name, partly through fear that they might make a spectacle of themselves.

The main reason for the vital change in the law was that the leaders of some newer ethnic groups did not wish to renounce loyalty to their own homeland. The Hawke Government gave in to them. We should realise that multiculturalism, as often practised in Canberra, is a new form of colonialism, in which we are the colony of every nation on earth.

The Hawke Government to its credit has made many minor changes to the citizenship law in the interests of clarity, national self-respect and all-round fairness to migrants. Some of the major changes, however, rouse alarm.

Whereas most governments insist that migrants should spend many years living in the nation before they can be admitted formally as citizens, we jump to the other extreme. A short residence here is deemed to be enough. Indeed many birds of passage are no sooner admitted to Australian citizenship than they fly away. Hong Kong has thousands of them. Like the oil tankers of Panama and Liberia they fly a flag of convenience.

Despite their solemn and sincere oath "to fulfil my duties as an Australian citizen" they immediately abandon their duties while retaining the privileges. Surely that type of absentee migrant should be granted the right of permanent residence but not yet the citizenship.

Until 1984 our law permitted migrants to apply for citizenship after they had lived here for three full years. The aggregate of three years of residence could be spread over the previous eight years. This three-year qualification, already low by world standards, was disliked by the Hawke Government. In 1984 it was reduced to two years.

In essence an applicant for citizenship today must "have lived in Australia as a permanent resident for 12 months in the preceding 2 years, and 2 years in the preceding five". In contrast, five years is demanded by the United States and France. Many nations demand ten years.

Our Government, in reducing the residential requirement from three years to two, explained that in the modern world migrants move about much. But people should not expect citizenship of a nation - along with the right to vote and to shape the nation's destiny - when they know little more than a migratory bird about their new land.

In Parliament not one of the speakers who supported this radical proposal for a mere two years' residence could offer a valid reason. Dr Andrew Theophanous explained that some migrant groups wanted citizenship for their countrymen as soon as they reached Australia, others were willing to wait only six months, and that therefore the two-year proposal was a "compromise". No supporting speaker made the vital democratic point that the opinion of the majority of Australians on a topic of importance should really form a crucial part of any "compromise" reached.

It was the same Parliament that watered down the requirement that new citizens should speak English. The previous rule was that new citizens should speak "adequate" English, by which was really meant "inadequate" English. In 1984 this was reduced to "basic" English. The immigration minister, Mr West, did not specify what he meant by "basic" English, except to indicate that it was more primitive than "adequate" English. On such whim and evasion is based our citizenship law.

Naturally, new migrants do not wish an ignorance of English to be held against them. But most of those objectors come from nations which insist that a knowledge of the native language must be a pre-requisite of citizenship. They should therefore explain why they want one rule for their homeland and another for Australia, with they themselves the beneficiaries in both lands.

Mr West tried to justify the down-grading of English with the words: "The government does not wish to deny citizenship to those with limited English who have lived in Australia for some time and would take pride in becoming citizens." That is not an argument; it is simply an admission of surrender to an effective lobby.

Labor backbenchers hurried to Mr West's rescue. Mr Peter Staples vowed that if migrants want citizenship, "what right do we have to deny it?". To his extraordinary question the answer is simple. A government worthy of the name has every right to deny citizenship to groups of people who are not yet ready for it.

The question is not whether the new migrants are in some way superior or inferior to Australians. It is a question of whether at this early stage they deserve an equal say with the existing citizens in shaping national policies.

As a result of these changes an applicant for citizenship has to pass only an elementary test in the English language. The Federal Government's interviewing officers are instructed, when applicants have limited English, to speak slowly and carefully, looking directly at them while speaking.

They first ask them to respond in simple English to questions in simple English about personal particulars. The applicant for citizenship next must answer "yes" or "no" or reply in simple words to factual questions about the responsibilities and rights of Australian citizenship.

Many migrants who possess few words of English are coached by articulate friends in how to answer these questions. Why should they not be coached? Our laws are so naive, the test is so rudimentary, that coaching is useful.

Our law-makers in their enthusiasm have deemed that large numbers of applicants do not even have to pass this kindergarten test. Any migrant over the age of fifty is exempt. The wife or husband of a younger migrant can be totally bereft of English and pass the test simply by virtue of the fact that the spouse passes it.

The language test is stunningly simple. In Australia last year, from February through to December, an army of migrants speaking every major language under the sun attended a citizenship interview, and only 247 were rejected because they did not understand the smattering of English required of them.

The issue at stake is not whether these migrants should receive welfare services or the right of continuing residence. They should. The issue is whether they should receive, a mere two years after reaching the country, and with scant knowledge of its language and laws and institutions, an equal right to determine its future.

There are strong reasons for delaying the citizenship of people who have difficulty in understanding the public discussion which is the essence of democracy. But Senator Alice Zakharov would fervently disagree. In the Senate she argued that to penalise people because they know little English is "inbuilt discrimination". Maybe it is. But Parliament itself sensibly encourages "inbuilt discrimination" by holding all its sessions in the English language.

The argument for not yet enfranchising a migrant who knows little English and has lived here for only two years is similar to the argument for not granting the vote to a 15-year-old. Neither category of person is fully capable - there will be many exceptions - of carrying out the duties of citizenship.

Of course you may object that all migrants deserve a vote because they pay taxes and have a stake in the nation. The simple answer to that objection is that in some ethnic groups a big proportion of migrants who seek citizenship after two years in the land are unemployed and pay no tax. Furthermore the 15-year-olds hold a greater stake in the nation, measured by the years that they will live in Australia.

There is a strong case for suggesting that people who know only a foreign language should fulfil a longer residential requirement than those migrants whose knowledge of English will help them to exercise their new citizenship.

It may appear unfair to penalise a would-be citizen on the grounds of language. On the other hand it is not fair to penalise existing citizens - and to weaken the nation - by lowering the standard and conditions of citizenship.

The impetus to weaken Australian citizenship comes partly from Labor's desire - and its desire is shared by other parties - to woo the ethnic vote. There is also an understandable concern in Canberra that maybe 40 per cent of migrants who are now eligible to become citizens have not applied. The FitzGerald committee on immigration concluded last year that citizenship was declining in symbolic value and was in fact "of little material value".

The fact remains that many migrants have valid reasons for refusing to become Australian citizens. We should respect their reluctance. Some are not sure whether they wish to remain permanently in Australia. Others will lose their right to make a long stay or to work in their own homeland - for instance Malaysia - if they become Australian citizens.

In essence the FitzGerald committee, like the Prime Minister, worried about the people who should become citizens but don't. We should rather worry about the people who should not become citizens but do.

Earlier this year every letterbox in Australia received a thoughtful letter from Mr Hawke urging all eligible migrants to become citizens and to accept equal responsibilities and rights with all other Australians. He added that it is "acceptance of those responsibilities that determines whether you are truly an Australian".

He forgets that he has so altered the conditions of citizenship that citizens no longer have equal responsibilities. Three specific duties - as distinct from oaths and affirmations - are formally demanded of new citizens. They have to vote; they have to be willing to serve on a jury; and they have to be willing to defend Australia, should the need arise.

And yet those citizens who speak token English cannot serve on a jury and cannot serve in the armed forces. They cannot, as a general rule, even vote as effectively as the majority of those who understand the language of national debate and dissemination.

Australia's unusual system of compulsory voting was designed for a nation where voters shared the same language and culture. Mr Hawke's citizenship laws have quietly undermined the case for compulsory voting. Why dragoon a new voter who knows little about the land, whose loyalties may lie elsewhere, and whose knowledge of English can be scribbled on a postage stamp?

People who have lived here only two years and know no English should not be compelled to vote. They should positively be forbidden to vote. In essence, our present citizenship laws mock our democratic tradition and our claim to be a sovereign and independent nation.

Australia now possesses two kinds of citizen. Firstly it has true citizens, and secondly it has those citizens who through no fault of their own are sham citizens. They are sham citizens because they cannot carry out all their civic responsibilities, as officially defined.

We should warmly welcome true citizens, no matter whether they come originally from Albania or Vietnam, no matter whether their native language is Filipino or Gaelic. But no migrant, whether from Manchester or Minsk, should become citizens prematurely, thus becoming sham or second-rate citizens.

It is a sound axiom of national life that citizenship should be granted in such a way that it satisfies both those who seek it and those who already have it. If new citizenship laws are too lenient, or too servile towards other nations, they weaken citizenship itself.

Citizenship is not a special favour to be awarded on the whim of the party presently in power. It is a precious asset belonging to the whole nation. It belongs to every committed Australian whose future lies in this land.

A campaign to confer citizenship on the easiest of terms robs those who already possess it. Most Australian citizens do not realise what they have lost in recent years.

<u>Weekend Australian</u>, 27-28 May 1989

Part IV

1990

52

The Infantile Custom of Compulsory Voting

Nearly every axiom of Australian politics has been X-rayed in the past twenty years, but the idea of compulsory voting has been surprisingly immune from serious attack. And yet it often relies on arguments that are more likely to be used in an infant school than a parliament.

We are one of the few peoples in the world who are compelled to vote, and almost certainly we are compelled to vote more frequently than the people of any other nation. And yet the reasons behind this curious example of political compulsion are rarely aired in public. If they were made public, most civic-minded Australians would probably express some puzzlement and even indignation.

Of all our electoral traditions, the frequent elections and the gerrymander have been debated with special intensity in recent years, but some of the suspicion of frequent elections is, I suspect, really a criticism of compulsory voting.

A great many people do not like being compelled to vote, nor being forced to do so frequently by political leaders who themselves fail again and again to carry out their parallel duty of completing the full three-year term for which they won election. If it is legitimate for paid politicians to skimp their duty, why is it illegitimate for mere citizens to skimp a lesser duty?

I was taken by surprise when, looking up the parliamentary debates, I found why compulsory voting was introduced in 1924. The experiment might have had a smidgen of justification then, but two-thirds of a century later it has to be classed a failure in nearly every respect.

Compulsory voting was imposed by a federal parliament in a hurry. It was imposed without that serious debate which precedes nearly every far-reaching political innovation.

The early enthusiast for compulsory voting was the Labor Party. It was just beginning its first long innings in Queensland; there, voting became compulsory in 1915 and Labor concluded that its share of the vote thereby increased. Whether it did gain from compulsory voting was a moot point, but the belief took root.

In federal parliament in 1915, Labor tried to push through a Bill that would have compelled every adult Australian to vote at federal referendums. The conservatives, suspecting that compulsion did not aid their side of politics, opposed it. Finally, the new law stipulated that only people living within five miles (8 km) of a polling booth had to vote.

The first referendum in which all electors had to vote was on the wartime question of whether Australian men should be compelled to join the armed forces and fight against Germany. Here was a compulsory poll on the topic of compulsion itself. This referendum of 1916 set in motion the process that split and temporarily crippled the Labor Party.

While Labor was in Opposition, the prospects seemed remote of enacting a law to compel people to vote in elections as distinct from referendums. And yet the law was passed, in extraordinary circumstances.

After a decade in which politics had been exciting, the issues ceased to be momentous and political differences were no longer clear-cut; fewer people voted. Between the elections of 1919 and 1922, the number of electors who actually voted fell from 72 per cent to a mere 59 per cent. There was much tut-tutting about the lack of responsibility of the voter who stayed home on polling day, but many must have stayed home for the simple reason that election day in 1922 was on Saturday, December 16.

That was an astonishingly - maybe deliberately - inconvenient day for voting. Many people said that it was one of their preparation days for Christmas because on the following weekend they would have the rare privilege - in that era of fewer holidays - of a very long break consisting of a holiday on Saturday afternoon and on Sunday, followed by Monday for Christmas Day and Tuesday for Boxing Day. Election day, therefore, found so many busily preparing for a special holiday that naturally they were tempted to forget their opportunity to vote.

Never, perhaps, in federal history has an election day fallen on such an inconvenient weekend for voters. It was therefore rather unfair for politicians who had selected that day to blame voters for ignoring it, and to decide henceforth to compel them to vote.

There were other oddities surrounding the decision to make voting compulsory. The poor turnout on polling day in 1922 had favoured the right-wing parties, if it favoured any party. Why, then, did they themselves decide to change the law and turn voting into a compulsory task? If they had actually lost and had come to the conclusion that they had lost partly because of a meagre turnout of voters, their sudden and unexpected support for the principle of compulsory voting would have been understandable.

A few non-Labor backbenchers, more than the leaders, were eager to bring in compulsory voting and, for some reason, their own Bruce-Page government let them have their way. Herbert Payne, who had sat almost continuously in the Tasmanian and then the federal parliament for more than twenty years, a senator noted more for his informed conversations on gardens than on politics, brought in the principle of compulsory voting as a private member's Bill in July 1924.

As only two private Bills had become law in the history of the Commonwealth, he seemed to be running uphill. His Bill had a dream passage through the Senate. He introduced it at 6.15 pm on July 17, the House adjourned for dinner at 6.30 pm, he resumed his short and simply argued speech at 8 pm, and by 9.11 pm the matter had been decided.

There was virtually no debate, and the only senior politician who spoke, Senator Gardiner, admitted that while it was the Labor Party's policy and he was the Labor leader in the Senate, he did not think much of the idea.

One week later, in the Lower House, the new member for Perth, Edward Mann, introduced the Bill. Mann had won his seat by only 214 votes. Perhaps the feeble turnout of voters - less than fifty per cent had voted in Western Australia - made this chemist think he might be do better under compulsory voting. Curiously, it did not save him from electoral defeat, and he was eventually to become a strong-voiced national broadcaster, a kind of Derryn Hinch of the air waves.

In the perilous years of World War II, his emphatic commentaries on the plight of the nation, delivered anonymously under the name of "The Watchman", attracted lunchtime crowds to those radio shops where his program could be heard. But the voice of "The Watchman" was even more influential in 1924: he spoke in favour of compulsory voting for only sixteen minutes, and that was enough. His only determined opponent was a new member of his own party, a South Australian returned soldier named John Duncan Hughes, who spoke for half an hour.

In both Houses, the Labor members contributed little to the debate. They were quietly happy to see their own policy introduced by opponents who had hitherto shunned it.

If there is any merit in compulsory voting, then it should be applied more to the proceedings of Parliament than to the events on election day. But neither in the Senate nor the Representatives was a vote formally taken. We do not even know how many members were absent from each House, let alone how many supported the Bill when it was passed.

It is not easy to defend a law that extols compulsory voting as an axiom of politics and inflicts it on the voter but exempts the parliamentarian. No penalty is extracted from a politician, no please-explain letter reaches him when he fails to vote on an important Bill even though he is present in the building.

It would probably be unreasonable to impose such a law on politicians: their task is difficult enough. None the less, it seems harsh to demand higher standards of duty from the electors than from the politicians, and to demand those high standards in the name of making democracy purer and more complete.

The politicians, in theory, are the servants, the people the masters. It is inconsistent that the master is not permitted to fine the servants for what is really a more serious dereliction of voting duty.

The conversion of the right-wing parties to compulsory voting had happened almost overnight. No other important innovation in Commonwealth elections has become law with so little discussion. Several newspapers of the day were not impressed, calling the new law a blot on democracy, a way of increasing the quantity of votes while decreasing their quality.

The law compelling all electors to vote was far from secure. As it was the result of a miracle, or a temporary loss of concentration, it was vulnerable.

This brings us to the second miracle, that this law, which had danced its way across the floor of Parliament almost unobstructed, lasts to this day.

Indeed, the events in Parliament in July 1924 were a turning point in the attitude to voting, and every State eventually adopted the idea, South Australia in 1942 being the last. Even local government became converts.

It remains a law because, presumably, it suits the main political parties most of the time. It saves them the trouble, on election eve, of organising ways to entice as many as possible of their own supporters to the polling booth. It eliminates the parties' dual problem of persuading us not only whom to vote for but also to attend the poll on election day and deliver that vote.

It is probable that compulsory voting gives some advantage to the big political parties at the expense of the independents and the smaller parties. The ignorant voter, the reluctant voter, may be slightly more likely than a serious citizen to support a big party rather than a smaller party or an independent candidate.

Whether compulsion favours Labor rather than Liberal is not easily answered. Labor had originally called for compulsory voting in the belief that it would thereby gain the victory in nearly all elections, but the belief was too optimistic.

The federal election of 1925 herded nearly every adult voter to a polling booth for the first time, but there was no sign that Labor gained from their presence. Perhaps it even lost because far more of the new voters were women, and women of that time tended to be slightly more conservative, other things being equal. Not for the first time had an earnest reform backfired into the face of its initial sponsor.

Those citizens who believe we should have the most sensible voting system are entitled to ask for reasons that serve the nation's interest as well as the interest of the main political parties. Senator Payne himself tried to give reasons for compulsory voting that were national rather than partisan.

Boldly he said that "in a short time there will be a wonderful improvement in the political knowledge of the people". The short time has become a long time: no observer has yet detected a wonderful improvement in our political knowledge. Maybe there has been a slight improvement since 1924. If so, it has probably come more from the media and schools than from compulsory voting.

The prime argument of Senator Payne has proved to be a delusion. He, being an earthy man on most issues, would agree with this verdict if he were alive. Compulsory voting has not forced Australians "to take a keener interest in the welfare of their country". Instead, they have taken a keen interest in avoiding the fine imposed on those neglecting to vote.

Payne also relied a little on the notion that since all adults were already compelled to place their name on an electoral roll, it was "the natural corollary that they should now be compelled to vote".

It is hardly a convincing argument. There is no necessary reason why all the people whose names are in the telephone book should be compelled to use the phone every week. There is no good reason why all those who are assigned a tax file number should, because of that reason alone, be compelled to pay income tax in that year.

The senator also argued that Australia could only become a true democracy if Parliament reflected the will of every citizen. This was an observation rather than a relevant argument. If it were an argument, the next step towards creating a true democracy would be to compel all citizens not only to vote but also to be a member of Parliament for a week for two.

Similarly, if the will of citizens is to be decisive, as Senator Payne maintained, then perhaps the people should be directly consulted in order to see whether they themselves actually approved of the idea of compulsory voting.

The arguments for compulsory voting, as expressed in Parliament, were frail. Even today, the Federal Government, while believing in the system, shows all the signs of a fair-weather believer. Few laws carry such a minor penalty for infringement. Indeed, the penalty has shrunk.

In 1924 a non-voter could be fined up to 2 pounds. A large sum in the paypacket of that day, it equalled half a week's wages for a typical man in a factory and equalled the whole week's wages for an adult woman in a factory. Today, a neglectful voter who actually appears before a magistrate is fined from $5 to $50 or placed on a good-behaviour bond.

Therefore, the maximum fine is less than one day's wages for the typical factory worker.

The Federal Government is sensible in imposing light penalties; after all, why rock such an unseaworthy boat for the sake of a little extra revenue? Harsh penalties against those who failed to vote might lead to a reform movement designed to abolish the system.

The Australian Electoral Commission, while diligent, is not punitive. Voters whose excuse is deemed unsatisfactory are required to pay $20 - it is called a deposit, but if paid it serves to end the matter.

Surprisingly few of those who fail to vote are actually fined. At the 1988 referendum on the question of changing the Constitution, 228,707 electors in Victoria alone failed to vote. Of these, about 177,000 were asked to explain. The avalanche of explanations was examined. After all the sorting out of excuses, just over 10,000 people were issued with letters requesting a $20 deposit, or unofficial fine. Presumably nearly all paid. Of those who refused, 1,100 were prosecuted.

The low level of fine or penalty reflects the fact that compulsion is to some extent a matter of bluff. The authorities who govern us do not think that the failure to vote is a dereliction of civic duty as serious as, say, returning to a parking meter ten minutes after it has expired.

The governments themselves have silently proclaimed by their light and diminishing penalties that a failure to vote is not a serious failure. Those who are overseas on polling day are not compelled to vote. Most of those who are travelling interstate on polling day are exempt.

These travellers, and they exist in numbers that were unimaginable in 1924, include some of the best-informed and most civic-minded people in the nation. Senator Payne would agree that their absence from the polling booths means that the will of the people is no longer so adequately represented on polling day.

People of "unsound mind" are not compelled to vote. In contrast, voting is compulsory for hundreds of thousands of people who have no view about the state of both the government and the nation. People who, while of sound mind, have no mind on the politics of the day, should have the right to vote but not be compelled to exercise it.

Don Chipp, founder of the Australian Democrats, recently reminisced about the seventeen elections in which he had taken part. He said that anyone handing out "how to vote" cards at a federal election would hear people say: "What's this, mate? This is the local council election?" He added, whether rightly or not, that the result of the next federal election could be decided by what he called "these morons".

Most of these confused or apathetic people, of course, are far from morons, and partly for that reason do not wish to vote on a set of issues they do not at present understand.

Those who dislike being compelled to vote seem to have a temporary loophole, apart from long-distance travel. They can carefully neglect to place their name on the electoral roll. While enrolment is actually compulsory, at least a quarter of a million eligible Australians at any one time are on no electoral roll. They are actively pursued, but few are prosecuted.

Compulsory voting has now been supplemented by another form of compulsion. A compulsory levy is imposed on our vote once the vote has been recorded. We must be the only nation in the world that extracts cash from those who fail to vote and simultaneously pays cash to the parties which receive each vote. After the 1987 election, the political parties received just over $1 from the public purse as a reward for each citizen who gave them the vote.

As for the genuine arguments in favour of compulsory voting, their weight is insufficient to balance the arguments on the opposite side. The main idea of 1924, that compulsory voting would revolutionise the people's knowledge of politics, has proved false.

On the other hand, supporters of compulsory voting employ an argument not used but probably felt in 1924. They fear that there may come an election day when, through some rare combination of human and climatic causes, very few people go to the polling booth. In other words, what if compulsory voting came to an end, a new federal election was held and such a tiny proportion of people went to the polls that their votes thrust into power a dangerous scatter-brained party unwanted by the mass of Australians? Such a happening is highly unlikely.

A few other nations have flirted with compulsory voting, and their experience suggests that most people will vote irrespective of whether voting is voluntary or compulsory. The Netherlands abolished compulsory voting in the early 1970s, and the turnout on polling days fell by only sixteen per cent. Some nations - for example, Austria and Sweden - have huge attendance at the polls without a penalty.

If Australia abolished compulsory voting, it is probable that about eighty per cent of the eligible population would vote in the average federal election of the '90s, and perhaps even more would vote in an election where vital issues were believed to be at stake.

Compulsory voting implies that a democracy is a kind of ship which can remain afloat no matter how many blindfolded crew it carries. Democracy, however, is no less vulnerable than other political systems: it should not be burdened by the hit-or-miss attitude, the acceptance of the third rate, which is an integral part of compulsory voting.

We glimpse the fragility of democratic government and how easily it can be toppled if we realise that our relatively young nation is one of the oldest continuous democracies in the world.

The essence of democracy is that every citizen is encouraged to accept some responsibility for the direction of the nation. Compulsory voting, while pretending to enthrone the people's responsibility, mocks it. It implies that citizens do not have to be responsible but merely have to attend the polling booth.

In a democracy, all voters are equal but not all are responsible. Compulsory voting ignores that elementary truth.

The Australian, 21 February 1990

53

Sounding an Alarm Bell for Australia's Foreign Debt

How do you ring an alarm bell without making it too loud? Australia's economy and standard of living are approaching a danger zone. If we reach that danger zone, we can conceivably survive in it for many years, surviving precariously at times. On the other hand once the economy is inside that danger zone, it can easily be toppled by the rush of local or global events.

Twice in the last hundred or so years we have been inside that danger zone. Each time we were toppled, and the human hardship was on the large scale. While we, the Australians of 1990, have not yet entered the danger zone, we are close to it.

The essence of Australia's dilemma is that it is not competitive enough. We are easily defeated by too many other nations. The penalty is the money we now owe to overseas interests and individuals.

Our big household of 17 million people, our nation, has come to depend on overseas borrowings for part of its spending money. In the 1980s we borrowed so much that our annual repayments of interest, if we continue to borrow, could well lead to a harsh fall in our standard of living and our national esteem.

Our present way of life is coming to depend too much on the over-use of international plastic money. What will happen, then, if our nation's credit card is temporarily withdrawn? Already our credit rating as a nation has been downgraded.

If we were as lacklustre in international sport as we now are in most of our economic activities, a howl of outrage would arise from the front of 4 million television sets. There would be a simmer of indignation as the cry of "Gold, Gold" permanently gave way to the cry of "Last" or "Second Last". But in the economic contest between nations, as distinct from sport, the scoreboard is not read so easily. The final score can be complicated. It can be camouflaged by technical terms and decimal points. And all those billions are hard to imagine. As this kind of national scoreboard also carries political implications, people do not always agree that the final score is correct.

Signs of slow economic decline were visible even before the Hawke era. In 1960 the income of the average Australian - as economists measure it - had been ranked at about the fourth highest in the world. Then other nations, one by one, ran past us. By 1987 we came only 16th. Using this measurement of GDP per capita, we enjoyed an average income about twice as high as that of Japan, Austria and Italy in 1960, but today we stand below those nations. And this has happened in just over a quarter of a century.

While I believe our present standard of living, our quality of life, is higher than these figures indicate, the figures tell an important truth. In relative terms we are losing the race. We are performing poorly, by earlier standards.

Debt is a mirror of this decline. We are increasingly reluctant to save; instead we borrow from foreigners. In the 1970s the typical Australian household saved 12 per cent of its income. A decade later the typical household saves only 8 per cent.

Our net overseas debt was so small, just ten years ago, that it was rarely discussed in public. By 1989 it had passed 100 billion dollars. It continues to rise, month after month. We are now so accustomed to these monthly rises that we applaud when the rise in overseas debt is less than we expected. Like a spectator on the beach, we cheer because the mouth of the drowning man is only half-filled with water.

Have we been here before? Has our nation faced a similar plight?

We have not yet opened our eyes to the seriousness of the economic situation. We do not realise that we are probably approaching a danger zone. By luck, by sane government or by the efforts of the people we may succeed in sailing past that danger. But what happens if we continue to ignore the danger?

Delving as far back as the gold rushes of 1851 I can find only two short periods that were more worrying than the present. The first period began about the mid-1880s and spread into the 1890s. We usually call it the bank crash or the 1890s depression. The other hazardous period began in the late 1920s and became the World Depression.

In both periods the cost of paying the interest on debts was high, even by our standards. Today, Australia's net payment of interest and dividends to overseas sources amounts to about 20 per cent of our export revenue. In contrast, this percentage had exceeded 25 per cent for much of the 1880s. By the years 1890-1-2 it was closer to 35 per cent. At the peak of the 1890s crisis, about 40 per cent of Australia's export revenue was mortgaged to the paying of interest and dividends.

Again in the 1920s Australia borrowed overseas on a risky scale. Interest and dividend payments rose to 21 per cent of export revenue in 1921-22. They reached 28 per cent at the end of the decade. As the world depression deepened, the percentage rose even higher.

The percentage of interest and dividend payments to export revenue is a vital indicator. The percentage of 25 is often seen in international financial circles as the start of the danger zone. Australia in the next two years could reach that zone. To step from 20 to 25 per cent is not difficult. After all, Australia had jumped from 4 to 16 per cent in a mere five years of the last decade. Whether Australia will make the risky step past 25 remains to be seen. Once that step is taken, the experience of Argentina and Mexico suggests that the burden of paying the interest and the principal begins to choke the normal avenues open to economic recovery. The economic decline of New Zealand is a lesson nearer home.

So we are close to the edge of the danger zone of debt. Twice Australia has been pummelled after it entered the danger zone. The first pummelling was in the early 1890s. Export prices fell, new borrowings fell. Financial panic set in. Thirteen of the 22 trading or note-issuing banks in Australia closed their doors for many weeks and most were reconstructed. Half of all Australian bank-deposits were in the locked banks. Neither England nor the United States in modern times has experienced a banking disaster of that magnitude. Melbourne, then the biggest city in Australia, was hit the hardest. People poured from Victoria. In the years 1891-1906 it lost more people through emigration than it had gained through immigration in the previous thirty years.

Australia's other debt crisis came in the early 1930s. Whereas the first was signalled by banking failures, the second was marked by an alarming level of unemployment. In the year 1932 just over 30 per cent of Australian breadwinners were out of work. Unlike the 1890s this was a world-wide depression; but Australia's ability to cope with it was gravely impaired by its heavy overseas debt. Australia was very vulnerable even before the tidal wave of world events arrived. Even if there had been no world depression, Australia could have stumbled.

It is fair to suggest that the debt crises of the 1890s and 1930s have much in common with our economic dilemma today. I do not wish to be alarmist. At the moment our overseas debts are definitely not as serious as those of the two earlier ill-fated periods. Even if they were as serious, we have no reason to expect a replay of the bank failures of 1893 or the massive unemployment of the early 1930s. History rarely repeats itself exactly. An economic crisis can do enough damage without being a repetition of earlier crises.

In summary, the extent of our overseas debts already places us in an unenviable position. It is our third worst situation in the last 130 years.

Twice in our history, severe pressures on our balance of payments have helped to catapult our parents and grandparents into a whirlpool far more dislocating then they could have expected. We should at least be alert to the danger. The irony of the depression of the 1890s is that it could have been minimised if bankers and politicians had thought a debt crisis could lead to a banking panic. They said, "It can't happen here". Most emphatic of the optimists was Henry Gyles Turner who was the head of the rising Commercial Bank of Australia - an earlier version of our present State Bank of Victoria. He thought Australia led the world in its prudent and cautious banking attitudes.

As a heavy overseas debt shaped these two earlier depressions, how did Australians manage to work their way out of debt? They traded their way out of trouble. That's the modern, glamorous way of expressing it but in fact they sweated their way out of trouble. They reduced their imports and increased their exports. Unfortunately, if we stumbled into a depression only half as serious, I doubt whether we could expect to "trade our way out" very easily.

Those old-time depressions offered their own painful cure. We will not, we dare not, emulate that cure because it consisted of massive unemployment. We forget that the extent of unemployment experienced in the early 1930s rapidly cut down the import bill which had been a major cause of the earlier crisis. Thus in the year 1928-29, Australia's total imports cost 130 million pounds. They cost only 51 million pounds, three years later. In case you think that changes in money, including the first major currency depreciation in our history, exaggerated the extent of this fall, let me specify how the actual tonnages of imports fell away.

In the two years after 1929-30, imports of motor-car chassis fell from 62,000 to 4,000. In the same two years the imports of electrical cables and wires fell from 15,000 to 2,000 tons. The import of petrol - the nation's consumption of petrol - was almost cut in half. The imports of Scotch whisky fell to a mere one-sixth. And in this era of the sardine sandwich, even the imports of tinned fish were halved.

Fortunately we will probably not again see unemployment so massive as that of the 1930s. The other side of the coin is that we will not be able, in a future debt crisis, to fight our way to solvency with such ruthless cuts in imports. Incidentally it was the fall in the standard of living that mainly cut the imports. This sobering truth, self-evident to an earlier generation of Australians, comes to our generation as a surprise.

Nor are we certain to ease a future debt crisis with the kind of speedy recovery in exports seen in the past. Australians worked their way out of the 1890s depression with a remarkable surge in gold exports and with sharp and quick increases in grain and such new exports as butter and frozen meat. In the 1930s depression, despite the falling prices of the main export commodities, there was a mighty increase in the volume of exports in the following two years,. Of the ten main exports in 1929-30, eight recorded leaps in actual volume in the following two years. The recovery of export prices came much later. Export prices did not even commence their recovery until the middle of 1933.

Earlier governments, faced with tooth-ache, simply pulled out the tooth. Today we are ostensibly more benevolent. Unwilling to yank out the tooth, we might well have to endure the pain and inconvenience for a much longer period. And yet Australia, compared to the days of the T-model Ford, has a far larger capacity to lift itself from a debt crisis. The problem will be to galvanise that capacity and to persuade us all that it must be done.

The idea of painlessly solving the debt problem is still foremost in our minds. It should not be: we tried it in the last few years, and we failed.

In 1985 and 1986 several members of the Federal Ministry courageously pointed to our mounting overseas debt. Mr Dawkins and his Department of Trade produced an excellent report on our failure, our relative failure compared to most other nations, to increase our share of exports. It was in May 1986 that Mr Keating, as Treasurer, courageously said we were in danger of becoming a banana republic.

For the next year at least it seemed that our debt problem might be tackled. Then from 1987 to 1989 came a jump in export prices - the kind of jump for which the early 1890s and 1930s had prayed. In theory it should have gone a considerable way towards restoring our balance of payments to respectability. Instead, it fostered a flood of imports. We are now standing in a worse position than in May 1986.

A banana republic distinguishes itself by lying under a tree and hoping its problems will go away. We are now closer to that state of somnolence than we were in 1986.

It is vital to ask whether overseas debts which are mainly raised by the private sector are especially hazardous to a nation. If the total debt becomes too high it does not greatly matter whether it is private or public debt. Thus in the late 1920s most of our overseas debt had been incurred by State and Federal Governments. They paid about 70 per cent of the cost of servicing those debts. The payment of the fixed interest by governments during the world depression of the early 1930s proved a burden for all Australians. That is why J.T. Lang, the Premier of NSW, tried to repudiate the payment of interest due in London, thus provoking a political crisis with its foretaste of 1975.

We also know that in the run-up to the 1890s depression, just over half of Australia's debt was being written on the nation's red ledger by the private sector. In the year 1890 the private sector sent overseas 6 of the 11.7 million pounds needed to pay interest and dividends. The payment of this big sum indirectly proved a heavy burden for all Australians.

In the Great Debate last Sunday night Mr Hawke seemed to wipe his hands of the debt problem by saying that the debt was mainly in the private sector. "The Government", he said, "had virtually paid off its overseas debts." He failed to add that the State Governments and the Federal Statutory Authorities still had a small mountain of debt. As for the large mountain of debt owed by the private sector, he implied that its origins lay outside the responsibility of his Government.

Does Mr Hawke know what happens in international finance? It was true of 100 years ago and it is almost certainly true of today: the world at large sees Australia as a unity. The world lumps our debts together. It does not see our balance of payments as in part healthy and in part sick. It sees it in aggregate, and in the aggregate it is sick. Our total debt and our burden in paying the interest on the debt is what concerns the overseas people who lent it and must ultimately decide whether to continue lending.

In 1891, when Australia faced a debt crisis not unlike our own, the bankers of England did not say: "Why worry! After all, half the debt is owed by banks, city developers and pastoral companies such as Goldsbroughs and Elders!" In fact London was worried partly because the private sector in Australia owed such big sums. Even the Australian trading banks held, for every thousand pounds of deposits collected in their own land, another 370 pounds collected mostly on the short-term from the British Isles.

London would probably have been less worried if all the Australian debt had been incurred by NSW, Victoria and the other governments in Australia. London knew that as a general rule, governments were less likely than private institutions to default. The Federal Government is unduly complacent if it really believes that private sector debt, when very high, does not endanger a nation's credit rating.

There is another way in which Mr Hawke tends to hide his share of responsibility for Australia's fast-increasing debt: he says it mainly arose through decisions made in the private sector. And yet he has no hesitation in claiming a large part of the credit for the new jobs created in the private sector in the last seven years. He cannot logically disown responsibility for the massive overseas debts but claim the credit for the new jobs, so many of which have been created by the debt.

Those who listened to Mr Hawke in the Great Debate on Sunday night would be entitled to conclude that he accepts little responsibility for the explosion of debt and places no high priority on curbing that explosion. I assume that Mr Keating, if privately questioned, would place a higher priority on the debt issue.

Both the Labor Party and the Coalition, it must be said, view our heavy overseas debt with more concern than do the Democrats. That party is now so immersed in protecting the environment that the balance of nature takes complete precedence over the balance of payments. Perhaps not before in Federal history has a political party come before the people with an earnest promise to accelerate the nation's economic decline.

There is still time to tackle the problem of debt. In tackling it the support of public opinion is vital. Never has a Federal Government spent so much money on so many schemes of propaganda and public instruction as this Government. The debt, however, has not been a noticeable part of such schemes. And yet the debt affects everyone. It especially affects the next generation of Australians who in the end may be forced to pay the interest on what we continue to borrow.

Meanwhile we can hope that something will turn up. We can also dream of a new surge in export prices. But the recent surge in export prices did not rescue us. It is better that we rescue ourselves, using common sense and determination.

> Opening Address to the Debt Summit, organised
> by the Business Council of Australia, Regent Hotel,
> Melbourne, 1 March 1990

54

Gallipoli: A Battle for a Mammoth Prize

Gallipoli is often called the foundation stone of a nation, but to each generation of Australians its gold lettering shines anew or fades.

Whereas most Australians in 1915 believed that the landing at Gallipoli was the foundation stone, many of their grandchildren living in the years of the Vietnam war, about half a century later, thought it was a crumbling stone. Some spat on it.

A "foundation stone" grows or shrinks according to changing ideologies. From time to time it is bound to shrink simply because we can barely conceive of the kind of Australia that hailed the news of the landing at Gallipoli with jubilation.

Australians then felt keenly their isolation from Europe. They wanted to be noticed by Europe. They also wished that they could quickly learn what was happening in the war in Europe.

There was no long-distance wireless to transmit the news from the beaches of Gallipoli to Australian cities, lonely huts and railway sidings. The news was four days old before it reached Australia, having crossed the world by telegraph lines and cables. Almost a fortnight passed before the first long eyewitness report of gunfire and bayonets and the hills "ablaze with bursting shells" appeared in Australian newspapers.

Most Australians felt pride when they first read how their own soldiers had landed on a rugged beach against high odds and were fighting to hold the tiny strip of Turkish territory. Those at home not only admired the Anzacs' courage and competence. They also believed ardently that they were fighting on the side of justice and right.

Something else helped make that first Anzac Day so memorable. Hundreds of thousands of Australians had unconsciously been waiting even before the war for such an event. Without knowing what event was needed they longed for Australia to parade in triumph before the nations of Europe. Here at last, they decided, was that triumph.

The Melbourne *Argus*, one of Australia's best-known daily newspapers, proclaimed that Australia had "in one moment stepped into the world-wide arena in the full stature of great manhood".

The seeds of the Australian nation lay in a convict colony, and those seeds still had an unpalatable taste more than a century after the First Fleet entered Sydney Harbour. Most Australians felt uneasy or embarrassed by their nation's convict origins. The idea of privately confiding, let alone publicly announcing, that one's own great-grandmother had been a convict was unthinkable.

With the invasion on April 25, 1915, Australian nationalists felt that at last they could stand high in the eyes of the world or at least that part of the world whose opinion they valued.

Of course Australian troops had fought on foreign soil long before World War I. They had fought the Boers in South Africa, winning a row of Victoria Crosses. The fault with the Boer War, however, was that it resembled a contest in a minor sporting league. In contrast, Gallipoli was a match of the day in the world's premier league.

Today it would be widely argued in senior schools that a nation surely should not have to engage in a major war to achieve respect among nations. But in the schools once attended by most of the Australian soldiers who fought at Gallipoli, wars between nations were viewed in a different light. War was seen as a heroic theatre for human conduct. War was seen as the most influential moulder of nations.

The books read aloud in schools then gave far more space to Trafalgar and Waterloo and other battles than they give today. Whereas writers of history books in, say, 1900 devoted too much attention to the influence of victorious wars, the writers of today's school textbooks devote too little.

Today, few Australians view war through the eyes of 1915 or even the eyes of 1940. One sign of the profound change in attitudes is the recent rise of the generalisation - spurred by the post-war economic miracles in West Germany and Japan - that it now pays to lose a war. Such an idea had no supporters on the eve of World War I. Being nonsensical, it should have no supporters today.

Likewise, we have painfully learnt that war can be infinitely more devastating than the world's peoples of 1914 had envisaged. On the Western Front the mighty German gun, Big Bertha, was a mere firecracker compared to the weakest nuclear missiles in today's stockpiles. In 1914 the world's biggest naval guns on the armour-clad decks of the huge Dreadnought battle-cruisers were mere popguns compared to weapons carried by nuclear submarines today.

We do not easily grasp the mental attitudes that instantly converted the news from Gallipoli into such a momentous concept for Australia - the idea that the young nation overnight had come of age. Today, the Western world tends to see war as only one of the ways in which a nation can show it stands tall among other nations. Economic success is another form of competition, and sport has almost become a partial substitute for war.

Sport, however, lacked international stature in 1914. While Australia was second to none in the emphasis it placed on sporting success, its opportunities were still meagre.

International sport was then an infant. The Olympic Games, revived in Athens in 1896, were not yet glamorous. Intercontinental football matches were a rarity. The Davis Cup was new and a target of few nations. International contests in golf and yachting were of little consequence, and the America's Cup was unknown to the average newspaper reader in Europe.

Perhaps there were only three sports in which Australians in 1914 enjoyed a reasonably long record of international competition - professional prize-fighting, professional sculling and Test cricket. None of these could have been called truly international. To defeat England in Test cricket gave rise to national rejoicing in Australia, but that news rarely found its way into the newspapers of Jamaica and Ceylon, let alone Berlin, Paris and St Petersburg.

War had more of the characteristics of a sporting contest then than now. The battlefield of Gallipoli was like a modern Olympic Games to spectators living in the safety of Australia, and it was of compelling interest both to people excited by sport and people bored by sport.

Gallipoli offered dozens of gold medals to the athletes that won. It was a race with a mammoth prize. The aim of the assault on Gallipoli and the narrow seaway of the Dardanelles was to capture Constantinople, to remove Turkey from the German alliance, and to open the way for supplies to be shipped from Britain and France to the Black Sea and so by rail to the huge but poorly equipped Russian armies.

If only Russia, at present cut off from her allies, could be helped, the war might quickly be ended, with Russia from the east and Britain and France from the west squeezing Germany into submission. This was the bold strategy that directed the landing by British, French, Australian and New Zealand troops on different strips of Turkish coast and the accompanying plan that, when called upon, the Russian forces would approach from the Black Sea.

The actual landing by Australian and New Zealand troops on the shallow water of the cliff-lined beach of Gallipoli conveyed a special glamour, partly because it evoked old-time wars in which the individual soldier and his human qualities were not dwarfed by the equipment of war.

In the recollections of the London journalist who sent to Australia the first long story of the landing, the events during the first weeks at Gallipoli had been far more newsworthy than the fighting year after year on the main field of war, the Western Front in France. Whereas the Western Front and its trench warfare had an "eternal sameness", Gallipoli experienced unusual events, landings from open boats, battleships shelling armies perched on the narrow peninsula, and other events "which no one ever believed could occur under modern conditions of warfare".

The London journalist was Ellis Ashmead-Bartlett and, in assessing the event whose first days he alone was permitted to report, he gave high praise to the Australian soldiers. That he was an experienced reporter of recent wars, having seen the Japanese fighting the Russians in 1904 and the Italians fighting the Turks in 1911, gave his words additional authority and even impartiality in the eyes of Australians.

If an Australian correspondent had been the only reporter of the Anzacs' landing, his praise would have cut no ice in the English-speaking world. But here instead was an independent witness, a man who knew so little about Australia that (to the astonishment of a Melbourne journalist by whom he was interviewed) he did not even know that Melbourne possessed a network of cable trams.

No wonder his Australian readers were proud to learn of the feats performed by soldiers from "this race of athletes" and the cheerful courage of those who were wounded. "There has been no finer feat in this war than this sudden landing in the dark," wrote Ashmead-Bartlett. His words appeared in nearly every Australian daily newspaper on Saturday, May 8, 1915.

How the first news of the fighting actually reached Australia strongly affected the way in which the event was interpreted. If the soldiers had fought in a theatre of war of little importance their heroism would not necessarily have fired the imagination of people at home. Already an Australian force had captured German New Guinea and their deeds caused no sensation.

If the Anzacs had been instantly routed by the entrenched Turks and driven back into the sea, the defeat - contrary to those who see defeat as a crucial ingredient of the Anzac legend - would not have made Australia's moulders of opinion see Gallipoli as a birthplace of the nation.

Furthermore, if the Australian diggers at the first landing had mingled with troops of many nations, their achievements might not have been so easily singled out for praise. Instead, the Australians and New Zealanders - often called Australasians in the first reports - occupied their own distinct stretch of the rugged coast. Nobody could attribute their achievement to another army. All these facts combined to make the Australian soldiers more noticeable and memorable.

Today it is often said that Gallipoli became a legend mainly because it was a failure. It is often said that events most celebrated in Australian folklore - whether the Eureka Stockade, the death of the explorers Burke and Wills, or the Anzac landing - capture our feelings precisely because they were defeats, and that this pattern tells us something important about the Australian character.

I hesitate to accept this pattern. Gallipoli became an Australian landmark long before it could be interpreted in any sense as a failure or defeat. The positive, not the negative, facets of the military campaign initially enthralled Australians. Even the final withdrawal of all the Allied troops from Gallipoli at the end of 1915 can hardly constitute a dramatic failure.

The withdrawal, a remarkable organisational feat, was begun not as an acceptance of defeat but as an admission that the fighting was now a stalemate. In the final scoreboard Gallipoli could well be summed up by a reasonably impartial Australian umpire as an impressive draw because it was played on the enemy's home ground.

Gallipoli also became a landmark partly because Australians, while fighting on Britain's side, saw themselves as different and even superior in fighting terms. Australian critics could blame Britain for the inability of the invaders to achieve the goal.

If the Australian prime minister and Australian generals had made those mistakes and blunders that flawed the invasion of Turkey, most Australian people would not have felt such national pride. But the British had made the controversial decision of when and how to attack. In the eyes of many Australian soldiers and civilians the British generals and privates were equally inadequate. This was an additional source of Australian pride. As Keith Murdoch of the Melbourne *Herald* wrote, after visiting Gallipoli in the fifth month of the fighting: "To be an Australian is the greatest privilege the world has to offer".

Whether we like the idea or not, war has again and again been seen as the great auditor, the special testing time, of a nation's strength and fibre. The Australian people in 1915, applying this idea to their own nation, were delighted with the result.

They were inclined, however, to overlook the important fact that success in war depends on military equipment and strong supply lines as well as on the courage and stamina of those who fight. Gallipoli was much more a test of the Australian soldiers than of their nations's ability to equip them, feed them and keep the ammunition flowing.

It has long been forgotten - for the Anzac legend, like every legend, is selective - that the Anzacs in the initial month pushed back the Turks not only by exerting their bravery and skill but by using the technology supplied by Britain and other nations. In May 1915 they were even surprising the

Turks with fire from the latest trench mortars, made in Japan.

World War II was to be a more realistic auditor of Australia's military balance sheet and fighting qualities. The fall of Singapore, which directly and indirectly was to exceed Gallipoli in taking the lives of Australian servicemen, showed the importance of military equipment on land, sea and air. The Japanese in 1941-42 were superior to the Australians in equipment and not inferior in courage.

The fall of Singapore is also relevant in an assessment of Gallipoli because it shows that failure is not necessarily the crucial ingredient of those historic events in which Australians take pride. If failure was important then the fall of Singapore, that stupendous failure, would long ago have supplanted Gallipoli in our imagination. But it is Gallipoli that became the legend and remains so.

The Australian, special edition, 24 April 1990

55

Immigration: Australia's Rag Doll

Australia's immigration policy once served our economic and political interests but now it shuns or neglects those interests. At one time it was designed to serve the whole nation but now it serves mainly the needs and ideologies of minorities.

The minorities are powerful partly because they have stolen the high moral ground. Believing that they are upholding high principles, they denounce their opponents as "racist" and therefore immoral. Consequently most people with some self respect and some standing - and professional politicians fall into this category - say they are reluctant to speak out publicly against the immigration policy. I understand their reluctance.

The high principles said to underlie the present immigration policy are violated too often to be called principles. Likewise Canberra's appeal to morality on ethnic and racial matters is too often the easy triumph of hypocrisy over morality.

Significantly, many politicians and commentators now say that they welcome a public debate on immigration - a subject they once said was taboo. But they insist that under no condition will they accept a debate on those areas where high principles must continue to reign. They are sadly mistaken. Those areas must be debated if only to show that their high principles are low.

The first weakness of Australia's immigration policy is that it is not a coherent policy but a rag doll hastily made of bits and pieces. In contrast, the immigration policy of the period 1945 to 1970 was generally successful because it was a coherent policy that served Australia's needs.

Australia then had an accepted motive for building up its population. It believed that a high population would enable the continent to be defended more effectively. It believed that a higher population would strengthen the manufacturing base, then deemed so important to equip the defence forces. Today the defence and manufacturing motives have largely faded away. A new political and economic rationale for large-scale immigration has not taken the place of the old.

Likewise in the years 1945 to 1970 immigration was justified by a continuing shortage of labour. Newcomers quickly gained jobs. Today, however, large numbers of the new migrants live entirely on the public purse and contribute nothing to the nation.

We are importing too many unemployed and too many who in the medium term remain unemployable. Such a statement is not anti-migrant. It is essentially a criticism of politicians of all parties who for too long were blind to elementary facts or nervous of an ethnic backlash if they took those facts seriously. Today many politicians, to their credit, are thinking twice about this policy.

For too long we have been fed the story that the migrants are needed because they work so hard, whereas old Australians do not. But how can migrants in aggregate be working hard when so many are idle? In the 1980s, for probably the first time in Australia's history, we have recruited an alarming proportion of migrants who long after their arrival do no work but receive large public subsidies.

In March this year, 24 per cent of Lebanese in the workforce were out of work. More than 17 per cent of Vietnamese in the so-called workforce had no work. To a much lesser degree the same can be said of New Zealanders with 7.7 per cent unemployment, compared to 6.2 per cent for Australian-born people.

The total taxpayers' subsidy for these migrants who cannot cope is enormous. The figure has never once appeared in the annual report of the immigration department. Presumably it would be too devastating.

In lean economic times it is madness to run immigration in such a way that a large slice of the program simply turns Sydney and Melbourne into sheltered workshops for the relatives of migrants, many of whom have themselves been on the dole since the day they arrived.

Homeless Australians are partly the victims of this policy. Many Australian youngsters whose poverty was to be abolished in 1990 are also victims. As new migrants, especially refugees, often receive a high priority for public housing and as such housing is now scarce, some groups must suffer if others are to gain. It is the Australian homeless who too often wait in the queue while the new migrant jumps ahead of them.

The present migration policy, in effect, discriminates against the Australian homeless. It is one of the ironies of a government which claims to oppose all ethnic discrimination that it has no hesitation in discriminating against Australian Australians.

It is right that Mr Hawke should shed tears for new migrants arriving here with nothing. But his tears are really crocodile tears when he thereby elbows aside - as he must, when money is scarce - many Australians with an equal right to be helped.

Overall, the economic effects of large-scale immigration are harmful for a nation entering a crisis in its balance of payments. The new migrants of the last decade - no matter where they come from - have done little to increase exports and much to increase imports. In short they have aggravated the overseas debt and the high interest rates.

I am not blaming the migrants. I blame the political parties in Canberra which continue to invite them in such large numbers, knowing only too well that this must weaken a frail economy.

For the Hawke Government to argue that in the next few years it can simultaneously rescue us from our import-export crisis, preserve the natural environment and maintain a high level of immigration is folly. Its policies are on a collision course and millions of Australians will be hurt.

Admittedly there is a school of economic make-believe which argues that business migrants help our balance of payments by bringing in big sums. In Tuesday's *The Australian*, Professor Nancy Viviani explained that business migrants in 1988 actually brought $3 billion to Australia. What she did not tell us is that part of this money could well increase our overseas debt. Nor did she explain that business migration in 1988 was sometimes genuine and sometimes a confidence trick, being too often a device for gaining Australian passports by bringing money here and later taking it away again. The former minister for immigration, Senator Ray, deserves praise for trying to improve a laxly-supervised system.

There seems to be no end to the arguments clutched at by the advocates of heavy immigration. In the last couple of years they have argued that our population will become dangerously old without a strong influx of migrants. This argument is faulty. By the time the present 9-year-olds reach retirement age, the over-65s will probably form about one in five of Australia's population - irrespective of whether immigration runs at a fast or slow pace.

It might conceivably be in the interests of Australia to aim for a much larger population within the lifetime of children now at school. While I have an open mind on Australia's optimum population, I am wary of the glib promise that our main economic ills will be automatically healed through the presence of a bigger population and consequently a bigger home market. A larger population can bring more headaches than it cures.

Meanwhile the economic arguments in favour of the present level of immigration in the next three or five years are feeble indeed. We have enough problems without importing migrants who, often through no fault of their own, contribute nothing in their first few years and may contribute nothing in their first decade.

Of course, tens of thousands of the migrants coming in the 1980s from Europe and Asia and Africa and Oceania work well, provide valuable skills and experience, accept the responsibilities of citizenship and will ultimately be proud to be Australian. But what they contribute is gravely weakened by the big minority who are chosen because Australian political parties pander to ethnic pressure groups rather than carefully consider the nation's needs.

That Australia should bring a proportion of migrants from Asia is obvious. More Australians should learn Asian languages, study Asian history and trade more with Asia when the opportunities arise. But it is slightly odd that those who advocate the superiority of Asian life should be so deaf to some of Asia's weaknesses and so blind to some of the secrets of Asian success.

Most Asian nations, for example, suffer from ethnic rivalries and tensions. And yet the politicians who shape our immigration policy ignore those tensions and are arrogant enough to think that they can create here a new nation of tribes which automatically avoids the pitfalls that even the wisest leaders in Asia have been unable to avoid.

The twin questions of learning from Asia and living with Asia are vital to our future. Throughout the 1980s they have not been freely discussed because of the taboo imposed by a medley of politicians, intellectuals, media commentators, ethnic leaders and bureaucrats.

These opinion-leaders insist that their own opinions are morally superior. That is why they view opponents with contempt. Significantly, church leaders who share many of their opinions are more reluctant to claim moral superiority for themselves. They know the dangers of hypocrisy.

From these seemingly moral heights many talented people in the Labor and Liberal parties, the media and the universities affirm as the highest of high principles that they oppose discrimination on grounds of race, culture and nationality. They say that the present immigration policy reflects these high principles and must continue to do so.

This argument is a delusion. When a clear cut exception is pointed out to them - for instance the favoured position of New Zealand migrants or the unfavoured position of Afghans - they promptly abandon their own precious principle with the feeble excuse that these are special exceptions. Such lofty principles should admit no exceptions.

Similarly, while they insist that non-discrimination is a sacred principle - and the difference between themselves and their opponents - they usually abandon this sacred principle inside Australia. Clearly the liberties of the average Australian include the right to discriminate in selecting a marriage partner, church, club, sporting team, weekly newspaper or school. Very often that discrimination is made on racial-ethnic grounds and will presumably continue to be so made.

Those who insist on the morality of non-discrimination have had no hesitation in violating their own sacred principle in dealing with Aborigines. It is not a question of whether their policy towards Aborigines is in the nation's interest - parts of it are probably wise. What is curious is that their Aboriginal policy, which they treat as equally sacred, actually overturns the sacred principles invoked in choosing migrants.

If our leaders of high principle were to be accused of inconsistency they would say proudly they were practising affirmative action. And yet by their own definition - the definition they are quick to apply to others - they surely are practising both hypocrisy and racism.

The use of special labels as defensive and offensive weapons has become a hallmark of this influential group. Thus an identical attitude or prejudice is made legitimate for themselves and illegitimate, indeed shameful, for their opponents.

When traditional Australians argue that Asian migrants should be welcome but that the ethnic mix of the nation should not be altered too quickly, they are called racists. But when ethnic minorities lobby politicians to enlist as many new migrants as possible from their own race, this is applauded as multiculturalism.

Some historians looking back on our era will probably marvel at the fragile economic arguments used to justify the present migration policy. Even more they will wonder at the self-deception of whose who defend the policy largely in the name of ethics and morality.

The sooner we understand that we are being bamboozled by special words and are being swayed by hypocrisy, the sooner can a wide range of legitimate views on immigration be debated.

Weekend Australian, 2-3 June 1990

56

John Cain: A Tall Tree Felled

John Cain is like a tall tree that has just been chopped down with a couple of blows of the axe. Almost immediately we have forgotten how tall the tree was.

In the wake of the succession of disasters that surrounded his last two years, his reputation is now fragile. It will become even more fragile when the full extent of Victoria's financial woes is spelt out to Victorian voters. And yet the fact remains that he has claims to his share of fame, and those claims are easily forgotten at the moment.

Since the 1850s, only four politicians have enjoyed a long reign at the top of Bourke Street. John Cain joins Albert Dunstan of the Country (National) Party and two Liberals, Sir Henry Bolte and Sir Rupert Hamer, as the only premier who managed to survive for eight years in a political climate that traditionally was as thundery as Port Moresby's today.

For the Labor Party, Mr Cain's success in Victorian elections must have seemed a miracle. Until his victory in 1982, the Labor Party was far less successful in Victoria than even the National Party in holding office. It was ironical that in the most industrialised of the Australian states, the Labor Party had for so long been ineffective at the state level. Even the gerrymander could not be blamed, because at most elections Labor used to receive well under 45 per cent and often less than 40 per cent of the vote.

John Cain eventually held office for almost as long as the total of all the previous Labor premiers of Victoria. As a man who is Labor to the toe-nails - indeed he is the only son of the only Labor premier with a reasonable record of success - he is entitled to feel pride in his electoral achievement.

He came to office when Australia was approaching the highest level of unemployment since the bread-and-dripping days of the 1930s, and his Government boasted year after year that it boldly coped with this serious problem. There was validity in his boast. Month after month the unemployment figures in Victoria were the envy of every state capital city.

The question of why Cain coped so well with unemployment has a variety of answers. One is clear-cut. Mr Cain and his colleagues set out to make jobs, especially in the public sector. People were almost tumbling over each other in his expanding Government departments, until dozens of floors in expensive buildings were rented to provide desks and filing cabinets for all.

The problem with a job-creation scheme on this lavish scale is that it is also a devastating tax-creation scheme. The new jobs were for long applauded. The taxes and the borrowings needed to pay for the new jobs are only now becoming evident to Victorians.

Side by side with the impressive employment statistics in Victoria, which Mr Cain rightly paraded in each election campaign, was another set of figures that, through the laxity of the Opposition, were rarely placed before the public. Victoria was performing poorly in the population stakes. Between 1976 and 1986, Victoria's population grew at a snail's pace compared with that of Western Australia and Queensland. Even New South Wales far outgrew Victoria, thus reversing the population trend for the period of 1945-70.

Mr Cain inherited a Victoria in relative decline, but, if anything, he accentuated the decline. He must have been pleased to see a reversal in the year ended June 1989, when Victoria suddenly outpaced New South Wales in its rate of population increase. But the grim news of financial failure during the past few months will probably push Victoria back again to the tail of the field.

Personally, Mr Cain had many of the hallmarks of a traditional Victorian politician from the conservative side.

He was against too much gambling and too much drinking. He waged war against smoking.

In his own use of public money he was frugal. He would not have dreamt of calling on a jet to take him to a football match. He liked to travel "economy" and did not fully realise that free champagne was being given to everyone at the other end of the aircraft called Victoria.

While his Government did many useful things, it created more financial muddles than probably any government in Victoria since at least the 1880s. He had to accept the responsibility and yesterday he did. But we, the public, still do not know enough to determine how much of the blame should fairly be fixed on his own Government and how much on Canberra.

The nation's main economic decisions are made in Canberra. Much of the trouble in Victoria would not have arisen if Canberra had not been so faint-hearted and so irresponsible in many of its decisions. Ironically, Victoria is a few steps nearer the banana republic of which Mr Keating vividly gave warning four years ago, a warning he clearly did not take seriously. Australia's economic future would have been enhanced if yesterday Mr Keating rather than Mr Cain had fallen.

The Age, 8 August 1990

57

In Honour of a High Priestess

Kathleen Fitzpatrick, who was buried yesterday, was one of the few prominent women in public life in an era when no woman in Australia had yet become a judge, a premier, a head of a government department, a divine, a captain of industry or a professor. Yet so many men who later attained those positions were influenced by her, indeed deeply impressed by her.

She had a wonderful mastery of the spoken and written word. While she did not reach in the course of a whole year an audience as large as that reached almost every week by Menzies and Whitlam, she was probably their equal in speech and prose, in timing and sense of theatre. At the same time she remained indelibly feminine.

She reached her largest listening audiences just after the Second World War when she lectured two or three times a week to an overflow audience of first-year students at Melbourne University. Many had just returned from New Guinea and the islands and still wore, on wintry afternoons, their old great-coats. Irrespective of their background, they knew that they were in a kind of intellectual church and that she was the high priestess and that a reverential silence was called for. She lectured - no, she held court - on Elizabethan and Puritan England.

Her voice was closer to an educated English than Australian voice: the kind of voice that some associated in Australia with superiority. But she claimed no superiority over her audience, and indeed in all her speaking and writing during more than half a century of taking part in public life she did not sing or even half-sing her own praises. She did not boast: she had no need to boast.

Of course she was a remote figure, standing aloft on the lecture platform. There was a wide gulf between her and the students; and although her charm and her fine mind and her eloquence easily bridged that gulf, the bridge seemed only temporary, a drawbridge that was pulled up as soon as she had completed the last sentence of each lecture.

Kathleen Fitzpatrick was born in the gold town of Omeo in 1905. Her father, H.A. Pitt, was the clerk of courts but during the 1930s depression he headed the Treasury in Victoria in that parsimonious era when such a high official virtually had to count the state's petty cash each Friday night. Of his daughter's childhood and schooldays we now know much. Her autobiography, *Solid Bluestone Foundations*, will one day be ranked as one of the most perceptive of Australian books.

After studying at Melbourne and Oxford and after a brief marriage to the talented historian and radical, Brian Fitzpatrick, she lectured in English and then history, becoming a leading member of Melbourne University's department of history when, under Professor R.M. Crawford, it was possibly the most celebrated and influential of all the social science and humanities departments in Australia. Soon she became the best-known woman academic in the university, perhaps in any Australian university, having been promoted to associate professor of history in 1948.

Her first book appeared a year later, a study of the famous Arctic explorer Sir John Franklin during the six years in which he was Governor of Tasmania. She had a soft spot for hero-adventurers and turned to the Australian explorers, becoming an authority on the Burke and Wills expedition and producing for the World's Classics a book called *Australian Explorers*.

She liked a grand opening, and her book on Franklin begins with the observation that "the heart-shaped island of Tasmania hangs like a pendant", while her book on explorers begins with the proclamation that "the island-continent of Australia is the most ancient land on earth" and the last refuge of "the vegetable works of the third day of creation". The hallmark of her prose is lucidity and rhythm and a power of observation.

Resigning from the university in her 50s, she went to her house overlooking the sea at Cinema Point on the Great Ocean Road, where she worked on a long book, never published, on the American novelist Henry James. Returning eventually to Melbourne, to an apartment overlooking the Botanic Garden, she again became prominent for a decade or more, writing books, occasionally sitting on a committee, and observing with polished sentences the state of the nation and the absurd or endearing things that happen to people.

She received many honours. The one she would have valued the most was not adequately given her during her lifetime but is beyond dispute: she was a rare sculptor with words.

The Age, 1 September 1990

58

Dreaming of Black and White: Collingwood's Strange Story

Collingwood is the most famous club in Australian football. Much of its fame rests on achievements that were wonderful in their day, but some of the fame stems from a black and white dreamtime.

The record books are peppered with the name of Collingwood. It appears again and again in lists of premierships, tallies of games won and crowds attending, and lists of heroes quaintly called "champions of the colony" or "true boot artists". Even the boots and footballs chosen by most Australian-rules players were made in Collingwood factories whose smoking chimneys once formed the skyline of the suburb.

Founded in 1892, a year of acute depression in Victoria, Collingwood is older than almost every senior club in such celebrated football nations as Argentina and Germany, the finalists in this year's world cup of soccer. And yet Melbourne is really such an old football city that Collingwood, by local standards, is a youngster. Of the twelve clubs which, until recently, constituted the Victorian Football League, Collingwood has to be called the youngest or at best the second youngest. That makes its achievements the more remarkable.

Citizens and sportsmen of Collingwood formed their club partly out of civic pride. At a time when big crowds were already attending matches in Melbourne's parks on Saturday afternoons, Collingwood was the only major suburb without a first-grade football club. While it already possessed that huge town hall - even more impressive today, following the widening of Hoddle Street - it had no sporting team worth barracking for.

Admittedly, Collingwood was home to a promising football club called Britannia and a cricket team called the Capulets but they played only in minor leagues; and the ground they played on, a smaller version of the present Victoria Park, was ankle deep in slush in wet winter and roughly grassed in dry summer. It remained a muddy ground for decades.

The president of the football club for its first twenty seasons, the politician William Beazley, lived with his widowed mother right beside the oval. He had arrived from London as a toddler or baby in arms, learned his trade as saddler and harness-maker and then become an estate agent and politician, being variously a member of early Liberal and Labor parties at a time when in inner suburbs the two parties overlapped. One of his wishes was that the new football club would keep the local larrikins off the streets. His wish was more than answered, and they poured into Victoria Park or wherever Collingwood was playing.

After a lean opening year the team rose quickly in the Victorian Football Association, which then ran senior football. Led at first by old Britannia players who had first tried their hand with Fitzroy, Collingwood then appointed a Carlton stalwart, Bill Strickland, as captain and did not look back.

The team's first hope of a premiership came in 1896 when it headed the ladder with South Melbourne. At the start of October these teams played a deciding match - the first grand final in Victoria - at the East Melbourne cricket ground which then stood opposite the present AFL headquarters in Jolimont. In front of a big crowd,

Collingwood won. It had already agreed to join the group of strong clubs which next year broke away to form the Victorian Football League.

Even then Collingwood played in black and white. These colours often look superb - partly because they seem to combine the right proportions of white and black - but originally they must have seemed second best to their new supporters.

At that time most football teams loved garish colours - especially in their caps and socks - but nearly all the favourite combinations of colours were already taken by Melbourne's other senior teams. White was a popular colour but black was not. A perusal of colours worn by football teams in Victoria about 1880 shows that only the country teams of Creswick and Echuca wore black and white.

The early Collingwood committee is said to have adopted the club colours after a supporter returned from Adelaide impressed with the black and white magpie on the South Australia coat of arms. If true it adds a quizzical aside to the recent episode when Port Adelaide, wishing to join the AFL but retain its colours and emblems, was informed that Collingwood had the prior claim.

Many of the strong football clubs did not worry about emblems and mascots; but Collingwood, when photographing its first premiership team of 1896, arranged for a painting of a magpie standing on a football to appear alongside the players. In that photo, Collingwood's colours do not look spectacular because the black stripes of the jumper were wider than the white, and the stripes themselves were not symmetrical.

The Magpie team soon commanded local loyalty and eventually fanaticism but it was never - contrary to the prevailing legend - a club exclusively for local players and supporters. In one of the early premiership teams half of the players came from country districts. As early as 1930, most supporters of Collingwood lived in such suburbs as

Preston, Northcote, Thornbury, Alphington, Ivanhoe and Kew, travelling to Victoria Park on foot or train or tram, or coming straight from Saturday-morning work. Perhaps they had once lived in Collingwood and their football loyalty remained behind.

They came to see Collingwood play mainly because it was their kind of club. It was run by people they knew or knew of, people who at some stage of life had had to battle.

The first Magpie hero was "Dick" Lee. A son of the head trainer, he topped the League's goal-kicking list in ten separate years, though his annual tally of goals was no higher than that reached by today's best forwards as early as the Queen's Birthday weekend. Lee gained the ball with clever ruses, and even from the picket fence on the half forward flank he could sometimes score goals with his place kicks.

Everyone swore by Lee's courage as well as his cleverness. In Collingwood's little Hall of Fame is a leather shinguard, about a foot long, with buckles at each end. It was made specially for Dick by the local factory of T.W. Sherrin in order to protect a kick-wound which stayed open and unhealed, it is said, for more than two years.

During the playing years of "Dick" Lee (1906-22), Collingwood was not quite the dominating team it later became. Somehow a myth has arisen that Collingwood was on top from the start: the product of a special spirit in that industrial suburb with its cobblestone lanes and skinny children. Fitzroy, however, has a stronger claim to be classed as *the* team in the first thirty years of the VFL. By 1910 it had won four flags - one more than Carlton or Collingwood. These three rivals from the northern suburbs, playing on ovals so close together, took it in turns to win 16 of the first 23 VFL premierships.

The long-awaited match of the year was often between the Maroons and the Magpies; and busy Smith Street - then one of the city's busiest shopping streets as well as the border between Fitzroy and Collingwood - would buzz with jeers and physical skirmishes on the Friday evening before the two teams clashed. The Fitzroy team more than held its own. By the end of 1925 it was clearly the leading team in VFL history. It had won seven flags compared to six by Essendon and five each by Carlton and Collingwood.

Then the Magpie soared. Between 1927 and 1930 it won four premierships in a row. The Collingwood of the late 1920s was that rarity, a side of champions as well as a champion side. Its talented ruckman Sid Coventry won the Brownlow in 1927, Albert Collier won it in 1929, and his brother Harry the rover was equal first in 1930 though he lost the medal on a countback.

Meanwhile the final member of these pairs of brothers, Gordon "Nuts" Coventry, was breaking all records at full forward with a league record of 83 goals in 1926 and, three years later, an astonishing tally of 124 goals kicked in the course of a season shorter than today's. He would have kicked even more but for the fact that in the 1929 grand final he acted as decoy and led the men minding him far from the goal square, enabling his unguarded team-mates to kick the winning goals.

In 1935-36 Collingwood won another two flags in a row, giving them six premierships in the space of ten years and an even larger army of supporters. The word now frequently used of Collingwood's teamwork was "machine". It was a well-oiled football machine which, once in motion, was not easily stopped.

Collingwood was henceforth the team to beat, the team with tradition, the team with a halo, the team to be jeered at by supporters of other clubs. Amazingly it continues to hold that role, less because of the team's success on the field in the last 50 years than because of the super-confidence and loyalty of its legion of supporters.

Towards the end of the heyday of the Magpies the name whispered with awe was "Jock" (James) McHale. Born in Sydney, the son of an Irish-born constable, McHale was one of those who made Collingwood but were themselves not made in Collingwood. His links were just beyond the suburb's boundaries for he went to Catholic schools in North Fitzroy and Coburg and finally to CBC in Victoria Parade before joining McCracken's brewery - McCracken was a high official of Essendon and eventually president of the VFL.

For Collingwood, Jock McHale played for some twelve years without missing a game. He was Mr Fitness and when he became the coach he insisted that his players must be fit. In the eyes of some observers that was to be his finest contribution to the club.

From before the First War until after the Second War (from 1913 until 1950) he coached Collingwood. Even Allan Jeans, who has just retired after half a lifetime as coach of St Kilda and Hawthorn, is still 153 games behind old Jock's coaching record.

It is doubtful, however, whether the McHale era and the Jeans era can sensibly be compared. For the first 15 or 20 years of McHales's coaching career a coach was not normally expected to be all-seeing and all-knowing. He did not send a stream of messages onto the field during the match. He usually did not alter players' positions even once during the course of a match.

It was a sign of the coach's lowlier status that in some of the Collingwood's premier teams McHale was not assigned a place of a honour in the framed official photographs. He had about the same status as a senior member of the committee. The fact that coaches are now deemed more important - sometimes too important - is partly due to him.

McHale's picture was not often in the daily newspapers (unless in the cartoons) during much of his coaching career. Rarely did he give interviews. It was not that his command of words was inadequate: he was a persuasive and even emotional speaker to his huddle of players.

His era now seems old-fashioned and unhurried. Who knows what he would think of modern coaches who, wearing neither tie nor jacket, hurry out - not a moment to lose - to address their players at the interval? To see Mr McHale, in his best suit and wide-brimmed hat, walking with leisurely steps onto the arena to address his team at three-quarter time was like seeing a respectable shopkeeper or factory foreman setting out for a Sunday afternoon stroll.

Overall he demanded less of his players than a modern coach would demand, but he did expect them to win. They happily obliged, winning eight premierships and becoming the runner-up ten times while he was coach.

The victories of Collingwood were so unusual that the envious looked for reasons. How, they asked, could a relatively poor suburb do so well? The legend arose that John Wren, Victoria's unofficial czar of gambling and a great "fixer" in politics and other facets of daily life, was the hidden financier.

In his youth Wren had played local football with the Star of Collingwood and other junior teams while employed as a cutter of leather at Whybrow's boot factory in Clifton Hill. Later he became a generous donor to Collingwood, making special gifts and even arranging during the depression of the early 1930s for a cluster of players to receive jobs at the Carlton brewery.

But Wren's money, while welcome, was not as vital to Collingwood's success as the folklore maintains. This is the verdict of Richard Stremski whose book *Kill for Collingwood* is probably the best history of the politics of any sporting and social institution in Australia.

John Wren certainly was not the ever-present backer of Collingwood. True, he twice gave the sum of 50 pounds to Gordon Coventry for kicking a record bag of 16 goals against Hawthorn and then 17 against Fitzroy. In the era when clubs paid players three pounds a match a lump sum of 50 pounds was as much as Coventry would normally receive for playing in the first seventeen games of the season. But such gestures were not often made by Wren to Collingwood's stars.

Amongst the richer, rival League clubs were supporters who also quietly gave money to star players. How else could South Melbourne have recruited its "foreign legion" of interstate stars who helped it to reach four grand finals in succession between 1933 and 1936?

Now and then a star player was lured away by a financial offer which John Wren, if he were really the backstairs financier of Collingwood, could have easily outbid. For example, Albert Collier at the height of his fame, with years of rib-pounding football ahead of him, was enticed to the now-forgotten Hobart team of Cananore. A roll of banknotes from Wren could have kept him at Collingwood but the roll was not forthcoming. A hundred footballers in other Victorian clubs must have sighed with relief when the fearsome Collier boarded the steamship for Tasmania.

The legend depicts the old Collingwood as roped together by a primitive loyalty. In part this was true but some brilliant players - before and after the Albert Collier episode - decided that all the camaraderie and loyalty they received at Victoria Park was no compensation for the chance of playing elsewhere for an extra two or three pounds a week.

Thus, early in the Second World War there were headlines when the two wonder boys, Todd and Fothergill, were separately enticed to Williamstown in the Victorian Football Association. It was a shock to all Magpie supporters to see such stars - their best playing days ahead of them - crossing "without a clearance" in an era when not many players, let alone champion players, changed clubs.

Incidentally Des Fothergill, the war almost over, returned to play briefly with Collingwood, having put on stones in weight. In his lumbering way he could still turn the football into a personal yo-yo. Even those of us who do not barrack for Collingwood marvelled at this reincarnation and glimpsed what Fothergill must have been like when in successive years he was judged best footballer in the VFL and the VFA.

John Wren, looking down from his mansion on the hill at Kew, could have easily outbid the Victorian and interstate clubs which successfully poached Albert Collier, Billy Libbis, Marcus Boyall, Des Fothergill and other Magpie stars. But Collingwood's committee was unusually wary of surrendering undue power to extreme individualists, whether they were star players wanting more money or rich supporters willing to slip gifts into the hands of favourite players.

The club demanded the highest loyalty from everyone in the club. That was the secret of its success. In turn its victories on the field brought it money and more loyalty. It is the level of loyalty and dedication given to Collingwood which makes it stand out. In its greatest years, in its spirit, it was as much like a religious order as a sporting club.

Of Collingwood's grand total of thirteen premierships won during almost one century of VFL and AFL football, nearly half had been won in the course of those superlative years between 1927 and 1936. The greatness of Collingwood belongs primarily to that one period of ten years.

A club of remarkable consistency in most decades, its mystique came largely from its success in those ten years. Thereafter a cloak of invincibility seemed to drape its whole history, though the cloak eventually became slightly faded and ill-fitting in the eyes of all but the most ardent Magpie supporters.

At the end of 1936 the club had a tally of 11 VFL premierships compared to the 7 of Fitzroy and the 6 of Essendon. This proved to be a long-term lead, enough to last for almost half a century. During that time Collingwood added only two more flags - by defeating Geelong in 1953 and Melbourne in 1958. Ironically Collingwood did not top the home-and-home ladder in either of those two triumphant years, and yet it has since experienced at least five years in which it was superior during the whole year, only to fail in the finals.

Even as recently as the start of the 1980s Collingwood held the most VFL flags, a total of thirteen, though its lead over its rivals was now perilous. Soon that lead was overtaken and passed. Today the list of League premierships reads:

Carlton	15
Essendon	14
Collingwood	13
Melbourne	12
Richmond	10

To win a mere two premierships in the last half century is small reward for all the fine teams that Collingwood fielded during that long period. And yet the club has come so close to success so often in that period. With the aid of a mere four straight kicks on a few Grand Final Days in recent memory, Collingwood would still be the clear leader on the League's list of aggregate premierships.

While we all want our team to win, the next choice is to be runner-up. By that test Collingwood has given enormous pleasure - as well as disappointment - to its barrackers. Since 1897, according to Graeme Atkinson in his *Complete Book of V.F.L Finals,* Collingwood has finished either first or second on 36 occasions. Next come Carlton and Essendon, each with a mere 24. Collingwood's record as far and away the leading runner-up is largely a creation of the last thirty years.

The best teams in that "Colliwobble era" - the teams that almost won the flag - have carried out a function which is easily overlooked. They have kept alive in most of the supporters a loyalty which would definitely have faded away if Collingwood instead had finished in the bottom half of the ladder in most seasons of the 1960s, 1970s and 1980s.

Above all, those teams of the "Colliwobble era" really recruited the new generation of Collingwood barrackers, the kids who wave those black and white flags as big as sails, who try to go to bed wearing Collingwood jumpers, who spend half their waking hours imagining that they are Peter Daicos about to kick the winning goal next Saturday, and whose own fathers can almost remember the last time Collingwood won a flag.

The Sunday Herald, 30 September 1990

59

A Grand Final Breakfast

Mr Bob Ansett, Prime Minister, Premier, Other Distinguished Guests.

Australian-rules football is old, much older than we realise.

When the final of the world cup of soccer was staged in Rome this year, the two finalists were traditional footballing nations: Argentina and Germany. And yet the oldest football team in Argentina is not a old as Essendon. Even some of our younger clubs like Fitzroy and Footscray have a longer history than the oldest recorded football team in Germany, FC Dresden, founded in 1889. Come to think of it, Carlton is older than the original Italian club, and North Melbourne is older than any football club in Ireland. Even in the fatherland of soccer, the English Football League has no club as old as Melbourne and Geelong.

Grand final day in Melbourne is the annual climax of something unusual, a competition with a history all of its own. I am pretty safe in saying that there is no senior football competition in the world as old as Victorian football.

Remarkably, the grand final is still played in the same park where our code of football was born. When this afternoon you walk to the Melbourne Cricket Ground you can see trees which were already there in the goldrush years of the 1850s. The pioneer footballers played around those trees. What continuity in a nation which is sometimes said to have no history!

In the whole world there is no other football field where the past and present so mingle. This afternoon, countless old players and spectators will be there in spirit. Tommy Wills will be there, silent in the crowd, marvelling at the skills of Aboriginal players - he was the first to train them seriously in any sport. Harrison will be there; and his eyes will be alight when he sees players bouncing the ball as they race along the grass, for back in the 1860s he provoked the bouncing rule that still prevails.

If skinny hands stretch up in the packed crowd behind the goalposts and try to mark the ball, perhaps that's Dick Lee or John Coleman or Lindsay White or Roy Cazaly. And if you're in the front row this afternoon, and an old man just behind hands you a 100 dollar note to give to a Collingwood player who has just kicked a goal, don't forget to say "Thank You, Mr Wren".*

Footballers who died in the world wars will be there, just for the day. Perhaps Ron Barassi's dad will be back, along with a host of forgotten heroes from Gallipoli, France, Tobruk, Ambon. They say Australia is too young to have a history - don't you believe it.

Those who are very much alive will be there, a hundred thousand of them from every corner of Australia, from Arnhem Land and Kalgoorlie and the Five Mile Creek - and even the Ten Mile Creek. They will come from every occupation, people of almost every age. If you're lucky you might even meet a barracker who recalls how, as a lad 79 years ago, he saw Essendon play Collingwood when last they met on grand final day in this same arena.

One of the triumphs of Australian-rules football, almost from the start, has been its ability to embrace every section of society, Catholic and Protestant, the prosperous and the poor, players with names like Jesaulenko and Schimmelbusch as well as Smith (both Norm and Len). Many people think that Melbourne as a city possesses a unity which Sydney lacks: the longtime popularity of Australian-rules is an important reason for that unity.

The men who founded this game, who made the early rules, thought that football was more than a game. They believed that football had something else to offer a nation. If they were alive they would still believe so. As a State, and as a nation, we are now caught by economic troubles; and the main cause of the troubles is simple. In economic life we are not competitive enough. In our markets overseas, in our markets here, we are too easily defeated by other nations.

On this day of days every footballer will run his heart out; both teams will give everything they possess. Aren't they giving us a hint, a lesson? They are reminding us all that, with more effort, with more skill, Australia can ultimately triumph over these troubles.

So, long live our game. And long live Australia.

Address to the 25th annual breakfast of the North Melbourne Football Club, Southern Cross Hotel, 6 October 1990

* At half time at the football that afternoon an oldish man approached me, saying with grave courtesy that he had heard my speech on television and wished to make one correction. The 100-dollar note passed down by John Wren, he said, was obviously for the umpire!

60

Canberra is Becoming a Parasite City

Lower interest rates will do little to cure the nation's long-lasting economic illness. Compared to other nations with which we like to be compared, we are in economic decline. On present evidence our decline will continue, and yet with the aid of common sense we could easily become prosperous again. Most international observers are conscious of Australia's long fall down the world's economic ladder. In Australia we tend to shut our eyes to the fall. Canberra especially shuts its eyes. Canberra's blindness and arrogance is my theme today.

Never has the federal capital been so important to the nation. It has to provide leadership in the most difficult time that Australia has had to face since the world depression. Let's not kid ourselves by comparing this situation with the recession of 1982-83. Let's not divert ourselves by discussing the technicality of whether this is or is not a recession. Admittedly the unemployment is not yet as severe as in the early 1980s. But there is an enormous difference between the underlying vigour of Australia's economy in 1982 compared to today. Moreover, in the recession of the early 1980s a major drought had been inflicted on us, whereas today most of our wounds are self-inflicted. The easing of the drought did much to revive the economy in 1983. Today, in debt-laden Australia, we need more than rain.

Canberra, and Sydney and Melbourne, are at the core of our problems. They do not pull their weight in the national economy. They are massive importers and pitiful exporters at a time when we need fewer imports and more exports. And yet there is no awareness by most people that the big cities are increasingly bludging on the nation.

Canberra is a special problem. It is becoming Parasite City. I respect Canberra's role and many of its past achievements. We originally needed a Canberra because of the rivalry between Sydney and Melbourne. But Canberra is becoming such a liability that I wonder whether we almost need to think of selecting another city as capital. Canberra is now the symbol of national complacency. A product of the postwar era of seemingly effortless national progress, it is still trying to live in that vanished world.

These sound like harsh words about a city that holds so many important institutions, that holds large numbers of talented and dedicated Australians, and that is beginning at last to appear like a capital city rather than a country town. But I am certain that the founders of the Australian federation would be appalled if they could see the spirit ruling Canberra in this year of difficulties. It was in 1901 that King O'Malley, virtually the father of Canberra, expressed his hopes to the very first federal parliament. He hoped that the federal capital, still unborn, would be "capable of nurturing a sympathetic and noble-minded people worthy to be the central pivot of this southern empire of Australia". He would surely agree that today the combined forces of the parliament and bureaucracy are proving to be neither noble-minded nor sympathetic.

The defect of Canberra is that, while so modern, it behaves like a medieval city. It has surrounded itself with a moat. Rather than serving Australia, it somehow keeps Australia at arm's length. This did not matter so much in prosperous years. In lean years this isolation is a hazard for the whole nation.

For the first time Canberra, as a fully-fledged capital city, has to fight a growing crisis in our balance of payments and our overseas debt. The last time Australia faced a similar problem - in the early 1930s - Canberra was a tiny makeshift capital. Most of the Commonwealth civil servants had not yet moved to Canberra, and most of the federal ministers spent their time away from Canberra.

While Canberra is now the capital city in every sense of the phrase, it has tended to lose touch with ordinary Australians. It is engrossed in its own self-contained world. It has its own mood and atmosphere, its own priorities.

It has a vested interest in a fat public service. In the nation's continuing export crisis, Canberra has another defect. It produces hardly any exports. It is not even a port which ships the exports. The world has few other capital cities that are several steps removed from a crisis in the balance of payments. Canberra carries out vital functions but its rewards are out of all proportion to its importance. It has the highest average income of any large city in Australia. It would be in the national interest if that honour was held by a city which did far more than Canberra to tackle the nation's problems.

As an exporter Canberra cannot even compete with most outback towns. This year I visited in Western Australia a tiny gold town with a population of sixty, of whom about five are infants. It is highly mechanised and the few people work long hours. Way out in the mulga and not even marked on most maps, it will probably produce more revenue from exporting goods than Canberra's 300,000 people will produce this year. That would not matter so much if Canberra understood the difficulties of the exporting industries but Canberra does not adequately understand them. The towns in the outback and the bush are our work heroes, and the hope of Australia's sick economy. Unfortunately the TV gives Canberra the glamour every evening.

Canberra has another weakness. Its parliament is largely composed of capital-city members, but nearly all our capital cities are weak in producing exports. In the federal parliament only a tiny proportion of members represent electorates that pull their weight as exporters. The task of increasing exports has few well-informed advocates in the federal parliament and very few in the federal ministry. This helps to explain why Canberra's system of rewards favours public servants and punishes exporters.

The towns and industries in the frontline of our economy carry an additional burden. They help finance the privileges which Canberra and the bureaucracies in all the state capitals have quietly claimed.

I am not singling out the present government and leaders of the public service. They largely inherited their special financial privileges from those few sunny months when Mr McMahon was promising everyone the world and Mr Whitlam was quickly outbidding him. So in 1972 and 1973 Canberra was given the world, with the assurance that the rest of Australia would be similarly treated. The rest of Australia is still waiting. It will always be waiting.

Commonwealth superannuation was reshaped in the early 1970s in the name of pace-making: "Let us blaze the trail for others to follow". But how can you blaze a trail which by definition will always be too narrow to accommodate most Australians? Judged by the arguments used to introduce them, all the public superannuation schemes - with their firm promises of indexed pensions normally exceeding 50% of retiring salary - are beyond the resources of the nation. They are also unfair. Nothing would do more for the public morale today than to reduce these costly privileges.

A basic principle in a democracy is that the politicians and bureaucrats are the servants of the people, sharing their hardships and sharing their prosperity. But the federal government over the years has so arranged its affairs that its civil servants and its parliamentarians are protected by superannuation schemes of incredible security and generosity. From these schemes the public are excluded. They are merely people whose taxes have to finance the pensions.

No private industry, profession or trade can even approach the present or proposed Canberra pensions or, for that matter, the parallel State government pensions and retirement payouts. The politicians' pensions are an eye-opener. They are infinitely more attractive than their annual salary and allowances. If a vital aim of a good salary is to attract good candidates to parliament then the present package is an utter failure. Few people outside Canberra know about the startlingly high pension as distinct from the moderate salary.

Politicians who won a federal seat during the swing to Labor in 1983 are now entitled, if they resign, to a pension for life. Their indexed pension equals half of the parliamentary salary. These politicians contribute to the pension fund a sum equal to one year of salary. For that small investment, they receive a large and increasing pension for life. It would be better for the nation if politicians were paid a high salary and were seen to receive a high salary. It would be better if, like other citizens, they then contributed to a normal superannuation scheme and took the risks which everyone in the private sector has to face. Today, federal politicians know that once they leave parliament they can receive automatic immunity from the downturns of the economy. That is dangerous for the well-being of the nation. It also diminishes the standing of politicians, and in a democracy such a diminution is unwise.

Not everything in Federal Pensionland is generous. Short-term public servants were at one time shabbily treated, and some top servants were not well rewarded by the Commonwealth superannuation scheme. Furthermore, this year a leaner super scheme - underwritten if necessary by massive public subsidies - is being offered to existing public servants though not forced upon them. Canberra clings to its privileges while the rest of Australia suffers.

Most of Canberra can hope to retire with unusual economic security after a working life of unparalleled security. Amidst the new policy that Australia as a whole - from banks to car-manufacturers - must face a competitive market, one city is largely exempted: its name is Canberra. It is hardly wise in lean times - and we are probably facing a decade of numerous disappointments - that the national leaders who prescribe nasty medicine should themselves refuse to swallow it. When their advisers and those who advise the advisers also refuse to swallow the medicine they prescribe, then something is drastically wrong.

The cost of this golden accord between the state and federal parliaments and the public services is astronomical. Nobody knows the exact cost for the whole nation. If calculated and then revealed, it would cause a sensation. In Victoria alone we do know that the state government has a liability of $16 billion for its contributions - promised but not yet paid - to its various pension schemes. If these schemes had been terminated on 30 June 1990, and if nobody henceforth could join them, and if the Victorian government decreed that it was under no obligation to make further contributions to the funds, its own liability would be $16 billion. In other words the taxpayers already face that liability.

In all States and in the Commonwealth the total liability or debt of these privileged superannuation schemes already exceeds $55 billion, according to my very conservative estimate. When a public company announces a loss of a mere $1 billion there is a financial sensation. Here is a mega-sensation. Governmental superannuation for its favoured sons and daughters is utterly bankrupt - unless other taxpayers pour in huge sums to buttress a benefit to which they themselves can never be entitled.

Mr Hawke and Mr Keating have rightly drawn attention to the enormous overseas debts incurred by Australian businesses. They have been appropriately silent about the enormous debts incurred inside Australia by all governments for their own superannuation schemes, schemes from which Mr Hawke and Keating will be happy beneficiaries. I offer this chilling fact. If by chance the federal government magically stabilised Australia's foreign debt, that colossal debt would, in the lifetime of most people now in the public service, be exceeded by the indebtedness of the present governmental schemes of superannuation. And that debt - unlike the foreign debt - must be made directly by the taxpayers.

To call this a scandal would be correct but provocative. The privileges of politicians and the public service should be radically reshaped, doing justice to the public sector, doing justice to special groups such as the judiciary and armed forces, and, above all, doing justice to the nation as a whole.

The same skilled axe should descend on all State schemes. Nothing is more important than the principle that those who govern should share in the lean times, especially if their mistakes have helped to create the lean times.

An address to the Conference, "Who Governs Australia", Burswood Convention Centre, Perth, 19 October 1990

61

The Quality of Life in Australia

I gratefully accepted the kind invitation of the Jennings Group, through the Australian Centre at the University of Melbourne, to give this public lecture. Sometime later, when I grasped the implications of the topic they had chosen, my spirits sank a little. I realised that I had never written even a couple of pages directly on the theme of the quality of life in Australia.

At one time or other we all pass judgment about the quality of life and especially the parts that annoy us. Nearly every parent thinks about the quality of life occasionally. Every candidate for public office thinks about it, even if only to attack opponents.

The early Australian governors held strong views about the quality of life. Lachlan Macquarie, landing in lonely Sydney in 1809, was dismayed to find that agriculture was languishing, public buildings were mouldering, roads in poor repair, and the country even 40 miles from Sydney quite impenetrable. Like all leaders eager to distance himself from his predecessors, Macquarie exaggerated; but he spoke much truth. He added that public life was torn by factionalism, that public revenue was "unknown", and that there was "no public credit nor private confidence". It sounds like Victoria in 1990.

He made the significant comment that he found "the morals of the great mass of the population in the lowest state of debasement, and religious worship almost totally neglected". Without doubt, most leaders in the nineteenth century regarded the morals of the Australian people as a more desirable component of the quality of life than we do today.

Long after Macquarie had completed his twelve years and sailed away, the quality of life remained of concern to Australian leaders. The quality of life they sought to give their people was primarily materialist. Mr Ben Chifley, the first of the post-war prime ministers, spoke in June 1949 of "the light on the hill". His phrase is remembered amongst the Labor faithful but its concrete meaning is almost forgotten. He wanted for all Australians the following goals:

1   high and rising standards of living

2   comprehensive social security

3   rapid development of our national resources

4   adequate defence.

Nearly every member of the Labor Party in 1949 would have agreed with those four priorities and the Liberals under R.G. Menzies would have agreed strongly with three and a half of them. But what is paradise for one political group can eventually become an urgent target for reform. Today, many radicals, including some of the more ardent Greens, would gladly switch off Chifley's "light on the hill" by deleting priorities 1, 3 and 4 and replacing them with a static or falling standard of living, a moratorium on the development of national resources, and less spending on defence. Nothing shows so clearly how traditional ideas of the quality of life can be overturned. Disagreement about what constitutes the good life is one of the main reasons, though rarely mentioned, for our present economic difficulties.

Most Australians who return after a first tour of Europe or Asia usually exclaim, when the jetlag is over, "This is God's own country". They might argue what is the most God-like quality, but they would agree on most components of the quality of life.

Nearly all Australians want a sense of security; they want their nation to be free from war. They wish their own person and property and possessions to be free from depredation, whether bushfires, robberies or revolutions. They want sound health and a long life. They hope that the sick and disabled will be cared for. They want education for their children though they have less faith than their parents had in schools and universities being the storehouses of wisdom. They want adequate and interesting food. They want shelter, especially in a wet winter and hot summer and they relish a house they can call "home". They demand leisure and the freedom to use it in the way they wish. To be fed and sheltered and clothed, to be free from epidemics and from invasion, is to be at least half way towards a high quality of life.

Milk and Honey

Judged by material well-being, Australia's quality of life since at least 1840 has been fortunate. Indeed most of the history books of Australia written until the last fifteen years took pride in the people's material success. By this measure we were often a world leader, winning a high average income very early, winning short hours of work by world standards, gaining longevity: soon Australian children were noticeably taller and heavier in the eyes of migrants. As Australian people placed a high value on material well-being, the major political parties tended to define their opposition to each other largely in economic terms. In the last seventy years it is not easy to recall many elections fought on non-economic issues. Even when such issues were prominent - for example the Vietnam War in the 1966 federal election and the environment in the 1990 election - the traditional bread and beer and butter issues were still vital in determining which party won.

Compared to other nations a surprising proportion of the accepted turning-points in Australian history are economic events that mark the gains, or sometimes the losses, in the welfare of the average person. These milestones include the spread of the squatters and their sheep in the 1820s, the finding of rich gold in 1851, the settling of the selectors on small farms especially from the 1860s, the depression and drought of the 1890s and the accompanying birth of the Labor Party, the creation of Australia's common market and the Commonwealth of Australia in 1901, the appalling depression of the 1930s, and the immigration of the prosperous Menzie era. The world wars provided major milestones but the Second World War was as much an economic as a military and political milestone for Australia.

Many, many people missed out on a slice of the cake in the various eras of milk and honey. And yet in most years of the last 150 years the majority of Australians have constituted a fortunate people by material standards. We don't need to moralise and conclude, as we sometimes do, that we are therefore uniquely materialist amongst the world's nations. The cultivated man of letters, Edmund Gibbon, author of the *Decline and Fall of the Roman Empire,* was one of many who emphasised that prosperity was a crucial component of the quality of life, and was so in every era: "If a man were called to fix the period in the history of the world during which the condition of the human race was most happy and prosperous, he would, without hesitation, name that which elapsed from the death of Domitian to the accession of Commodus." He actually penned this high praise to the old Roman empire just before the town of Sydney was founded, but if he had lived a century later in, say, 1890 he would have revised that verdict. By 1890 he would have written that Australia was clearly far more prosperous than even Rome had been in the heyday of the Roman empire.

Three meals a day, a roof over the head, a day's work that was not too long, free school for the children, a generous number of holidays, a short working week: they might not sound grand achievements to us but in 1890 they were a cause of intense pride. I think that our two severe depressions - those of the 1890s and the 1930s - are such landmarks in Australian history because they were shocks to people who hitherto had mostly been so prosperous by world standards.

The 1970s and 1980s have proved to be two of Australia's less prosperous decades. In those decades our economy performed more poorly than that of most of the nations with which we like to compare ourselves. In the last two or three years the margin of our inadequacy has been alarmingly high. Even Canberra sometimes admits that.

As our quality of life as a nation has depended heavily on our prosperity, we should ask ourselves whether we are now entering a new era in which the quality of life could diminish. We can quickly climb the ladder of prosperity again; it is within our power if we have the will. But we deceive ourselves if we think that today we are doing anything but continuing to slip slowly down the ladder. The high interest rates prevailing for several years are sometimes seen in political circles as the highest obstacle. Painful as they are, they are simply the evidence of deeper economic troubles. To reduce interest rates will be a great relief for many struggling businesses and for hundreds of thousands of families paying off a house. But further falls in interest rates, while welcome, will probably do little to remedy a deeper defect.

In essence, our economy is not competitive by world standards, has not been competitive for most of the last decade, and will not become competitive again without major changes in public as well as parliamentary attitudes. Our present ills are as much cultural as economic in origin. They also stem more from Australia than from the world outside. In that sense they can easily be tackled if we have the determination to tackle them.

It is possible to maintain a high quality of life while the material standard of living is falling. It is possible but not easy. Australia has a widespread body of intellectual opinion that in theory would applaud our economic decline: many intellectuals see in Australia's traditionally high standard of living and its love of possessions and leisure the seedbed of philistinism. This argument, while true in part, overlooks one inescapable fact. Even the artistic and intellectual activity has to be underwritten, whether by private or public wealth. Poverty and hardship may be invigorating for artists, but wealth is also stimulating.

Would Nellie Melba have been famous as a singer of opera if her father had remained a poor Melbourne stonemason instead of becoming one of the city's richest building contractors, the Grollo of his era? Would Patrick White have become a successful novelist if his family had not made a rural fortune, part of which enabled him to write full-time in London when income from his books did not pay his rent? The same was true of the young Robert Helpmann, making the expensive journey from South Australia to London in the 1930s to study dancing. The arts needs patrons, public or private.

Some talents, like champagne bubbles, seem to rise effortlessly to the top but other talents do not easily overcome sustained adversity. In the arts, education, medical research and a variety of fields in which Australia has contributed to the world's knowledge or delight, money is a great help, especially if spent intelligently. Our economic decline, if it continues, will bring gain: a certain austerity and a diminished dependence on possessions. But it will probably harm many of those activities that are seen as a vital part of the quality of life in today's Australia.

Prosperity can also help in attacking poverty, as Archbishop Hollingworth courteously explained to the Prime Minister last week. Prosperity can redress the increasing neglect of hospitals. It is even relevant to education. I make this point, knowing that the education profession - from primary through to tertiary - is the home of powerful voices which for years have opposed most of the economic activities in which Australia excels: the very activities on which the financing of education will continue to depend.

There is a danger in striving too hard for prosperity and in valuing it too highly. Australia is no longer in such danger. Our risk is that unless we shake ourselves and our economic and social institutions we will sit close to the third world in the year 2010. A trip overseas, even to Bali, might become too costly - unless it is one way - for the great majority of Australians in the bottom half of the scale of incomes.

A Sense of Belonging

I see prosperity, widely shared, as a vital ingredient of the quality of life in Australia. I see another kind of security as equally important. This is more an emotional and mental form of security: it is simply the feeling that Australia is home.

Few changes have done more to improve the quality of life in Australia than the slow growth of a sense of belonging. The Aboriginals living their traditional life had a profound sense of belonging; the people and culture that supplanted the Aboriginals were slow to gain that feeling of belonging here. For the migrants from the British Isles and elsewhere, the sense that Australia was their home grew very slowly.

The climate in summer in many parts of the continent was far too hot for most migrants and for the first-generation of native-born. Even in Melbourne in the nineteenth century, summer and not winter was the feared season. The fear of the heat was partly subjective and - we have forgotten - it was partly rational. In Melbourne in the period 1853-1864 half of the total deaths were of children under the age of two. The hot months marked the peak of infantile deaths. They increased threefold in those months, largely through diarrhoea.

In Australia the vegetation was strange to English eyes - except perhaps the park-like grasslands. The light was seen as too glaring, and in much of the country the rain was sparse and erratic. For decades the early settlers believed that a continent much larger than India must have an inland sea: it could not all be dry. And when settlers began to live on the endless plains they were bewildered by a terrain which had virtually no parallel in the English-language books, pictures and imagery they brought with them. Mary Gilmore, brought up around Goulburn and Wagga in the era of the bullock dray, expressed it movingly when she wrote: "Europe has its peaks piercing the sky but we have the horizon".

The sense of the unfamiliar was increased by the way the seasons fell - a sweltering Christmas Day, and a 22nd June that was unbelievably short. It was a slow and incredibly difficult process of adjustment, prolonged by the isolation of Australia from Europe and the fact that few migrants ever achieved their wish to return to their old home unless as merchant seamen or as soldiers.

We have forgotten how difficult was the emotional adjustment. When about 1904 Dorothea Mackellar wrote her lines that now seem obvious - "I love a sunburnt country, a land of sweeping plains" - she was making a provocative statement. At least half of the Australians then did not love a sunburnt country. Farmers, housewives, bankers and general storekeepers certainly had no reason to prefer it to a green country!

Poor Adam Lindsay Gordon, the poet and steeplechase-rider, was famous in his day but is no longer famous. To the few who recall his poems he is often a misfit, an Englishmen who seemed metaphorically lost in the bush in the 1860s, a poet whom many nationalists do not forgive, because he described Australia as "a land where bright blossoms are scentless, and songless bright birds". And yet Adam Lindsay Gordon was a giant in the formidable task of making his generation feel a little more at home. More than anybody, he placed the wattle and the bush flowers on the altar of Australian affections.

While we now imagine that every migrant must have loved the wildflowers, we forget their nostalgia for what was familiar at home. Rachel Henning, writing near Sydney in 1855, noted that the arrival of an English letter, so long awaited, made her miserably homesick for a day. Even pretty wildflowers seen in the bush were of only faint passing interest whereas "at home every wildflower seemed like a friend to me".

Curiously, our national anthem belongs to the last century when most Australians, not feeling fully at home here, liked to pretend that their new land was more like the places they had come from. The official words of 'Advance Australia Fair' give the impression that the author had never been to Australia or, if he had, did not adventure further than Sydney's outer suburbs. The words, imposed on the nation by official edict as recently as the 1980s, might not last the distance.

We are all beneficiaries of these countless brave and lonely attempts by earlier Australians to feel at home and to express in paintings and the printed page, in gardens and architecture and games, their initial pride, their attempt to be at one with Australia. Our descendants in one hundred years' time, will feel even more at home than we do.

The strength of the green movement in Australia today is partly an outcome of this growing sense of belonging and partly the growth from other roots. This movement is so important for debates about the quality of life in Australia that it calls for a brief diagnosis. It mirrors the unprecedented economic development in Australia and the world since 1945 and the consequent pressure on sea and land and atmosphere. It is also aided by the declining appeal of communism and socialism, and one of its wings consists of people who find the greens a more effective vehicle than the pinks for the purposes of opposing their old enemy - international capitalism, especially in mining and paper-making and other resource-based industries.

The green crusade is also a reflection of the decline of orthodox Christianity. Many of the dedicated greens see Nature as a shrine, a theatre of wonder and harmony and beauty, indeed a new God. Some of the moral passion and righteousness in the greens comes from this religious source. Whereas mainstream Christianity in Australia with its emphasis on saving, working, and on the filling of each waking hour had been a dynamo of rapid economic development, this new religious offspring works in the opposite direction. And yet, traditional Christianity had room for greens. St Francis of Assisi was a half-green. One of the popular hymns of the English speaking world was "From Greenland's icy mountains" and its second verse marvelled at the beauty of Ceylon and its spicy breezes - "where every prospect pleases, and only man is vile." It is one of several oldtime hymns which could serve as an environmental-impact statement.

The green crusade in Australia consists of two main strands: the light greens and the dark greens. The light greens who provide the movement with the most support on election days have a genuine concern for the environment but also wish to see economic development. They want a rising standard of living: they also believe that nature sometimes deserves first priority. The light greens have a strong tradition in Australia. Banjo Paterson was a light green when almost a century ago he wrote of the " the wonderous glory of the everlasting stars" but Henry Lawson, now seen as the more nationalist writer, was really not a light green by Australian standards. It goes without saying that green is an imported political term, and is hardly suited to Dorothea Mackellar's "wide brown land" and Arthur Streeton's land of the golden summers.

In contrast to the numerous light greens, the few dark greens set the agenda. Small in number, they are the priests in what is a religious movement. They see the environment facing a crisis caused by greed and carelessness, and they believe that the traditional goal of economic development must be subordinated. They have already succeeded in declaring large tracts of Australia out of bounds for mining, logging, grazing and agriculture. Unfortunately their main targets are the very industries which produce about 80 per cent of our commodity exports. Nearly all their main targets are industries which are the most competitive in Australia, the industries which must become even stronger if we are to revive the economy in the short term and even the medium term.

The crisis in our balance of payments, the mountain of debt we owe to overseas nations, is a reflection of the capacity of Australia's cities to be more energetic in criticising others than in producing the national wealth that they so eagerly consume. In terms of paying our way as a nation, the sparsely-peopled outback and the inland are now the great work horses and the cities are too often the show ponies. The first step towards economic recovery is for the cities to accept that unpalatable fact and use their dominant voting power to reduce some of their own special privileges. And that brings me to a third component of the quality of life - democracy.

Democracy

We are amongst the oldest, continuous democracies in the world. By one definition Australia is the oldest because in 1902 it became the world's first nation to give women as well as men both the right to vote and the right to stand for parliament. I think, however, that at present we undervalue democracy and the liberties that spring from it. We are especially mistaken in assuming that a full-blooded parliamentary democracy is an easy method of government. Anybody can make it work, we now assume; and so our leaders express deep indignation when it is eroded, as in Fiji, or not fully implemented, as in South Africa and indeed in nearly all Africa.

I suspect that one major cause of our economic troubles is that we have devalued democracy while pretending to enthrone it. A parliamentary democracy, at every level, depends as much on asserting duties as on asserting rights, but in the last decade there has been a rush in Australia to claim rights and even more rights. The federal parliament tended to lead the way, even trying to introduce that confidence trick called the Bill of Rights. Many of the rights it promised to the Australian people were contradictory or fictitious for there can be no right without a corresponding duty.

In my view, democracy in Australia has also been harmed by degrading citizenship, the foundation stone of a democracy. I see no justification for granting citizenship and the voting right to people who have lived in Australia for only two years, do not speak the common language of political debate, and do not disown their previous citizenship. This new policy weakens the democracy for every Australian old and new. To grant the vote to those not yet ready for it, and then compel them to use it, is childish. All voters in a democracy are equal but not all are responsible. By its very nature a democracy depends on the voluntary fulfilling of responsibilities. Nothing belittles democracy more than to lower it to a hit-or-miss method of government in which the act of voting is no more thoughtful than the licking of an ice cream.

I glory in those Australians who, amidst all the upheavals and distractions of the gold rushes of the 1850s, tried to make democracy work. With little or no political experience and not even a record in municipal politics, they tried to be answerable to that global rarity - a parliament for which virtually all men had the right to vote. It is a sign of how easy we think it is to run a democracy that we no longer retain in our folk memory the occasional disasters of that experiment. It was John Martineau, a Unitarian clergyman of sound judgment, who described Victoria in the late 1860s as a new democracy where any bill could be passed if the sponsor spent enough money in bribing the members. We, of all people, should not see this form of government as easy for a new nation or always easy for ourselves. It relies partly on a sense of duty; but that word is not frequent in Australia's political vocabulary today.

Democracy has the advantage that more than any form of government it allows the people to overthrow peacefully an incompetent or inadequate regime. It is not necessarily the most effective form of government in the short term, for it often works in a slow, unstructured way. You may wish at present for more action - for one strong government for all Australia, for the abolition of states and upper houses, for a government which can hold office for five years. You may wish for leadership which works wonders, or promises to work wonders. But that type of political approach often has disadvantages? The failure of communism in the Soviet Union and eastern Europe is in many ways the failure of a system of government in which the mass of the people, being allotted little responsibility for the direction of society, accepted no responsibility. The failure of communism was the failure to tap hundreds of millions of people and all their talent, drive and skill. Perhaps that too, in lesser degree, is our present failure as a nation.

While I hope to see, in Canberra and all the state capitals, wiser leadership and a sense of direction in the next year, I place no less reliance on what the people can do by thinking and acting. We should realise that, living in a democracy, the nation's future is in our hands and our heads if only we use them. To me one of the attractive qualities in Australian life has been visible in the last month, in cities and small towns, in the columns of newspapers, in talkback radio and chance discussions at bus stops. That quality is an intense desire by young and old to discover the mistakes of the past and to find new ways of going ahead. That this quest seems to be stronger amongst the Australian people than in Canberra itself still gives me heart.

The inaugural Jennings Group lecture, organised by the Australian Centre of the University of Melbourne, and given at the Regent of Melbourne , 24 October 1990